NON SANZ DROICT.

M. William Shak-speare:

HIS
True Chronicle Historie of the life and death of King LEAR and his three Daughters.

With the vnfortunate life of Edgar, *sonne and heire to the Earle of* Gloster, *and his sullen and assumed humor of* TOM *of Bedlam :*

As it was played before the Kings Maiestie at Whitehall vpon S. Stephans night in Christmas Hollidayes.

By his Maiesties seruants playing vsually at the Gloabe on the Bancke-side.

LONDON,
Printed for *Nathaniel Butter,* and are to be sold at his shop in *Pauls* Church-yard at the signe of the Pide Bull neere S. *Austins* Gate. 1608.

Title page of Q1 (1608), the earliest version of *King Lear*

William Shakespeare

The Tragedy
of
King Lear

With New and Updated
Critical Essays
and a Revised Bibliography

Edited by Russell Fraser

THE SIGNET CLASSIC SHAKESPEARE
General Editor: Sylvan Barnet

$\mathcal{C}$

A SIGNET CLASSIC

This book is for Allan Macdonald
Requiescat a labore
Doloroso et amore

SIGNET CLASSIC
Published by New American Library, a division of
Penguin Putnam Inc., 375 Hudson Street,
New York, New York 10014, U.S.A.
Penguin Books Ltd, 80 Strand,
London WC2R 0RL, England
Penguin Books Australia Ltd, 250 Camberwell Road,
Camberwell, Victoria 3124, Australia
Penguin Books Canada Ltd, 10 Alcorn Avenue,
Toronto, Ontario, Canada M4V 3B2
Penguin Books (N.Z.) Ltd, Cnr Rosedale and Airborne Roads,
Albany, Auckland 1310, New Zealand

Penguin Books Ltd, Registered Offices:
Harmondsworth, Middlesex, England

Published by Signet Classic, an imprint of New American Library,
a division of Penguin Putnam Inc. The Signet Classic edition of *King Lear*
was first published in 1963, and an updated edition was published in 1986.

First Signet Classic Printing (Second Revised Edition), June 1998
15 14 13 12 11 10

Contents

Shakespeare: An Overview

Biographical Sketch

Between the record of his baptism in Stratford on 26 April 1564 and the record of his burial in Stratford on 25 April 1616, some forty official documents name Shakespeare, and many others name his parents, his children, and his grandchildren. Further, there are at least fifty literary references to him in the works of his contemporaries. More facts are known about William Shakespeare than about any other playwright of the period except Ben Jonson. The facts should, however, be distinguished from the legends. The latter, inevitably more engaging and better known, tell us that the Stratford boy killed a calf in high style, poached deer and rabbits, and was forced to flee to London, where he held horses outside a playhouse. These traditions are only traditions; they may be true, but no evidence supports them, and it is well to stick to the facts.

Mary Arden, the dramatist's mother, was the daughter of a substantial landowner; about 1557 she married John Shakespeare, a tanner, glove-maker, and trader in wool, grain, and other farm commodities. In 1557 John Shakespeare was a member of the council (the governing body of Stratford), in 1558 a constable of the borough, in 1561 one of the two town chamberlains, in 1565 an alderman (entitling him to the appellation of "Mr."), in 1568 high bailiff—the town's highest political office, equivalent to mayor. After 1577, for an unknown reason he drops out of local politics. What *is* known is that he had to mortgage his wife's property, and that he was involved in serious litigation.

The birthday of William Shakespeare, the third child and the eldest son of this locally prominent man, is unrecorded, but the Stratford parish register records that the infant was baptized on 26 April 1564. (It is quite possible that he was born on 23 April, but this date has probably been assigned by tradition because it is the date on which, fifty-two years later, he died, and perhaps because it is the feast day of St. George, patron saint of England.) The attendance records of the Stratford grammar school of the period are not extant, but it is reasonable to assume that the son of a prominent local official attended the free school—it had been established for the purpose of educating males precisely of his class—and received substantial training in Latin. The masters of the school from Shakespeare's seventh to fifteenth years held Oxford degrees; the Elizabethan curriculum excluded mathematics and the natural sciences but taught a good deal of Latin rhetoric, logic, and literature, including plays by Plautus, Terence, and Seneca.

On 27 November 1582 a marriage license was issued for the marriage of Shakespeare and Anne Hathaway, eight years his senior. The couple had a daughter, Susanna, in May 1583. Perhaps the marriage was necessary, but perhaps the couple had earlier engaged, in the presence of witnesses, in a formal "troth plight" which would render their children legitimate even if no further ceremony were performed. In February 1585, Anne Hathaway bore Shakespeare twins, Hamnet and Judith.

That Shakespeare was born is excellent; that he married and had children is pleasant; but that we know nothing about his departure from Stratford to London or about the beginning of his theatrical career is lamentable and must be admitted. We would gladly sacrifice details about his children's baptism for details about his earliest days in the theater. Perhaps the poaching episode is true (but it is first reported almost a century after Shakespeare's death), or perhaps he left Stratford to be a schoolmaster, as another tradition holds; perhaps he was moved (like Petruchio in *The Taming of the Shrew*) by

> Such wind as scatters young men through the world,
> To seek their fortunes farther than at home
> Where small experience grows.   (1.2.49–51)

In 1592, thanks to the cantankerousness of Robert Greene, we have our first reference, a snarling one, to Shakespeare as an actor and playwright. Greene, a graduate of St. John's College, Cambridge, had become a playwright and a pamphleteer in London, and in one of his pamphlets he warns three university-educated playwrights against an actor who has presumed to turn playwright:

> There is an upstart crow, beautified with our feathers, that with his *tiger's heart wrapped in a player's hide* supposes he is as well able to bombast out a blank verse as the best of you, and being an absolute Johannes-factotum [i.e., jack-of-all-trades] is in his own conceit the only Shake-scene in a country.

The reference to the player, as well as the allusion to Aesop's crow (who strutted in borrowed plumage, as an actor struts in fine words not his own), makes it clear that by this date Shakespeare had both acted and written. That Shakespeare is meant is indicated not only by *Shake-scene* but also by the parody of a line from one of Shakespeare's plays, *3 Henry VI*: "O, tiger's heart wrapped in a woman's hide" (1.4.137). If in 1592 Shakespeare was prominent enough to be attacked by an envious dramatist, he probably had served an apprenticeship in the theater for at least a few years.

In any case, although there are no extant references to Shakespeare between the record of the baptism of his twins in 1585 and Greene's hostile comment about "Shake-scene" in 1592, it is evident that during some of these "dark years" or "lost years" Shakespeare had acted and written. There are a number of subsequent references to him as an actor. Documents indicate that in 1598 he is a "principal comedian," in 1603 a "principal tragedian," in 1608 he is one of the "men players." (We do not have, however, any solid information about which roles he may have played; later traditions say he played Adam in *As You Like It* and the ghost in *Hamlet*, but nothing supports the assertions. Probably his role as dramatist came to supersede his role as actor.) The profession of actor was not for a gentleman, and it occasionally drew the scorn of university men like Greene who resented writing speeches for persons less educated than themselves, but it was respectable enough; players, if prosperous, were in effect members of the bourgeoisie, and there is nothing to suggest that Stratford considered William Shakespeare less than a solid citizen. When, in 1596, the Shakespeares were granted a coat of arms—i.e., the right to be considered gentlemen—the grant was made to Shakespeare's father, but probably William Shakespeare had arranged the matter on his own behalf. In subsequent transactions he is occasionally styled a gentleman.

Although in 1593 and 1594 Shakespeare published two narrative poems dedicated to the Earl of Southampton, *Venus and Adonis* and *The Rape of Lucrece*, and may well have written most or all of his sonnets in the middle nineties, Shakespeare's literary activity seems to have been almost entirely devoted to the theater. (It may be significant that the two narrative poems were written in years when the plague closed the theaters for several months.) In 1594 he was a charter member of a theatrical company called the Chamberlain's Men, which in 1603 became the royal company, the King's Men, making Shakespeare the king's playwright. Until he retired to Stratford (about 1611, apparently), he was with this remarkably stable company. From 1599 the company acted primarily at the Globe theater, in which Shakespeare held a one-tenth interest. Other Elizabethan dramatists are known to have acted, but no other is known also to have been entitled to a share of the profits.

Shakespeare's first eight published plays did not have his name on them, but this is not remarkable; the most popular play of the period, Thomas Kyd's *The Spanish Tragedy*, went through many editions without naming Kyd, and Kyd's authorship is known only because a book on the profession of acting happens to quote (and attribute to Kyd) some lines on the interest of Roman emperors in the drama. What is remarkable is that after 1598 Shakespeare's name commonly appears on printed plays—some of which are not his. Presumably his name was a drawing card, and publishers used it to attract potential buyers. Another indication of his popularity comes from Francis Meres, author of *Palladis Tamia: Wit's Treasury* (1598). In this anthology of snippets accompanied by an essay on literature, many playwrights are mentioned, but Shakespeare's name occurs more often than any other, and Shakespeare is the only play-wright whose plays are listed.

From his acting, his play writing, and his share in a playhouse, Shakespeare seems to have made considerable money. He put it to work, making substantial investments in Stratford real estate. As early as 1597 he bought New Place, the second-largest house in Stratford. His family moved in soon afterward, and the house remained in the family until a granddaughter died in 1670. When Shakespeare made his will in 1616, less than a month before he died, he sought to leave his property intact to his descendants. Of small bequests to relatives and to friends (including three actors, Richard Burbage, John Heminges, and Henry Condell), that to his wife of the second-best bed has provoked the most comment. It has sometimes been taken as a sign of an unhappy marriage (other supposed signs are the apparently hasty marriage, his wife's seniority of eight years, and his residence in London without his family). Perhaps the second-best bed was the bed the couple had slept in, the best bed being reserved for visitors. In any case, had Shakespeare not excepted it, the bed would have gone (with the rest of his household possessions) to his daughter and her husband.

On 25 April 1616 Shakespeare was buried within the chancel of the church at Stratford. An unattractive monument to his memory, placed on a wall near the grave, says that he died on 23 April. Over the grave itself are the lines, perhaps by Shakespeare, that (more than his literary fame) have kept his bones undisturbed in the crowded burial ground where old bones were often dislodged to make way for new:

> Good friend, for Jesus' sake forbear
> To dig the dust enclosed here.
> Blessed be the man that spares these stones
> And cursed be he that moves my bones.

A Note on the Anti-Stratfordians, Especially Baconians and Oxfordians

Not until 1769—more than a hundred and fifty years after Shakespeare's death—is there any record of anyone expressing doubt about Shakespeare's authorship of the plays and poems. In 1769, however, Herbert Lawrence nominated Francis Bacon (1561–1626) in *The Life and Adventures of Common Sense*. Since then, at least two dozen other nominees have been offered, including Christopher Marlowe, Sir Walter Raleigh, Queen Elizabeth I, and Edward de Vere, 17th earl of Oxford. The impulse behind all anti-Stratfordian movements is the scarcely concealed snobbish opinion that "the man from Stratford" simply could not have written the plays because he was a country fellow without a university education and without access to high society. Anyone, the argument goes, who used so many legal terms, medical terms, nautical terms, and so forth, and who showed some familiarity with classical writing, must have attended a university, and anyone who knew so much about courtly elegance and courtly deceit must himself have moved among courtiers. The plays do indeed reveal an author whose interests were exceptionally broad, but specialists in any given field—law, medicine, arms and armor, and so on—soon find that the plays do not reveal deep knowledge in specialized matters; indeed, the playwright often gets technical details wrong.

The claim on behalf of Bacon, forgotten almost as soon as it was put forth in 1769, was independently reasserted by Joseph C. Hart in 1848. In 1856 it was reaffirmed by W. H. Smith in a book, and also by Delia Bacon in an article; in 1857 Delia Bacon published a book, arguing that Francis Bacon had directed a group of intellectuals who wrote the plays.

Francis Bacon's claim has largely faded, perhaps because it was advanced with such evident craziness by Ignatius Donnelly, who in *The Great Cryptogram* (1888) claimed to break a code in the plays that proved Bacon had written not only the plays attributed to Shakespeare but also other Renaissance works, for instance the plays of Christopher Marlowe and the essays of Montaigne.

Consider the last two lines of the Epilogue in *The Tempest*:

As you from crimes would pardoned be,
Let your indulgence set me free.

What was Shakespeare—sorry, Francis Bacon, Baron Verulam—*really* saying in these two lines? According to Baconians, the lines are an anagram reading, "Tempest of Francis Bacon, Lord Verulam; do ye ne'er divulge me, ye words." Ingenious, and it is a pity that in the quotation the letter *a* appears only twice in the cryptogram, whereas in the deciphered message it appears three times. Oh, no problem; just alter "Verulam" to "Verul'm" and it works out very nicely.

Most people understand that with sufficient ingenuity one can torture any text and find in it what one wishes. For instance: Did Shakespeare have a hand in the King James Version of the Bible? It was nearing completion in 1610, when Shakespeare was forty-six years old. If you look at the 46th Psalm and count forward for forty-six words, you will find the word *shake*. Now if you go to the end of the psalm and count backward forty-six words, you will find the word *spear*. Clear evidence, according to some, that Shakespeare slyly left his mark in the book.

Bacon's candidacy has largely been replaced in the twentieth century by the candidacy of Edward de Vere (1550–1604), 17th earl of Oxford. The basic ideas behind the Oxford theory, advanced at greatest length by Dorothy and Charlton Ogburn in *This Star of England* (1952, rev. 1955), a book of 1297 pages, and by Charlton Ogburn in *The Mysterious William Shakespeare* (1984), a book of 892 pages, are these: (1) The man from Stratford could not possibly have had the mental equipment and the experience to have written the plays—only a courtier could have written them; (2) Oxford had the requisite background (social position, education, years at Queen Elizabeth's court); (3) Oxford did not wish his authorship to be known for two basic reasons: writing for the public theater was a vulgar pursuit, and the plays show so much courtly and royal disreputable behavior that they would have compromised Oxford's position at court. Oxfordians offer countless details to support the claim. For example, Hamlet's phrase "that ever I was born to set it right" (1.5.89) barely conceals "E. Ver, I was born to set it right," an unambiguous announcement of de Vere's authorship, according to *This Star of England* (p. 654). A second example: Consider Ber

Jonson's poem entitled "To the Memory of My Beloved
Master William Shakespeare," prefixed to the first collected
edition of Shakespeare's plays in 1623. According to Oxfordians, when Jonson in this poem speaks of the author of
the plays as the "swan of Avon," he is alluding not to William Shakespeare, who was born and died in Stratford-on-
Avon and who throughout his adult life owned property
there; rather, he is alluding to Oxford, who, the Ogburns say,
used "William Shakespeare" as his pen name, and whose
manor at Bilton was on the Avon River. Oxfordians do not
offer any evidence that Oxford took a pen name, and they do
not mention that Oxford had sold the manor in 1581, forty-
two years before Jonson wrote his poem. Surely a reference
to the Shakespeare who was born in Stratford, who had
returned to Stratford, and who had died there only seven
years before Jonson wrote the poem is more plausible. And
exactly why Jonson, who elsewhere also spoke of Shakespeare as a playwright, and why Heminges and Condell,
who had acted with Shakespeare for about twenty years,
should speak of Shakespeare as the author in their dedication
in the 1623 volume of collected plays is never adequately
explained by Oxfordians. Either Jonson, Heminges and
Condell, and numerous others were in on the conspiracy, or
they were all duped—equally unlikely alternatives. Another
difficulty in the Oxford theory is that Oxford died in 1604,
and some of the plays are clearly indebted to works and
events later than 1604. Among the Oxfordian responses are:
At his death Oxford left some plays, and in later years these
were touched up by hacks, who added the material that
points to later dates. *The Tempest*, almost universally
regarded as one of Shakespeare's greatest plays and pretty
clearly dated to 1611, does indeed date from a period after
the death of Oxford, but it is a crude piece of work that
should not be included in the canon of works by Oxford.

The anti-Stratfordians, in addition to assuming that the
author must have been a man of rank and a university man,
usually assume two conspiracies: (1) a conspiracy in Elizabethan and Jacobean times, in which a surprisingly large
number of persons connected with the theater knew that the
actor Shakespeare did not write the plays attributed to him
but for some reason or other pretended that he did; (2) a con-

spiracy of today's Stratfordians, the professors who teach Shakespeare in the colleges and universities, who are said to have a vested interest in preserving Shakespeare as the author of the plays they teach. In fact, (1) it is inconceivable that the secret of Shakespeare's non-authorship could have been preserved by all of the people who supposedly were in on the conspiracy, and (2) academic fame awaits any scholar today who can disprove Shakespeare's authorship.

The Stratfordian case is convincing not only because hundreds or even thousands of anti-Stratford arguments—of the sort that say "ever I was born" has the secret double meaning "E. Ver, I was born"—add up to nothing at all but also because irrefutable evidence connects the man from Stratford with the London theater and with the authorship of particular plays. The anti-Stratfordians do not seem to understand that it is not enough to dismiss the Stratford case by saying that a fellow from the provinces simply couldn't have written the plays. Nor do they understand that it is not enough to dismiss all of the evidence connecting Shakespeare with the plays by asserting that it is perjured.

The Shakespeare Canon

We return to William Shakespeare. Thirty-seven plays as well as some nondramatic poems are generally held to constitute the Shakespeare canon, the body of authentic works. The exact dates of composition of most of the works are highly uncertain, but evidence of a starting point and/or of a final limiting point often provides a framework for informed guessing. For example, *Richard II* cannot be earlier than 1595, the publication date of some material to which it is indebted; *The Merchant of Venice* cannot be later than 1598, the year Francis Meres mentioned it. Sometimes arguments for a date hang on an alleged topical allusion, such as the lines about the unseasonable weather in *A Midsummer Night's Dream*, 2.1.81–117, but such an allusion, if indeed it is an allusion to an event in the real world, can be variously interpreted, and in any case there is always the possibility that a topical allusion was inserted years later, to bring the play up to date. (The issue of alterations in a text between the time that Shakespeare drafted it and the time that it was printed—alterations due to censorship or playhouse practice or Shakespeare's own second thoughts—will be discussed in "The Play Text as a Collaboration" later in this overview.) Dates are often attributed on the basis of style, and although conjectures about style usually rest on other conjectures (such as Shakespeare's development as a playwright, or the appropriateness of lines to character), sooner or later one must rely on one's literary sense. There is no documentary proof, for example, that *Othello* is not as early as *Romeo and Juliet*, but one feels that *Othello* is a later, more mature work, and because the first record of its performance is 1604, one is glad enough to set its composition at that date and not push it back into Shakespeare's early years. (*Romeo and Juliet* was first published in 1597, but evidence suggests that it was written a little earlier.) The following chronology, then, is indebted not only to facts but also to informed guesswork and sensitivity. The dates, necessarily imprecise for some works, indicate something like a scholarly consensus concerning the time of original composition. Some plays show evidence of later revision.

Plays. The first collected edition of Shakespeare, published in 1623, included thirty-six plays. These are all accepted as Shakespeare's, though for one of them, *Henry VIII*, he is thought to have had a collaborator. A thirty-seventh play, *Pericles*, published in 1609 and attributed to Shakespeare on the title page, is also widely accepted as being partly by Shakespeare even though it is not included in the 1623 volume. Still another play not in the 1623 volume, *The Two Noble Kinsmen*, was first published in 1634, with a title page attributing it to John Fletcher and Shakespeare. Probably most students of the subject now believe that Shakespeare did indeed have a hand in it. Of the remaining plays attributed at one time or another to Shakespeare, only one, *Edward III*, anonymously published in 1596, is now regarded by some scholars as a serious candidate. The prevailing opinion, however, is that this rather simpleminded play is not Shakespeare's; at most he may have revised some passages, chiefly scenes with the Countess of

Salisbury. We include *The Two Noble Kinsmen* but do not include *Edward III* in the following list.

1588–94	*The Comedy of Errors*
1588–94	*Love's Labor's Lost*
1589–91	*2 Henry VI*
1590–91	*3 Henry VI*
1589–92	*1 Henry VI*
1592–93	*Richard III*
1589–94	*Titus Andronicus*
1593–94	*The Taming of the Shrew*
1592–94	*The Two Gentlemen of Verona*
1594–96	*Romeo and Juliet*
1595	*Richard II*
1595–96	*A Midsummer Night's Dream*
1596–97	*King John*
1594–96	*The Merchant of Venice*
1596–97	*1 Henry IV*
1597	*The Merry Wives of Windsor*
1597–98	*2 Henry IV*
1598–99	*Much Ado About Nothing*
1598–99	*Henry V*
1599	*Julius Caesar*
1599–1600	*As You Like It*
1599–1600	*Twelfth Night*
1600–1601	*Hamlet*
1601–1602	*Troilus and Cressida*
1602–1604	*All's Well That Ends Well*
1603–1604	*Othello*
1604	*Measure for Measure*
1605–1606	*King Lear*
1605–1606	*Macbeth*
1606–1607	*Antony and Cleopatra*
1605–1608	*Timon of Athens*
1607–1608	*Coriolanus*
1607–1608	*Pericles*
1609–10	*Cymbeline*
1610–11	*The Winter's Tale*
1611	*The Tempest*

| 1612–13 | *Henry VIII* |
| 1613 | *The Two Noble Kinsmen* |

Poems. In 1989 Donald W. Foster published a book in which he argued that "A Funeral Elegy for Master William Peter," published in 1612, ascribed only to the initials W.S., *may* be by Shakespeare. Foster later published an article in a scholarly journal, *PMLA* 111 (1996), in which he asserted the claim more positively. The evidence begins with the initials, and includes the fact that the publisher and the printer of the elegy had published Shakespeare's *Sonnets* in 1609. But such facts add up to rather little, especially because no one has found any connection between Shakespeare and William Peter (an Oxford graduate about whom little is known, who was murdered at the age of twenty-nine). The argument is based chiefly on statistical examinations of word patterns, which are said to correlate with Shakespeare's known work. Despite such correlations, however, many readers feel that the poem does not sound like Shakespeare. True, Shakespeare has a great range of styles, but his work is consistently imaginative and interesting. Many readers find neither of these qualities in "A Funeral Elegy."

1592–93	*Venus and Adonis*
1593–94	*The Rape of Lucrece*
1593–1600	*Sonnets*
1600–1601	*The Phoenix and the Turtle*

Shakespeare's English

1. Spelling and Pronunciation. From the philologist's point of view, Shakespeare's English is modern English. It requires footnotes, but the inexperienced reader can comprehend substantial passages with very little help, whereas for the same reader Chaucer's Middle English is a foreign language. By the beginning of the fifteenth century the chief grammatical changes in English had taken place, and the final unaccented *-e* of Middle English had been lost (though it survives even today in spelling, as in *name*); during the fifteenth century the dialect of London, the commercial and political center, gradually displaced the provincial dialects, at least in writing; by the end of the century, printing had helped to regularize and stabilize the language, especially spelling. Elizabethan spelling may seem erratic to us (there were dozens of spellings of *Shakespeare*, and a simple word like *been* was also spelled *beene* and *bin*), but it had much in common with our spelling. Elizabethan spelling was conservative in that for the most part it reflected an older pronunciation (Middle English) rather than the sound of the language as it was then spoken, just as our spelling continues to reflect medieval pronunciation—most obviously in the now silent but formerly pronounced letters in a word such as *knight*. Elizabethan pronunciation, though not identical with ours, was much closer to ours than to that of the Middle Ages. Incidentally, though no one can be certain about what Elizabethan English sounded like, specialists tend to believe it was rather like the speech of a modern stage Irishman (*time* apparently was pronounced *toime*, *old* pronounced *awld*, *day* pronounced *die*, and *join* pronounced *jine*) and not at all like the Oxford speech that most of us think it was.

An awareness of the difference between our pronunciation and Shakespeare's is crucial in three areas—in accent, or number of syllables (many metrically regular lines may look irregular to us); in rhymes (which may not look like rhymes); and in puns (which may not look like puns). Examples will be useful. Some words that were at least on occasion stressed differently from today are *aspèct*, *còmplete*, *fòrlorn*, *revènue*, and *sepùlcher*. Words that sometimes had an additional syllable are *emp[e]ress*, *Hen[e]ry*, *mon[e]th*, and *villain* (three syllables, *vil-lay-in*). An additional syllable is often found in possessives, like *moon*'s (pronounced *moones*) and in words ending in *-tion* or *-sion*. Words that had one less syllable than they now have are *needle* (pronounced *neel*) and *violet* (pronounced *vilet*). Among rhymes now lost are *one* with *loan*, *love* with *prove*, *beast* with *jest*, *eat* with *great*. (In reading, trust your sense of metrics and your ear, more than your eye.) An example of a pun that has become obliterated by a change in pronunciation is Falstaff's reply to Prince Hal's "Come, tell us your

reason" in *1 Henry IV*: "Give you a reason on compulsion?
If reasons were as plentiful as blackberries, I would give no
man a reason upon compulsion, I" (2.4.237–40). The *ea* in
reason was pronounced rather like a long *a,* like the *ai* in
raisin, hence the comparison with blackberries.

Puns are not merely attempts to be funny; like metaphors
they often involve bringing into a meaningful relationship
areas of experience normally seen as remote. In *2 Henry IV,*
when Feeble is conscripted, he stoically says, "I care not. A
man can die but once. We owe God a death" (3.2.242–43),
punning on *debt,* which was the way *death* was pronounced.
Here an enormously significant fact of life is put into simple
commercial imagery, suggesting its commonplace quality.
Shakespeare used the same pun earlier in *1 Henry IV,* when
Prince Hal says to Falstaff, "Why, thou owest God a death,"
and Falstaff replies, " 'Tis not due yet: I would be loath
to pay him before his day. What need I be so forward with
him that calls not on me?" (5.1.126–29).

Sometimes the puns reveal a delightful playfulness;
sometimes they reveal aggressiveness, as when, replying to
Claudius's "But now, my cousin Hamlet, and my son,"
Hamlet says, "A little more than kin, and less than kind!"
(1.2.64–65). These are Hamlet's first words in the play, and
we already hear him warring verbally against Claudius.
Hamlet's "less than kind" probably means (1) Hamlet is not
of Claudius's family or nature, *kind* having the sense it still
has in our word *mankind*; (2) Hamlet is not kindly (affectionately) disposed toward Claudius; (3) Claudius is not
naturally (but rather unnaturally, in a legal sense incestu-
ously) Hamlet's father. The puns evidently were not put in
as sops to the groundlings; they are an important way of
communicating a complex meaning.

2. *Vocabulary.* A conspicuous difficulty in reading Shakespeare is rooted in the fact that some of his words are no
longer in common use—for example, words concerned with
armor, astrology, clothing, coinage, hawking, horsemanship, law, medicine, sailing, and war. Shakespeare had a
large vocabulary—something near thirty thousand words—
but it was not so much a vocabulary of big words as a
vocabulary drawn from a wide range of life, and it is partly

his ability to call upon a great body of concrete language that gives his plays the sense of being in close contact with life. When the right word did not already exist, he made it up. Among words thought to be his coinages are *accommodation, all-knowing, amazement, bare-faced, countless, dexterously, dislocate, dwindle, fancy-free, frugal, indistinguishable, lackluster, laughable, overawe, premeditated, sea change, star-crossed*. Among those that have not survived are the verb *convive,* meaning to feast together, and *smilet,* a little smile.

Less overtly troublesome than the technical words but more treacherous are the words that seem readily intelligible to us but whose Elizabethan meanings differ from their modern ones. When Horatio describes the Ghost as an "erring spirit," he is saying not that the ghost has sinned or made an error but that it is wandering. Here is a short list of some of the most common words in Shakespeare's plays that often (but not always) have a meaning other than their most usual modern meaning:

'a	he
abuse	deceive
accident	occurrence
advertise	inform
an, and	if
annoy	harm
appeal	accuse
artificial	skillful
brave	fine, splendid
censure	opinion
cheer	(1) face (2) frame of mind
chorus	a single person who comments on the events
closet	small private room
competitor	partner
conceit	idea, imagination
cousin	kinsman
cunning	skillful
disaster	evil astrological influence
doom	judgment
entertain	receive into service

envy	malice
event	outcome
excrement	outgrowth (of hair)
fact	evil deed
fancy	(1) love (2) imagination
fell	cruel
fellow	(1) companion (2) low person (often an insulting term if addressed to someone of approximately equal rank)
fond	foolish
free	(1) innocent (2) generous
glass	mirror
hap, haply	chance, by chance
head	army
humor	(1) mood (2) bodily fluid thought to control one's psychology
imp	child
intelligence	news
kind	natural, acting according to nature
let	hinder
lewd	base
mere(ly)	utter(ly)
modern	commonplace
natural	a fool, an idiot
naughty	(1) wicked (2) worthless
next	nearest
nice	(1) trivial (2) fussy
noise	music
policy	(1) prudence (2) stratagem
presently	immediately
prevent	anticipate
proper	handsome
prove	test
quick	alive
sad	serious
saw	proverb
secure	without care, incautious
silly	innocent

sensible	capable of being perceived by the senses
shrewd	sharp
so	provided that
starve	die
still	always
success	that which follows
tall	brave
tell	count
tonight	last night
wanton	playful, careless
watch	keep awake
will	lust
wink	close both eyes
wit	mind, intelligence

All glosses, of course, are mere approximations; sometimes one of Shakespeare's words may hover between an older meaning and a modern one, and as we have seen, his words often have multiple meanings.

3. Grammar. A few matters of grammar may be surveyed, though it should be noted at the outset that Shakespeare sometimes made up his own grammar. As E.A. Abbott says in *A Shakespearian Grammar,* "Almost any part of speech can be used as any other part of speech": a noun as a verb ("he childed as I fathered"); a verb as a noun ("She hath made compare"); or an adverb as an adjective ("a seldom pleasure"). There are hundreds, perhaps thousands, of such instances in the plays, many of which at first glance would not seem at all irregular and would trouble only a pedant. Here are a few broad matters.

Nouns: The Elizabethans thought the *-s* genitive ending for nouns (as in *man's*) derived from *his*; thus the line " 'gainst the count his galleys I did some service," for "the count's galleys."

Adjectives: By Shakespeare's time adjectives had lost the endings that once indicated gender, number, and case. About the only difference between Shakespeare's adjectives and ours is the use of the now redundant *more* or *most* with the comparative ("some more fitter place") or superlative

("This was the most unkindest cut of all"). Like double comparatives and double superlatives, double negatives were acceptable; Mercutio "will not budge for no man's pleasure."

Pronouns: The greatest change was in pronouns. In Middle English *thou, thy,* and *thee* were used among familiars and in speaking to children and inferiors; *ye, your,* and *you* were used in speaking to superiors (servants to masters, nobles to the king) or to equals with whom the speaker was not familiar. Increasingly the "polite" forms were used in all direct address, regardless of rank, and the accusative *you* displaced the nominative *ye.* Shakespeare sometimes uses *ye* instead of *you,* but even in Shakespeare's day *ye* was archaic, and it occurs mostly in rhetorical appeals.

Thou, thy, and *thee* were not completely displaced, however, and Shakespeare occasionally makes significant use of them, sometimes to connote familiarity or intimacy and sometimes to connote contempt. In *Twelfth Night* Sir Toby advises Sir Andrew to insult Cesario by addressing him as *thou:* "If thou thou'st him some thrice, it shall not be amiss" (3.2.46–47). In *Othello* when Brabantio is addressing an unidentified voice in the dark he says, "What are you?" (1.1.91), but when the voice identifies itself as the foolish suitor Roderigo, Brabantio uses the contemptuous form, saying, "I have charged thee not to haunt about my doors" (93). He uses this form for a while, but later in the scene, when he comes to regard Roderigo as an ally, he shifts back to the polite *you,* beginning in line 163, "What said she to you?" and on to the end of the scene. For reasons not yet satisfactorily explained, Elizabethans used *thou* in addresses to God—"O God, thy arm was here," the king says in *Henry V* (4.8.108)—and to supernatural characters such as ghosts and witches. A subtle variation occurs in *Hamlet.* When Hamlet first talks with the Ghost in 1.5, he uses *thou,* but when he sees the Ghost in his mother's room, in 3.4, he uses *you,* presumably because he is now convinced that the Ghost is not a counterfeit but is his father.

Perhaps the most unusual use of pronouns, from our point of view, is the neuter singular. In place of our *its, his* was often used, as in "How far that little candle throws *his* beams." But the use of a masculine pronoun for a neuter noun came to seem unnatural, and so *it* was used for the possessive as well as the nominative: "The hedge-sparrow fed the cuckoo so long / That it had it head bit off by it young." In the late sixteenth century the possessive form *its* developed, apparently by analogy with the *-s* ending used to indicate a genitive noun, as in *book*'s, but *its* was not yet common usage in Shakespeare's day. He seems to have used *its* only ten times, mostly in his later plays. Other usages, such as "you have seen Cassio and she together" or the substitution of *who* for *whom,* cause little problem even when noticed.

Verbs, Adverbs, and Prepositions: Verbs cause almost no difficulty: The third person singular present form commonly ends in *-s,* as in modern English (e.g., "He blesses"), but sometimes in *-eth* (Portia explains to Shylock that mercy "blesseth him that gives and him that takes"). Broadly speaking, the *-eth* ending was old-fashioned or dignified or "literary" rather than colloquial, except for the words *doth, hath,* and *saith.* The *-eth* ending (regularly used in the King James Bible, 1611) is very rare in Shakespeare's dramatic prose, though not surprisingly it occurs twice in the rather formal prose summary of the narrative poem *Lucrece.* Sometimes a plural subject, especially if it has collective force, takes a verb ending in *-s,* as in "My old bones aches." Some of our strong or irregular preterites (such as *broke*) have a different form in Shakespeare (*brake*); some verbs that now have a weak or regular preterite (such as *helped*) in Shakespeare have a strong or irregular preterite (*holp*). Some adverbs that today end in *-ly* were not inflected: "grievous sick," "wondrous strange." Finally, prepositions often are not the ones we expect: "We are such stuff as dreams are made on," "I have a king here to my flatterer."

Again, none of the differences (except meanings that have substantially changed or been lost) will cause much difficulty. But it must be confessed that for some elliptical passages there is no widespread agreement on meaning. Wise editors resist saying more than they know, and when they are uncertain they add a question mark to their gloss.

Shakespeare's Theater

In Shakespeare's infancy, Elizabethan actors performed wherever they could—in great halls, at court, in the courtyards of inns. These venues implied not only different audiences but also different playing conditions. The innyards must have made rather unsatisfactory theaters: on some days they were unavailable because carters bringing goods to London used them as depots; when available, they had to be rented from the innkeeper. In 1567, presumably to avoid such difficulties, and also to avoid regulation by the Common Council of London, which was not well disposed toward theatricals, one John Brayne, brother-in-law of the carpenter turned actor James Burbage, built the Red Lion in an eastern suburb of London. We know nothing about its shape or its capacity; we can say only that it may have been the first building in Europe constructed for the purpose of giving plays since the end of antiquity, a thousand years earlier. Even after the building of the Red Lion theatrical activity continued in London in makeshift circumstances, in marketplaces and inns, and always uneasily. In 1574 the Common Council required that plays and playing places in London be licensed because

> sundry great disorders and inconveniences have been found to ensue to this city by the inordinate haunting of great multitudes of people, specially youth, to plays, interludes, and shows, namely occasion of frays and quarrels, evil practices of incontinency in great inns having chambers and secret places adjoining to their open stages and galleries.

The Common Council ordered that innkeepers who wished licenses to hold performance put up a bond and make contributions to the poor.

The requirement that plays and innyard theaters be licensed, along with the other drawbacks of playing at inns and presumably along with the success of the Red Lion, led James Burbage to rent a plot of land northeast of the city walls, on property outside the jurisdiction of the city. Here he built England's second playhouse, called simply the Theatre. About all that is known of its construction is that it was wood. It soon had imitators, the most famous being the Globe (1599), essentially an amphitheater built across the Thames (again outside the city's jurisdiction), constructed with timbers of the Theatre, which had been dismantled when Burbage's lease ran out.

Admission to the theater was one penny, which allowed spectators to stand at the sides and front of the stage that jutted into the yard. An additional penny bought a seat in a covered part of the theater, and a third penny bought a more comfortable seat and a better location. It is notoriously difficult to translate prices into today's money, since some things that are inexpensive today would have been expensive in the past and vice versa—a pipeful of tobacco (imported, of course) cost a lot of money, about three pennies, and an orange (also imported) cost two or three times what a chicken cost—but perhaps we can get some idea of the low cost of the penny admission when we realize that a penny could also buy a pot of ale. An unskilled laborer made about five or sixpence a day, an artisan about twelve pence a day, and the hired actors (as opposed to the sharers in the company, such as Shakespeare) made about ten pence a performance. A printed play cost five or sixpence. Of course a visit to the theater (like a visit to a baseball game today) usually cost more than the admission since the spectator probably would also buy food and drink. Still, the low entrance fee meant that the theater was available to all except the very poorest people, rather as movies and most athletic events are today. Evidence indicates that the audience ranged from apprentices who somehow managed to scrape together the minimum entrance fee and to escape from their masters for a few hours, to prosperous members of the middle class and aristocrats who paid the additional fee for admission to the galleries. The exact proportion of men to women cannot be determined, but women of all classes certainly were present. Theaters were open every afternoon but Sundays for much of the year, except in times of plague, when they were closed because of fear of infection. By the way, no evidence suggests the presence of toilet facilities. Presumably the patrons relieved themselves by making a quick trip to the fields surrounding the playhouses.

There are four important sources of information about the

structure of Elizabethan public playhouses—drawings, a contract, recent excavations, and stage directions in the plays. Of drawings, only the so-called de Witt drawing (c. 1596) of the Swan—really his friend Aernout van Buchell's copy of Johannes de Witt's drawing—is of much significance. The drawing, the only extant representation of the interior of an Elizabethan theater, shows an amphitheater of three tiers, with a stage jutting from a wall into the yard or

Johannes de Witt, a Continental visitor to London, made a drawing of the Swan theater in about the year 1596. The original drawing is lost; this is Aernout van Buchell's copy of it.

center of the building. The tiers are roofed, and part of the stage is covered by a roof that projects from the rear and is supported at its front on two posts, but the groundlings, who paid a penny to stand in front of the stage or at its sides, were exposed to the sky. (Performances in such a playhouse were held only in the daytime; artificial illumination was not used.) At the rear of the stage are two massive doors; above the stage is a gallery.

The second major source of information, the contract for the Fortune (built in 1600), specifies that although the Globe (built in 1599) is to be the model, the Fortune is to be square, eighty feet outside and fifty-five inside. The stage is to be forty-three feet broad, and is to extend into the middle of the yard, i.e., it is twenty-seven and a half feet deep.

The third source of information, the 1989 excavations of the Rose (built in 1587), indicate that the Rose was fourteen-sided, about seventy-two feet in diameter with an inner yard almost fifty feet in diameter. The stage at the Rose was about sixteen feet deep, thirty-seven feet wide at the rear, and twenty-seven feet wide downstage. The relatively small dimensions and the tapering stage, in contrast to the rectangular stage in the Swan drawing, surprised theater historians and have made them more cautious in generalizing about the Elizabethan theater. Excavations at the Globe have not yielded much information, though some historians believe that the fragmentary evidence suggests a larger theater, perhaps one hundred feet in diameter.

From the fourth chief source, stage directions in the plays, one learns that entrance to the stage was by the doors at the rear (*"Enter one citizen at one door, and another at the other"*). A curtain hanging across the doorway—or a curtain hanging between the two doorways—could provide a place where a character could conceal himself, as Polonius does, when he wishes to overhear the conversation between Hamlet and Gertrude. Similarly, withdrawing a curtain from the doorway could "discover" (reveal) a character or two. Such discovery scenes are very rare in Elizabethan drama, but a good example occurs in *The Tempest* (5.1.171), where a stage direction tells us, *"Here Prospero discovers Ferdinand and Miranda playing at chess."* There was also some sort of playing space "aloft" or "above" to represent, for instance, the top of a city's walls or a room above the street. Doubtless each theater had its own peculiarities, but perhaps we can talk about a "typical" Elizabethan theater if we realize that no theater need exactly fit the description, just as no mother is the average mother with 2.7 children.

This hypothetical theater is wooden, round, or polygonal (in *Henry V* Shakespeare calls it a "wooden *O*") capable of holding some eight hundred spectators who stood in the yard around the projecting elevated stage—these spectators were the "groundlings"—and some fifteen hundred additional spectators who sat in the three roofed galleries. The stage, protected by a "shadow" or "heavens" or roof, is entered from two doors; behind the doors is the "tiring house" (attiring house, i.e., dressing room), and above the stage is some sort of gallery that may sometimes hold spectators but can be used (for example) as the bedroom from which Romeo—according to a stage direction in one text—"goeth down." Some evidence suggests that a throne can be lowered onto the platform stage, perhaps from the "shadow"; certainly characters can descend from the stage through a trap or traps into the cellar or "hell." Sometimes this space beneath the stage accommodates a sound-effects man or musician (in *Antony and Cleopatra* "*music of the hautboys* [oboes] *is under the stage*") or an actor (in *Hamlet* the "*Ghost cries under the stage*"). Most characters simply walk on and off through the doors, but because there is no curtain in front of the platform, corpses will have to be carried off (Hamlet obligingly clears the stage of Polonius's corpse, when he says, "I'll lug the guts into the neighbor room"). Other characters may have fallen at the rear, where a curtain on a doorway could be drawn to conceal them.

Such may have been the "public theater," so called because its inexpensive admission made it available to a wide range of the populace. Another kind of theater has been called the "private theater" because its much greater admission charge (sixpence versus the penny for general admission at the public theater) limited its audience to the wealthy or the prodigal. The private theater was basically a large room, entirely roofed and therefore artificially illuminated, with a stage at one end. The theaters thus were distinct in two ways: One was essentially an amphitheater that catered to the general public; the other was a hall that catered to the wealthy. In 1576 a hall theater was established in Blackfriars, a Dominican priory in London that had been suppressed in 1538 and confiscated by the Crown and thus was not under the city's jurisdiction. All the actors in this Blackfriars theater were boys about eight to thirteen years old (in the public theaters similar boys played female parts; a boy Lady Macbeth played to a man Macbeth). Near the end of this section on Shakespeare's theater we will talk at some length about possible implications in this convention of using boys to play female roles, but for the moment we should say that it doubtless accounts for the relative lack of female roles in Elizabethan drama. Thus, in *A Midsummer Night's Dream*, out of twenty-one named roles, only four are female; in *Hamlet*, out of twenty-four, only two (Gertrude and Ophelia) are female. Many of Shakespeare's characters have fathers but no mothers—for instance, King Lear's daughters. We need not bring in Freud to explain the disparity; a dramatic company had only a few boys in it.

To return to the private theaters, in some of which all of the performers were children—the "eyrie of . . . little eyases" (nest of unfledged hawks—2.2.347–48) which Rosencrantz mentions when he and Guildenstern talk with Hamlet. The theater in Blackfriars had a precarious existence, and ceased operations in 1584. In 1596 James Burbage, who had already made theatrical history by building the Theatre, began to construct a second Blackfriars theater. He died in 1597, and for several years this second Blackfriars theater was used by a troupe of boys, but in 1608 two of Burbage's sons and five other actors (including Shakespeare) became joint operators of the theater, using it in the winter when the open-air Globe was unsuitable. Perhaps such a smaller theater, roofed, artificially illuminated, and with a tradition of a wealthy audience, exerted an influence in Shakespeare's late plays.

Performances in the private theaters may well have had intermissions during which music was played, but in the public theaters the action was probably uninterrupted, flowing from scene to scene almost without a break. Actors would enter, speak, exit, and others would immediately enter and establish (if necessary) the new locale by a few properties and by words and gestures. To indicate that the scene took place at night, a player or two would carry a torch. Here are some samples of Shakespeare establishing the scene:

This is Illyria, lady.   (*Twelfth Night*, 1.2.2)

Well, this is the Forest of Arden.   (*As You Like It*, 2.4.14)

This castle has a pleasant seat; the air
Nimbly and sweetly recommends itself
Unto our gentle senses.   (*Macbeth*, 1.6.1–3)

The west yet glimmers with some streaks of day.
                                          (*Macbeth*, 3.3.5)

Sometimes a speech will go far beyond evoking the minimal setting of place and time, and will, so to speak, evoke the social world in which the characters move. For instance, early in the first scene of *The Merchant of Venice* Salerio suggests an explanation for Antonio's melancholy. (In the following passage, *pageants* are decorated wagons, floats, and *cursy* is the verb "to curtsy," or "to bow.")

Your mind is tossing on the ocean,
There where your argosies with portly sail—
Like signiors and rich burghers on the flood,
Or as it were the pageants of the sea—
Do overpeer the petty traffickers
That cursy to them, do them reverence,
As they fly by them with their woven wings.   (1.1.8–14)

Late in the nineteenth century, when Henry Irving produced the play with elaborate illusionistic sets, the first scene showed a ship moored in the harbor, with fruit vendors and dock laborers, in an effort to evoke the bustling and exotic life of Venice. But Shakespeare's words give us this exotic, rich world of commerce in his highly descriptive language when Salerio speaks of "argosies with portly sail" that fly with "woven wings"; equally important, through Salerio Shakespeare conveys a sense of the orderly, hierarchical society in which the lesser ships, "the petty traffickers," curtsy and thereby "do . . . reverence" to their superiors, the merchant prince's ships, which are "Like signiors and rich burghers."

On the other hand, it is a mistake to think that except for verbal pictures the Elizabethan stage was bare. Although Shakespeare's Chorus in *Henry V* calls the stage an "unworthy scaffold" (Prologue 1.10) and urges the spectators to "eke out our performance with your mind" (Prologue 3.35), there was considerable spectacle. The last act of *Macbeth,* for instance, has five stage directions calling for *"drum and colors,"* and another sort of appeal to the eye is indicated by the stage direction *"Enter Macduff, with Macbeth's head."* Some scenery and properties may have been substantial; doubtless a throne was used, but the pillars supporting the roof would have served for the trees on which Orlando pins his poems in *As You Like It.*

Having talked about the public theater—"this wooden *O*"—at some length, we should mention again that Shakespeare's plays were performed also in other locales. Alvin Kernan, in *Shakespeare, the King's Playwright: Theater in the Stuart Court 1603–1613* (1995) points out that "several of [Shakespeare's] plays contain brief theatrical performances, set always in a court or some noble house. When Shakespeare portrayed a theater, he did not, except for the choruses in *Henry V*, imagine a public theater" (p. 195). (Examples include episodes in *The Taming of the Shrew*, *A Midsummer Night's Dream*, *Hamlet*, and *The Tempest*.)

A Note on the Use of Boy Actors in Female Roles

Until fairly recently, scholars were content to mention that the convention existed; they sometimes also mentioned that it continued the medieval practice of using males in female roles, and that other theaters, notably in ancient Greece and in China and Japan, also used males in female roles. (In classical Noh drama in Japan, males still play the female roles.) Prudery may have been at the root of the academic failure to talk much about the use of boy actors, or maybe there really is not much more to say than that it was a convention of a male-centered culture (Stephen Green-

blatt's view, in *Shakespearean Negotiations* [1988]). Further, the very nature of a convention is that it is not thought
about: Hamlet is a Dane and Julius Caesar is a Roman, but
in Shakespeare's plays they speak English, and we in the
audience never give this odd fact a thought. Similarly, a
character may speak in the presence of others and we understand, again without thinking about it, that he or she is not
heard by the figures on the stage (the aside); a character
alone on the stage may speak (the soliloquy), and we do
not take the character to be unhinged; in a realistic (box)
set, the fourth wall, which allows us to see what is going on,
is miraculously missing. The no-nonsense view, then, is
that the boy actor was an accepted convention, accepted
unthinkingly—just as today we know that Kenneth Branagh
is not Hamlet, Al Pacino is not Richard III, and Denzel Wash-
ington is not the Prince of Aragon. In this view, the audience
takes the performer for the role, and that is that; such is the
argument we now make for race-free casting, in which
African-Americans and Asians can play roles of persons
who lived in medieval Denmark and ancient Rome. But
gender perhaps is different, at least today. It is a matter of
abundant academic study: The Elizabethan theater is now
sometimes called a transvestite theater, and we hear much
about cross-dressing.

Shakespeare himself in a very few passages calls attention
to the use of boys in female roles. At the end of *As You Like
It* the boy who played Rosalind addresses the audience, and
says, "O men, . . . if I were a woman, I would kiss as many
of you as had beards that pleased me." But this is in the Epilogue; the plot is over, and the actor is stepping out of the
play and into the audience's everyday world. A second reference to the practice of boys playing female roles occurs in
Antony and Cleopatra, when Cleopatra imagines that she
and Antony will be the subject of crude plays, her role being
performed by a boy:

> The quick comedians
> Extemporally will stage us, and present
> Our Alexandrian revels: Antony
> Shall be brought drunken forth, and I shall see
> Some squeaking Cleopatra boy my greatness.   (5.2.216–20)

In a few other passages, Shakespeare is more indirect. For instance, in *Twelfth Night* Viola, played of course by a boy, disguises herself as a young man and seeks service in the house of a lord. She enlists the help of a Captain, and (by way of explaining away her voice and her beardlessness) says,

> I'll serve this duke
> Thou shalt present me as an eunuch to him.   (1.2.55–56)

In *Hamlet*, when the players arrive in 2.2, Hamlet jokes with the boy who plays a female role. The boy has grown since Hamlet last saw him: "By'r Lady, your ladyship is nearer to heaven than when I saw you last by the altitude of a chopine" (a lady's thick-soled shoe). He goes on: "Pray God your voice . . . be not cracked" (434–38).

Exactly how sexual, how erotic, this material was and is, is now much disputed. Again, the use of boys may have been unnoticed, or rather not thought about—an unexamined convention—by most or all spectators most of the time, perhaps *all* of the time, except when Shakespeare calls the convention to the attention of the audience, as in the passages just quoted. Still, an occasional bit seems to invite erotic thoughts. The clearest example is the name that Rosalind takes in *As You Like It*, Ganymede—the beautiful youth whom Zeus abducted. Did boys dressed to play female roles carry homoerotic appeal for straight men (Lisa Jardine's view, in *Still Harping on Daughters* [1983]), or for gay men, or for some or all women in the audience? Further, when the boy actor played a woman who (for the purposes of the plot) disguised herself as a male, as Rosalind, Viola, and Portia do—so we get a boy playing a woman playing a man—what sort of appeal was generated, and for what sort of spectator?

Some scholars have argued that the convention empowered women by letting female characters display a freedom unavailable in Renaissance patriarchal society; the convention, it is said, undermined rigid gender distinctions. In this view, the convention (along with plots in which female characters for a while disguised themselves as young men) allowed Shakespeare to say what some modern gender

critics say: Gender is a constructed role rather than a bio-
logical given, something we make, rather than a fixed binary
opposition of male and female (see Juliet Dusinberre, in
Shakespeare and the Nature of Women [1975]). On the other
hand, some scholars have maintained that the male disguise
assumed by some female characters serves only to reaffirm
traditional social distinctions since female characters who
don male garb (notably Portia in *The Merchant of Venice*
and Rosalind in *As You Like It*) return to their female garb
and at least implicitly (these critics say) reaffirm the status
quo. (For this last view, see Clara Claiborne Park, in an
essay in *The Woman's Part*, ed. Carolyn Ruth Swift Lenz et
al. [1980].) Perhaps no one answer is right for all plays; in
As You Like It cross-dressing empowers Rosalind, but in
Twelfth Night cross-dressing comically traps Viola.

Shakespeare's Dramatic Language: Costumes, Gestures and Silences; Prose and Poetry

Because Shakespeare was a dramatist, not merely a poet,
he worked not only with language but also with costume,
sound effects, gestures, and even silences. We have already
discussed some kinds of spectacle in the preceding section,
and now we will begin with other aspects of visual language;
a theater, after all, is literally a "place for seeing." Consider
the opening stage direction in *The Tempest*, the first play in
the first published collection of Shakespeare's plays: *"A
tempestuous noise of thunder and Lightning heard: Enter a
Ship-master, and a Boteswain."*

Costumes: What did that shipmaster and that boatswain
wear? Doubtless they wore something that identified them
as men of the sea. Not much is known about the costumes
that Elizabethan actors wore, but at least three points are
clear: (1) many of the costumes were splendid versions of
contemporary Elizabethan dress; (2) some attempts were
made to approximate the dress of certain occupations and of
antique or exotic characters such as Romans, Turks, and
Jews; (3) some costumes indicated that the wearer was

supernatural. Evidence for elaborate Elizabethan clothing can be found in the plays themselves and in contemporary comments about the "sumptuous" players who wore the discarded clothing of noblemen, as well as in account books that itemize such things as "a scarlet cloak with two broad gold laces, with gold buttons down the sides."

The attempts at approximation of the dress of certain occupations and nationalities also can be documented from the plays themselves, and it derives additional confirmation from a drawing of the first scene of Shakespeare's *Titus Andronicus*—the only extant Elizabethan picture of an identifiable episode in a play. (See pp. xxxviii–xxxix.) The drawing, probably done in 1594 or 1595, shows Queen Tamora pleading for mercy. She wears a somewhat medieval-looking robe and a crown; Titus wears a toga and a wreath, but two soldiers behind him wear costumes fairly close to Elizabethan dress. We do not know, however, if the drawing represents an actual stage production in the public theater, or perhaps a private production, or maybe only a reader's visualization of an episode. Further, there is some conflicting evidence: In *Julius Caesar* a reference is made to Caesar's doublet (a close-fitting jacket), which, if taken literally, suggests that even the protagonist did not wear Roman clothing; and certainly the lesser characters, who are said to wear hats, did not wear Roman garb.

It should be mentioned, too, that even ordinary clothing can be symbolic: Hamlet's "inky cloak," for example, sets him apart from the brightly dressed members of Claudius's court and symbolizes his mourning; the fresh clothes that are put on King Lear partly symbolize his return to sanity. Consider, too, the removal of disguises near the end of some plays. For instance, Rosalind in *As You Like It* and Portia and Nerissa in *The Merchant of Venice* remove their male attire, thus again becoming fully themselves.

Gestures and Silences: Gestures are an important part of a dramatist's language. King Lear kneels before his daughter Cordelia for a benediction (4.7.57–59), an act of humility that contrasts with his earlier speeches banishing her and that contrasts also with a comparable gesture, his ironic

kneeling before Regan (2.4.153–55). Northumberland's failure to kneel before King Richard II (3.3.71–72) speaks volumes. As for silences, consider a moment in *Coriolanus*: Before the protagonist yields to his mother's entreaties (5.3.182), there is this stage direction: *"Holds her by the hand, silent."* Another example of "speech in dumbness" occurs in *Macbeth*, when Macduff learns that his wife and children have been murdered. He is silent at first, as Malcolm's speech indicates: "What, man! Ne'er pull your hat upon your brows. Give sorrow words" (4.3.208–09). (For a discussion of such moments, see Philip C. McGuire's *Speechless Dialect: Shakespeare's Open Silences* [1985].)

Of course when we think of Shakespeare's work, we think primarily of his language, both the poetry and the prose.

Prose: Although two of his plays (*Richard II* and *King John*) have no prose at all, about half the others have at least one quarter of the dialogue in prose, and some have notably more: *1 Henry IV* and *2 Henry IV*, about half; *As You Like It*

and *Twelfth Night*, a little more than half; *Much Ado About Nothing*, more than three quarters; and *The Merry Wives of Windsor*, a little more than five sixths. We should remember that despite Molière's joke about M. Jourdain, who was amazed to learn that he spoke prose, most of us do not speak prose. Rather, we normally utter repetitive, shapeless, and often ungrammatical torrents; prose is something very different—a sort of literary imitation of speech at its most coherent.

Today we may think of prose as "natural" for drama; or even if we think that poetry is appropriate for high tragedy we may still think that prose is the right medium for comedy. Greek, Roman, and early English comedies, however, were written in verse. In fact, prose was not generally considered a literary medium in England until the late fifteenth century; Chaucer tells even his bawdy stories in verse. By the end of the 1580s, however, prose had established itself on the English comic stage. In tragedy, Marlowe made some use of prose, not simply in the speeches of clownish servants but even in the speech of a tragic hero, Doctor Faustus. Still, before Shakespeare, prose normally was used in the theater only for special circumstances: (1) letters and proclamations, to set them off from the poetic dialogue; (2) mad characters, to indicate that normal thinking has become disordered; and (3) low comedy, or speeches uttered by clowns even when they are not being comic. Shakespeare made use of these conventions, but he also went far beyond them. Sometimes he begins a scene in prose and then shifts into verse as the emotion is heightened; or conversely, he may shift from verse to prose when a speaker is lowering the emotional level, as when Brutus speaks in the Forum.

Shakespeare's prose usually is not prosaic. Hamlet's prose includes not only small talk with Rosencrantz and Guildenstern but also princely reflections on "What a piece of work is a man" (2.2.312). In conversation with Ophelia, he shifts from light talk in verse to a passionate prose denunciation of women (3.1.103), though the shift to prose here is perhaps also intended to suggest the possibility of madness. (Consult Brian Vickers, *The Artistry of Shakespeare's Prose* [1968].)

Poetry: Drama in rhyme in England goes back to the Middle Ages, but by Shakespeare's day rhyme no longer dominated poetic drama; a finer medium, blank verse (strictly speaking, unrhymed lines of ten syllables, with the stress on every second syllable) had been adopted. But before looking at unrhymed poetry, a few things should be said about the chief uses of rhyme in Shakespeare's plays. (1) A couplet (a pair of rhyming lines) is sometimes used to convey emotional heightening at the end of a blank verse speech; (2) characters sometimes speak a couplet as they leave the stage, suggesting closure; (3) except in the latest plays, scenes fairly often conclude with a couplet, and sometimes, as in *Richard II*, 2.1.145–46, the entrance of a new character within a scene is preceded by a couplet, which wraps up the earlier portion of that scene; (4) speeches of two characters occasionally are linked by rhyme, most notably in *Romeo and Juliet*, 1.5.95–108, where the lovers speak a sonnet between them; elsewhere a taunting reply occasionally rhymes with the previous speaker's last line; (5) speeches with sententious or gnomic remarks are sometimes in rhyme, as in the duke's speech in *Othello* (1.3.199–206); (6) speeches of sardonic mockery are sometimes in rhyme—for example, Iago's speech on women in *Othello* (2.1.146–58)—and they sometimes conclude with an emphatic couplet, as in Bolingbroke's speech on comforting words in *Richard II* (1.3.301–2); (7) some characters are associated with rhyme, such as the fairies in *A Midsummer Night's Dream*; (8) in the early plays, especially *The Comedy of Errors* and *The Taming of the Shrew*, comic scenes that in later plays would be in prose are in jingling rhymes; (9) prologues, choruses, plays-within-the-play, inscriptions, vows, epilogues, and so on are often in rhyme, and the songs in the plays are rhymed.

Neither prose nor rhyme immediately comes to mind when we first think of Shakespeare's medium: It is blank verse, unrhymed iambic pentameter. (In a mechanically exact line there are five iambic feet. An iambic foot consists of two syllables, the second accented, as in *away*; five feet make a pentameter line. Thus, a strict line of iambic pentameter contains ten syllables, the even syllables being stressed more heavily than the odd syllables. Fortunately, Shakespeare usually varies the line somewhat.) The first speech in *A Midsummer Night's Dream*, spoken by Duke Theseus to his betrothed, is an example of blank verse:

> Now, fair Hippolyta, our nuptial hour
> Draws on apace. Four happy days bring in
> Another moon; but, O, methinks, how slow
> This old moon wanes! She lingers my desires,
> Like to a stepdame, or a dowager,
> Long withering out a young man's revenue.   (1.1.1–6)

As this passage shows, Shakespeare's blank verse is not mechanically unvarying. Though the predominant foot is the iamb (as in *apace* or *desires*), there are numerous variations. In the first line the stress can be placed on "fair," as the regular metrical pattern suggests, but it is likely that "Now" gets almost as much emphasis; probably in the second line "Draws" is more heavily emphasized than "on," giving us a trochee (a stressed syllable followed by an unstressed one); and in the fourth line each word in the phrase "This old moon wanes" is probably stressed fairly heavily, conveying by two spondees (two feet, each of two stresses) the oppressive tedium that Theseus feels.

In Shakespeare's early plays much of the blank verse is end-stopped (that is, it has a heavy pause at the end of each line), but he later developed the ability to write iambic pentameter verse paragraphs (rather than lines) that give the illusion of speech. His chief techniques are (1) enjambing, i.e., running the thought beyond the single line, as in the first three lines of the speech just quoted; (2) occasionally replacing an iamb with another foot; (3) varying the position of the chief pause (the caesura) within a line; (4) adding an occasional unstressed syllable at the end of a line, traditionally called a feminine ending; (5) and beginning or ending a speech with a half line.

Shakespeare's mature blank verse has much of the rhythmic flexibility of his prose; both the language, though richly figurative and sometimes dense, and the syntax seem natural. It is also often highly appropriate to a particular character. Consider, for instance, this speech from *Hamlet*, in which Claudius, King of Denmark ("the Dane"), speaks to Laertes:

> And now, Laertes, what's the news with you?
> You told us of some suit. What is't, Laertes?
> You cannot speak of reason to the Dane
> And lose your voice. What wouldst thou beg, Laertes,
> That shall not be my offer, not thy asking?   (1.2.42–46)

Notice the short sentences and the repetition of the name "Laertes," to whom the speech is addressed. Notice, too, the shift from the royal "us" in the second line to the more intimate "my" in the last line, and from "you" in the first three lines to the more intimate "thou" and "thy" in the last two lines. Claudius knows how to ingratiate himself with Laertes.

For a second example of the flexibility of Shakespeare's blank verse, consider a passage from *Macbeth*. Distressed by the doctor's inability to cure Lady Macbeth and by the imminent battle, Macbeth addresses some of his remarks to the doctor and others to the servant who is arming him. The entire speech, with its pauses, interruptions, and irresolution (in "Pull't off, I say," Macbeth orders the servant to remove the armor that the servant has been putting on him), catches Macbeth's disintegration. (In the first line, *physic* means "medicine," and in the fourth and fifth lines, *cast the water* means "analyze the urine.")

> Throw physic to the dogs, I'll none of it.
> Come, put mine armor on. Give me my staff.
> Seyton, send out.—Doctor, the thanes fly from me.—
> Come, sir, dispatch. If thou couldst, doctor, cast
> The water of my land, find her disease
> And purge it to a sound and pristine health,
> I would applaud thee to the very echo,
> That should applaud again.—Pull't off, I say.—
> What rhubarb, senna, or what purgative drug,
> Would scour these English hence? Hear'st thou of them?
>
> (5.3.47–56)

Blank verse, then, can be much more than unrhymed iambic pentameter, and even within a single play Shakespeare's blank verse often consists of several styles, depending on the speaker and on the speaker's emotion at the moment.

The Play Text as a Collaboration

Shakespeare's fellow dramatist Ben Jonson reported that the actors said of Shakespeare, "In his writing, whatsoever he penned, he never blotted out line," i.e., never crossed out material and revised his work while composing. None of Shakespeare's plays survives in manuscript (with the possible exception of a scene in *Sir Thomas More*), so we cannot fully evaluate the comment, but in a few instances the published work clearly shows that he revised his manuscript. Consider the following passage (shown here in facsimile) from the best early text of *Romeo and Juliet*, the Second Quarto (1599):

Ro. Would I were sleepe and peace so sweet to rest
The grey eyde morne smiles on the frowning night,
Checkring the Easterne Clouds with streaks of light,
And darknesse fleckted like a drunkard reeles,
From forth daies pathway, made by *Tytans* wheeles.
Hence will I to my ghostly Friers close cell,
His helpe to craue, and my deare hap to tell.

                                                       Exit.

     Enter Frier alone with a basket.   (night,
Fri. The grey-eyed morne smiles on the frowning
Checking the Easterne clowdes with streaks of light:
And fleckeld darknesse like a drunkard reeles,
From forth daies path, and *Titans* burning wheeles:
Now erethe sun aduance his burning eie,

Romeo rather elaborately tells us that the sun at dawn is
dispelling the night (morning is smiling, the eastern clouds
are checked with light, and the sun's chariot—Titan's
wheels—advances), and he will seek out his spiritual father,
the Friar. He exits and, oddly, the Friar enters and says pretty
much the same thing about the sun. Both speakers say that
"the gray-eyed morn smiles on the frowning night," but there
are small differences, perhaps having more to do with the
business of printing the book than with the author's
composition: For Romeo's "checkring," "fleckted," and
"pathway," we get the Friar's "checking," "fleckeld," and
"path." (Notice, by the way, the inconsistency in Elizabethan
spelling: Romeo's "clouds" become the Friar's "clowdes.")

Both versions must have been in the printer's copy, and it
seems safe to assume that both were in Shakespeare's manuscript. He must have written one version—let's say he first
wrote Romeo's closing lines for this scene—and then he
decided, no, it's better to give this lyrical passage to the
Friar, as the opening of a new scene, but he neglected to
delete the first version. Editors must make a choice, and they
may feel that the reasonable thing to do is to print the text as
Shakespeare intended it. But how can we know what he
intended? Almost all modern editors delete the lines from

Romeo's speech, and retain the Friar's lines. They don't do this because they know Shakespeare's intention, however. They give the lines to the Friar because the first published version (1597) of *Romeo and Juliet* gives only the Friar's version, and this text (though in many ways inferior to the 1599 text) is thought to derive from the memory of some actors, that is, it is thought to represent a performance, not just a script. Maybe during the course of rehearsals Shakespeare—an actor as well as an author—unilaterally decided that the Friar should speak the lines; if so (remember that we don't know this to be a fact) his final intention was to give the speech to the Friar. Maybe, however, the actors talked it over and settled on the Friar, with or without Shakespeare's approval. On the other hand, despite the 1597 version, one might argue (if only weakly) on behalf of giving the lines to Romeo rather than to the Friar, thus: (1) Romeo's comment on the coming of the daylight emphasizes his separation from Juliet, and (2) the figurative language seems more appropriate to Romeo than to the Friar. Having said this, in the Signet edition we have decided in this instance to draw on the evidence provided by earlier text and to give the lines to the Friar, on the grounds that since Q1 reflects a production, in the theater (at least on one occasion) the lines were spoken by the Friar.

A playwright sold a script to a theatrical company. The script thus belonged to the company, not the author, and author and company alike must have regarded this script not as a literary work but as the basis for a play that the actors would create on the stage. We speak of Shakespeare as the author of the plays, but readers should bear in mind that the texts they read, even when derived from a single text, such as the First Folio (1623), are inevitably the collaborative work not simply of Shakespeare with his company—doubtless during rehearsals the actors would suggest alterations—but also with other forces of the age. One force was governmental censorship. In 1606 parliament passed "an Act to restrain abuses of players," prohibiting the utterance of oaths and the name of God. So where the earliest text of *Othello* gives us "By heaven" (3.3.106), the first Folio gives "Alas," presumably reflecting the compliance of stage practice with the law. Similarly, the 1623 version of *King Lear* omits the oath "Fut" (probably from "By God's foot") at 1.2.142, again presumably reflecting the line as it was spoken on the stage. Editors who seek to give the reader the play that Shakespeare initially conceived—the "authentic" play conceived by the solitary Shakespeare—probably will restore the missing oaths and references to God. Other editors, who see the play as a collaborative work, a construction made not only by Shakespeare but also by actors and compositors and even government censors, may claim that what counts is the play as it was actually performed. Such editors regard the censored text as legitimate, since it is the play that was (presumably) finally put on. A performed text, they argue, has more historical reality than a text produced by an editor who has sought to get at what Shakespeare initially wrote. In this view, the text of a play is rather like the script of a film; the script is not the film, and the play text is not the performed play. Even if we want to talk about the play that Shakespeare "intended," we will find ourselves talking about a script that he handed over to a company with the intention that it be implemented by actors. The "intended" play is the one that the actors—we might almost say "society"—would help to construct.

Further, it is now widely held that a play is also the work of readers and spectators, who do not simply receive meaning, but who create it when they respond to the play. This idea is fully in accord with contemporary post-structuralist critical thinking, notably Roland Barthes's "The Death of the Author," in *Image-Music-Text* (1977) and Michel Foucault's "What Is an Author?," in *The Foucault Reader* (1984). The gist of the idea is that an author is not an isolated genius; rather, authors are subject to the politics and other social structures of their age. A dramatist especially is a worker in a collaborative project, working most obviously with actors—parts may be written for particular actors—but working also with the audience. Consider the words of Samuel Johnson, written to be spoken by the actor David Garrick at the opening of a theater in 1747:

> The stage but echoes back the public voice;
> The drama's laws, the drama's patrons give,
> For we that live to please, must please to live.

The audience—the public taste as understood by the playwright—helps to determine what the play is. Moreover, even members of the public who are not part of the playwright's immediate audience may exert an influence through censorship. We have already glanced at governmental censorship, but there are also other kinds. Take one of Shakespeare's most beloved characters, Falstaff, who appears in three of Shakespeare's plays, the two parts of *Henry IV* and *The Merry Wives of Windsor*. He appears with this name in the earliest printed version of the first of these plays, *1 Henry IV*, but we know that Shakespeare originally called him (after an historical figure) Sir John Oldcastle. Oldcastle appears in Shakespeare's source (partly reprinted in the Signet edition of *1 Henry IV*), and a trace of the name survives in Shakespeare's play, 1.2.43–44, where Prince Hal punningly addresses Falstaff as "my old lad of the castle." But for some reason—perhaps because the family of the historical Oldcastle complained—Shakespeare had to change the name. In short, the play as we have it was (at least in this detail) subject to some sort of censorship. If we think that a text should present what we take to be the author's intention, we probably will want to replace *Falstaff* with *Oldcastle*. But if we recognize that a play is a collaboration, we may welcome the change, even if it was forced on Shakespeare. Somehow *Falstaff*, with its hint of *false-staff*, i.e., inadequate prop, seems just right for this fat knight who, to our delight, entertains the young prince with untruths. We can go as far as saying that, at least so far as a play is concerned, an insistence on the author's original intention (even if we could know it) can sometimes impoverish the text.

The tiny example of Falstaff's name illustrates the point that the text we read is inevitably only a version—something in effect produced by the collaboration of the playwright with his actors, audiences, compositors, and editors—of a fluid text that Shakespeare once wrote, just as the *Hamlet* that we see on the screen starring Kenneth Branagh is not the *Hamlet* that Shakespeare saw in an open-air playhouse starring Richard Burbage. *Hamlet* itself, as we shall note in a moment, also exists in several versions. It is not surprising that there is now much talk about the *instability* of Shakespeare's texts.

Because he was not only a playwright but was also an actor and a shareholder in a theatrical company, Shakespeare probably was much involved with the translation of the play from a manuscript to a stage production. He may or may not have done some rewriting during rehearsals, and he may or may not have been happy with cuts that were made. Some plays, notably *Hamlet* and *King Lear*, are so long that it is most unlikely that the texts we read were acted in their entirety. Further, for both of these plays we have more than one early text that demands consideration. In *Hamlet*, the Second Quarto (1604) includes some two hundred lines not found in the Folio (1623). Among the passages missing from the Folio are two of Hamlet's reflective speeches, the "dram of evil" speech (1.4.13–38) and "How all occasions do inform against me" (4.4.32–66). Since the Folio has more numerous and often fuller stage directions, it certainly looks as though in the Folio we get a theatrical version of the play, a text whose cuts were probably made—this is only a hunch, of course—not because Shakespeare was changing his conception of Hamlet but because the playhouse demanded a modified play. (The problem is complicated, since the Folio not only cuts some of the Quarto but adds some material. Various explanations have been offered.)

Or take an example from *King Lear*. In the First and Second Quarto (1608, 1619), the final speech of the play is given to Albany, Lear's surviving son-in-law, but in the First Folio version (1623), the speech is given to Edgar. The Quarto version is in accord with tradition—usually the highest-ranking character in a tragedy speaks the final words. Why does the Folio give the speech to Edgar? One possible answer is this: The Folio version omits some of Albany's speeches in earlier scenes, so perhaps it was decided (by Shakespeare? by the players?) not to give the final lines to so pale a character. In fact, the discrepancies are so many between the two texts, that some scholars argue we do not simply have texts showing different theatrical productions. Rather, these scholars say, Shakespeare substantially revised the play, and we really have two versions of *King Lear* (and of *Othello* also, say some)—two different plays—not simply two texts, each of which is in some ways imperfect.

In this view, the 1608 version of *Lear* may derive from Shakespeare's manuscript, and the 1623 version may derive from his later revision. The Quartos have almost three hundred lines not in the Folio, and the Folio has about a hundred lines not in the Quartos. It used to be held that all the texts were imperfect in various ways and from various causes—some passages in the Quartos were thought to have been set from a manuscript that was not entirely legible, other passages were thought to have been set by a compositor who was new to setting plays, and still other passages were thought to have been provided by an actor who misremembered some of the lines. This traditional view held that an editor must draw on the Quartos and the Folio in order to get Shakespeare's "real" play. The new argument holds (although not without considerable strain) that we have two authentic plays, Shakespeare's early version (in the Quarto) and Shakespeare's—or his theatrical company's—revised version (in the Folio). Not only theatrical demands but also Shakespeare's own artistic sense, it is argued, called for extensive revisions. Even the titles vary: Q1 is called *True Chronicle Historie of the life and death of King Lear and his three Daughters*, whereas the Folio text is called *The Tragedie of King Lear*. To combine the two texts in order to produce what the editor thinks is the play that Shakespeare intended to write is, according to this view, to produce a text that is false to the history of the play. If the new view is correct, and we do have texts of two distinct versions of *Lear* rather than two imperfect versions of one play, it supports in a textual way the poststructuralist view that we cannot possibly have an unmediated vision of (in this case) a play by Shakespeare; we can only recognize a plurality of visions.

Editing Texts

Though eighteen of his plays were published during his lifetime, Shakespeare seems never to have supervised their publication. There is nothing unusual here; when a playwright sold a play to a theatrical company he surrendered his ownership to it. Normally a company would not publish the play, because to publish it meant to allow competitors to acquire the piece. Some plays did get published: Apparently hard-up actors sometimes pieced together a play for a publisher; sometimes a company in need of money sold a play; and sometimes a company allowed publication of a play that no longer drew audiences. That Shakespeare did not concern himself with publication is not remarkable; of his contemporaries, only Ben Jonson carefully supervised the publication of his own plays.

In 1623, seven years after Shakespeare's death, John Heminges and Henry Condell (two senior members of Shakespeare's company, who had worked with him for about twenty years) collected his plays—published and unpublished—into a large volume, of a kind called a folio. (A folio is a volume consisting of large sheets that have been folded once, each sheet thus making two leaves, or four pages. The size of the page of course depends on the size of the sheet—a folio can range in height from twelve to sixteen inches, and in width from eight to eleven; the pages in the 1623 edition of Shakespeare, commonly called the First Folio, are approximately thirteen inches tall and eight inches wide.) The eighteen plays published during Shakespeare's lifetime had been issued one play per volume in small formats called quartos. (Each sheet in a quarto has been folded twice, making four leaves, or eight pages, each page being about nine inches tall and seven inches wide, roughly the size of a large paperback.)

Heminges and Condell suggest in an address "To the great variety of readers" that the republished plays are presented in better form than in the quartos:

> Before you were abused with diverse stolen and surreptitious copies, maimed and deformed by the frauds and stealths of injurious impostors that exposed them; even those, are now offered to your view cured and perfect of their limbs, and all the rest absolute in their numbers, as he [i.e., Shakespeare] conceived them.

There is a good deal of truth to this statement, but some of the quarto versions are better than others; some are in fact preferable to the Folio text.

Whoever was assigned to prepare the texts for publication

in the first Folio seems to have taken the job seriously and yet not to have performed it with uniform care. The sources of the texts seem to have been, in general, good unpublished copies or the best published copies. The first play in the collection, *The Tempest*, is divided into acts and scenes, has unusually full stage directions and descriptions of spectacle, and concludes with a list of the characters, but the editor was not able (or willing) to present all of the succeeding texts so fully dressed. Later texts occasionally show signs of carelessness: in one scene of *Much Ado About Nothing* the names of actors, instead of characters, appear as speech prefixes, as they had in the Quarto, which the Folio reprints; proofreading throughout the Folio is spotty and apparently was done without reference to the printer's copy; the pagination of *Hamlet* jumps from 156 to 257. Further, the proofreading was done while the presses continued to print, so that each play in each volume contains a mix of corrected and uncorrected pages.

Modern editors of Shakespeare must first select their copy; no problem if the play exists only in the Folio, but a considerable problem if the relationship between a Quarto and the Folio—or an early Quarto and a later one—is unclear. In the case of *Romeo and Juliet*, the First Quarto (Q1), published in 1597, is vastly inferior to the Second (Q2), published in 1599. The basis of Q1 apparently is a version put together from memory by some actors. Not surprisingly, it garbles many passages and is much shorter than Q2. On the other hand, occasionally Q1 makes better sense than Q2. For instance, near the end of the play, when the parents have assembled and learned of the deaths of Romeo and Juliet, in Q2 the Prince says (5.3.208–9),

Come, *Montague;* for thou art early vp
To see thy sonne and heire, now earling downe.

The last three words of this speech surely do not make sense, and many editors turn to Q1, which instead of "now earling downe" has "more early downe." Some modern editors take only "early" from Q1, and print "now early down"; others take "more early," and print "more early down." Further, Q1 (though, again, quite clearly a garbled and abbreviated text) includes some stage directions that are not found in Q2, and today many editors who base their text on Q2 are glad to add these stage directions, because the directions help to give us a sense of what the play looked like on Shakespeare's stage. Thus, in 4.3.58, after Juliet drinks the potion, Q1 gives us this stage direction, not in Q2: *"She falls upon her bed within the curtains."*

In short, an editor's decisions do not end with the choice of a single copy text. First of all, editors must reckon with Elizabethan spelling. If they are not producing a facsimile, they probably modernize the spelling, but ought they to preserve the old forms of words that apparently were pronounced quite unlike their modern forms—*lanthorn, alablaster*? If they preserve these forms are they really preserving Shakespeare's forms or perhaps those of a compositor in the printing house? What is one to do when one finds *lanthorn* and *lantern* in adjacent lines? (The editors of this series in general, but not invariably, assume that words should be spelled in their modern form, unless, for instance, a rhyme is involved.) Elizabethan punctuation, too, presents problems. For example, in the First Folio, the only text for the play, Macbeth rejects his wife's idea that he can wash the blood from his hand (2.2.60–62):

> No: this my Hand will rather
> The multitudinous Seas incarnardine,
> Making the Greene one, Red.

Obviously an editor will remove the superfluous capitals, and will probably alter the spelling to "incarnadine," but what about the comma before "Red"? If we retain the comma, Macbeth is calling the sea "the green one." If we drop the comma, Macbeth is saying that his bloody hand will make the sea ("the Green") *uniformly* red.

An editor will sometimes have to change more than spelling and punctuation. Macbeth says to his wife (1.7.46–47):

> I dare do all that may become a man,
> Who dares no more, is none.

For two centuries editors have agreed that the second line is unsatisfactory, and have emended "no" to "do": "Who dares do more is none." But when in the same play (4.2.21–22) Ross says that fearful persons

> Floate vpon a wilde and violent Sea
> Each way, and moue,

need we emend the passage? On the assumption that the compositor misread the manuscript, some editors emend "each way, and move" to "and move each way"; others emend "move" to "none" (i.e., "Each way and none"). Other editors, however, let the passage stand as in the original. The editors of the Signet Classic Shakespeare have restrained themselves from making abundant emendations. In their minds they hear Samuel Johnson on the dangers of emendation: "I have adopted the Roman sentiment, that it is more honorable to save a citizen than to kill an enemy." Some departures (in addition to spelling, punctuation, and lineation) from the copy text have of course been made, but the original readings are listed in a note following the play, so that readers can evaluate the changes for themselves.

Following tradition, the editors of the Signet Classic Shakespeare have prefaced each play with a list of characters, and throughout the play have regularized the names of the speakers. Thus, in our text of *Romeo and Juliet*, all speeches by Juliet's mother are prefixed "Lady Capulet," although the 1599 Quarto of the play, which provides our copy text, uses at various points seven speech tags for this one character: *Capu. Wi.* (i.e., Capulet's wife), *Ca. Wi., Wi., Wife, Old La.* (i.e., Old Lady), *La.,* and *Mo.* (i.e., Mother). Similarly, in *All's Well That Ends Well,* the character whom we regularly call "Countess" is in the Folio (the copy text) variously identified as *Mother, Countess, Old Countess, Lady,* and *Old Lady.* Admittedly there is some loss in regularizing, since the various prefixes may give us a hint of the way Shakespeare (or a scribe who copied Shakespeare's manuscript) was thinking of the character in a particular scene—for instance, as a mother, or as an old lady. But too much can be made of these differing prefixes, since the social relationships implied are *not* always relevant to the given scene.

We have also added line numbers and in many cases act and scene divisions as well as indications of locale at the beginning of scenes. The Folio divided most of the plays into acts and some into scenes. Early eighteenth-century editors increased the divisions. These divisions, which provide a convenient way of referring to passages in the plays, have been retained, but when not in the text chosen as the basis for the Signet Classic text they are enclosed within square brackets, [ ], to indicate that they are editorial additions. Similarly, though no play of Shakespeare's was equipped with indications of the locale at the heads of scene divisions, locales have here been added in square brackets for the convenience of readers, who lack the information that costumes, properties, gestures, and scenery afford to spectators. Spectators can tell at a glance they are in the throne room, but without an editorial indication the reader may be puzzled for a while. It should be mentioned, incidentally, that there are a few authentic stage directions—perhaps Shakespeare's, perhaps a prompter's—that suggest locales, such as *"Enter Brutus in his orchard,"* and *"They go up into the Senate house."* It is hoped that the bracketed additions in the Signet text will provide readers with the sort of help provided by these two authentic directions, but it is equally hoped that the reader will remember that the stage was not loaded with scenery.

Shakespeare on the Stage

Each volume in the Signet Classic Shakespeare includes a brief stage (and sometimes film) history of the play. When we read about earlier productions, we are likely to find them eccentric, obviously wrongheaded—for instance, Nahum Tate's version of *King Lear*, with a happy ending, which held the stage for about a century and a half, from the late seventeenth century until the end of the first quarter of the nineteenth. We see engravings of David Garrick, the greatest actor of the eighteenth century, in eighteenth-century garb as King Lear, and we smile, thinking how absurd the production must have been. If we are more thoughtful, we say, with the English novelist L. P. Hartley, "The past is a foreign country: they do things differently there." But if the eighteenth-century staging is a foreign country, what of the plays of the late sixteenth and seventeenth centuries? A foreign language, a foreign theater, a foreign audience.

Probably all viewers of Shakespeare's plays, beginning with Shakespeare himself, at times have been unhappy with the plays on the stage. Consider three comments about production that we find in the plays themselves, which suggest Shakespeare's concerns. The Chorus in *Henry V* complains that the heroic story cannot possibly be adequately staged:

> But pardon, gentles all,
> The flat unraisèd spirits that hath dared
> On this unworthy scaffold to bring forth
> So great an object. Can this cockpit hold
> The vasty fields of France? Or may we cram
> Within this wooden *O* the very casques
> That did affright the air at Agincourt?
> . . . .
> Piece out our imperfections with your thoughts.
>
> (Prologue 1.8–14,23)

Second, here are a few sentences (which may or may not represent Shakespeare's own views) from Hamlet's longish lecture to the players:

> Speak the speech, I pray you, as I pronounced it to you, trippingly on the tongue. But if you mouth it, as many of our players do, I had as lief the town crier spoke my lines. . . . O, it offends me to the soul to hear a robustious periwig-pated fellow tear a passion to tatters, to very rags, to split the ears of the groundlings. . . . And let those that play your clowns speak no more than is set down for them, for there be of them that will themselves laugh, to set on some quantity of barren spectators to laugh too, though in the meantime some necessary question of the play be then to be considered. That's villainous and shows a most pitiful ambition in the fool that uses it. (3.2.1–47)

Finally, we can quote again from the passage cited earlier in this introduction, concerning the boy actors who played the female roles. Cleopatra imagines with horror a theatrical version of her activities with Antony:

> The quick comedians
> Extemporally will stage us, and present
> Our Alexandrian revels: Antony
> Shall be brought drunken forth, and I shall see
> Some squeaking Cleopatra boy my greatness
> I' th' posture of a whore.   (5.2.216–21)

It is impossible to know how much weight to put on such passages—perhaps Shakespeare was just being modest about his theater's abilities—but it is easy enough to think that he was unhappy with some aspects of Elizabethan production. Probably no production can fully satisfy a playwright, and for that matter, few productions can fully satisfy *us;* we regret this or that cut, this or that way of costuming the play, this or that bit of business.

One's first thought may be this: Why don't they just do "authentic" Shakespeare, "straight" Shakespeare, the play as Shakespeare wrote it? But as we read the plays—words written to be performed—it sometimes becomes clear that we do not know *how* to perform them. For instance, in *Antony and Cleopatra* Antony, the Roman general who has succumbed to Cleopatra and to Egyptian ways, says, "The nobleness of life / Is to do thus" (1.1.36–37). But what is "thus"? Does Antony at this point embrace Cleopatra? Does he embrace and kiss her? (There are, by the way, very few scenes of kissing on Shakespeare's stage, possibly because boys played the female roles.) Or does he make a sweeping gesture, indicating the Egyptian way of life?

This is not an isolated example; the plays are filled with lines that call for gestures, but we are not sure what the gestures should be. *Interpretation* is inevitable. Consider a passage in *Hamlet*. In 3.1, Polonius persuades his daughter, Ophelia, to talk to Hamlet while Polonius and Claudius eavesdrop. The two men conceal themselves, and Hamlet encounters Ophelia. At 3.1.131 Hamlet suddenly says to her, "Where's your father?" Why does Hamlet, apparently out of nowhere—they have not been talking about Polonius—ask this question? Is this an example of the "antic disposition" (fantastic behavior) that Hamlet earlier (1.5.172) had told Horatio and others—including us—he would display? That is, is the question about the whereabouts of her father a seemingly irrational one, like his earlier question (3.1.103) to Ophelia, "Ha, ha! Are you honest?" Or, on the other hand, has Hamlet (as in many productions) suddenly glimpsed Polonius's foot protruding from beneath a drapery at the rear? That is, does Hamlet ask the question because he has suddenly seen something suspicious and now is testing Ophelia? (By the way, in productions that do give Hamlet a physical cue, it is almost always Polonius rather than Claudius who provides the clue. This itself is an act of interpretation on the part of the director.) Or (a third possibility) does Hamlet get a clue from Ophelia, who inadvertently betrays the spies by nervously glancing at their place of hiding? This is the interpretation used in the BBC television version, where Ophelia glances in fear toward the hiding place just after Hamlet says "Why wouldst thou be a breeder of sinners?" (121–22). Hamlet, realizing that he is being observed, glances here and there *before* he asks "Where's your father?" The question thus is a climax to what he has been doing while speaking the preceding lines. Or (a fourth interpretation) does Hamlet suddenly, without the aid of any clue whatsoever, intuitively (insightfully, mysteriously, wonderfully) sense that someone is spying? Directors must decide, of course—and so must readers.

Recall, too, the preceding discussion of the texts of the plays, which argued that the texts—though they seem to be before us in permanent black on white—are unstable. The Signet text of *Hamlet*, which draws on the Second Quarto (1604) and the First Folio (1623) is considerably longer than any version staged in Shakespeare's time. Our version, even if spoken very briskly and played without any intermission, would take close to four hours, far beyond "the two hours' traffic of our stage" mentioned in the Prologue to *Romeo and Juliet*. (There are a few contemporary references to the duration of a play, but none mentions more than three hours.) Of Shakespeare's plays, only *The Comedy of Errors*, *Macbeth*, and *The Tempest* can be done in less than three hours without cutting. And even if we take a play that exists only in a short text, *Macbeth*, we cannot claim that we are experiencing the very play that Shakespeare conceived, partly because some of the Witches' songs almost surely are non-Shakespearean additions, and partly because we are not willing to watch the play performed without an intermission and with boys in the female roles.

Further, as the earlier discussion of costumes mentioned, the plays apparently were given chiefly in contemporary, that is, in Elizabethan dress. If today we give them in the costumes that Shakespeare probably saw, the plays seem not contemporary but curiously dated. Yet if we use our own dress, we find lines of dialogue that are at odds with what we see; we may feel that the language, so clearly not our own, is inappropriate coming out of people in today's dress. A common solution, incidentally, has been to set the plays in the nineteenth century, on the grounds that this attractively distances the plays (gives them a degree of foreignness, allowing for interesting costumes) and yet doesn't put them into a museum world of Elizabethan England.

Inevitably our productions are adaptations, *our* adaptations, and inevitably they will look dated, not in a century but in twenty years, or perhaps even in a decade. Still, we cannot escape from our own conceptions. As the director Peter Brook has said, in *The Empty Space* (1968):

> It is not only the hair-styles, costumes and make-ups that look dated. All the different elements of staging—the shorthands of behavior that stand for emotions; gestures, gesticulations and tones of voice—are all fluctuating on an invisible stock exchange all the time. . . . A living theatre that thinks it can stand aloof from anything as trivial as fashion will wilt. (p. 16)

As Brook indicates, it is through today's hairstyles, costumes, makeup, gestures, gesticulations, tones of voice— this includes our *conception* of earlier hairstyles, costumes, and so forth if we stage the play in a period other than our own—that we inevitably stage the plays.

It is a truism that every age invents its own Shakespeare, just as, for instance, every age has invented its own classical world. Our view of ancient Greece, a slave-holding society in which even free Athenian women were severely circumscribed, does not much resemble the Victorians' view of ancient Greece as a glorious democracy, just as, perhaps, our view of Victorianism itself does not much resemble theirs. We cannot claim that the Shakespeare on our stage is the true Shakespeare, but in our stage productions we find a Shakespeare that speaks to us, a Shakespeare that our ancestors doubtless did not know but one that seems to us to be the true Shakespeare—at least for a while.

Our age is remarkable for the wide variety of kinds of staging that it uses for Shakespeare, but one development deserves special mention. This is the now common practice of race-blind or color-blind or nontraditional casting, which allows persons who are not white to play in Shakespeare. Previously blacks performing in Shakespeare were limited to a mere three roles, Othello, Aaron (in *Titus Andronicus*), and the Prince of Morocco (in *The Merchant of Venice*), and there were no roles at all for Asians. Indeed, African-Americans rarely could play even one of these three roles, since they were not welcome in white companies. Ira Aldridge (c.1806–1867), a black actor of undoubted talent, was forced to make his living by performing Shakespeare in England and in Europe, where he could play not only Othello but also—in whiteface—other tragic roles such as King Lear. Paul Robeson (1898–1976) made theatrical history when he played Othello in London in 1930, and there was some talk about bringing the production to the United States, but there was more talk about whether American audiences would tolerate the sight of a black man—a real black man, not a white man in blackface—kissing and then killing a white woman. The idea was tried out in summer stock in 1942, the reviews were enthusiastic, and in the following year Robeson opened on Broadway in a production that ran an astounding 296 performances. An occasional all-black company sometimes performed Shakespeare's plays, but otherwise blacks (and other minority members) were in effect shut out from performing Shakespeare. Only since about 1970 has it been common for nonwhites to play major roles along with whites. Thus, in a 1996–97 production of *Antony and Cleopatra*, a white Cleopatra, Vanessa Redgrave, played opposite a black Antony, David Harewood.

Multiracial casting is now especially common at the New York Shakespeare Festival, founded in 1954 by Joseph Papp, and in England, where even siblings such as Claudio and Isabella in *Measure for Measure* or Lear's three daughters may be of different races. Probably most viewers today soon stop worrying about the lack of realism, and move beyond the color of the performers' skin to the quality of the performance.

Nontraditional casting is not only a matter of color or race; it includes sex. In the past, occasionally a distinguished woman of the theater has taken on a male role—Sarah Bernhardt (1844–1923) as Hamlet is perhaps the most famous example—but such performances were widely regarded as eccentric. Although today there have been some performances involving cross-dressing (a drag *As You Like It* staged by the National Theatre in England in 1966 and in the United States in 1974 has achieved considerable fame in the annals of stage history), what is more interesting is the casting of women in roles that traditionally are male but that need not be. Thus, a 1993–94 English production of *Henry V* used a woman—*not* cross-dressed—in the role of the governor of Harfleur. According to Peter Holland, who reviewed the production in *Shakespeare Survey* 48 (1995), "having a female Governor of Harfleur feminized the city and provided a direct response to the horrendous threat of rape and murder that Henry had offered, his language and her body in direct connection and opposition" (p. 210). Ten years from now the device may not play so effectively, but today it speaks to us. Shakespeare, born in the Elizabethan Age, has been dead nearly four hundred years, yet he is, as Ben Jonson said, "not of an age but for all time." We must understand, however, that he is "for all time" precisely because each age finds in his abundance something for itself and something of itself.

And here we come back to two issues discussed earlier in this introduction—the instability of the text and, curiously, the Bacon/Oxford heresy concerning the authorship of the plays. *Of course* Shakespeare wrote the plays, and we should daily fall on our knees to thank him for them—and yet there is something to the idea that he is not their only author. Every editor, every director and actor, and every reader to some degree shapes them, too, for when we edit, direct, act, or read, we inevitably become Shakespeare's collaborator and re-create the plays. The plays, one might say, are so cunningly contrived that they guide our responses, tell us how we ought to feel, and make a mark on us, but (for better or for worse) we also make a mark on them.

—SYLVAN BARNET
Tufts University

Introduction

In structure *Lear* differs significantly from the other tragedies of Shakespeare. It is like them in this. It dramatizes the fall of a hero who, assailed by the rebel passion, gives it sovereign sway and masterdom, and is in consequence destroyed. That is the case of Brutus, Othello, and Macbeth. But the resemblance is more ostensible than real. Ostensibly the play is one long denouement. In fact the declining action, which is the dogging of the hero to death, is complemented by a rising action, which is the hero's regeneration. As the tragic action moves down toward darkness, the more hopeful action that lives within it begins to emerge. This emergent, or renascent, action is a condition of the hero's loss of the world. The play fools us. Its primary story is not the descent of the King into Hell, but the ascent of the King as he climbs the Mountain of Purgatory and is fulfilled. The suspense the play develops is a function of the ascending action, which is not material but spiritual. Battles and thrones count for little. What does it profit a man if he gain the whole world and suffer the loss of his soul?

The rising and falling curves, the hero tasting his folly, the hero triumphing over it, intersect in the center of the play, in the fourth scene of Act 3. It is on the heath that Lear reaches his nadir. His characteristic utterance is the command: the wonted reversal follows: he is made less than the slave of a detested groom. These are the injuries that he himself has procured. So far the parallel is precise to the action of the other tragedies.

But now the crucial difference. It is also on the heath

that Lear is made pregnant to pity. That is another and an unexpected kind of reversal. "In boy, go first." These words, addressed to the Fool, who stands shivering in the rain before a hovel that is the refuge of a madman, constitute the real, as opposed to the apparent, hinge of the play. They do not signal the decay but the metamorphosis of the King, Lear the Socialist, got up in a red shirt. The great apostrophe to the poor follows at once:

> Poor naked wretches, wheresoe'er you are,
> That bide the pelting of this pitiless storm,
> How shall your houseless heads and unfed sides,
> Your looped and windowed raggedness, defend you
> From seasons such as these? O, I have ta'en
> Too little care of this!
>
> (28–33)

From this point, the action turns upward.

The structure of the subplot duplicates and so of course clarifies and confirms that of the central story. As the King is limed, and by his own folly, so are Gloucester and Edgar: "A credulous father, and a brother noble" (1.2.192). The one is, initially, an unthinking sensualist. The other, the younger, is initially a kind of clown: "and pat he comes like the catastrophe of the old comedy" (145–46). But the degradation of Gloucester is not ratified. He also undergoes a miraculous transformation. The critical point or pivot at which this transformation is announced is located, like Lear's, in the mathematical center of the play (3.3), which is also, with a fit symmetry, the symbolic center where meanings are clarified. The man who wants to please everyone and would have all well between the contending parties, is emboldened suddenly to choose. "If I die for it, as no less is threatened me, the King my old master must be relieved" (18–19). In that decision is his death, but also his salvation.

The retrieving of Edgar is more spectacular, if not so abruptly achieved. Edgar is conceded the chance to grow and prosper. He seizes his chance; he makes himself over. "Bear free and patient thoughts" (4.6.80). The dupe of the opening scenes is the philosopher who dominates in the close of the play.

This is not to pretend that the close is thereby made happy. "All's cheerless, dark, and deadly" (5.3.292). Kent's somber valediction is approved. If the kindness of the one daughter hints at the redemption of Nature, it does not take off entirely the general curse which twain have brought her to. The implication is uneasy in Edgar's assertion (as of one who is saying "what we ought to say") that man must obey the weight of the time. His flawed heart, on the evidence of the play, is too weak to support it. His nature cannot carry the affliction or the fear.

> What ribs of oak, when mountains melt on them,
> Can hold the mortise?   (*Othello*, 2.1)

Human beings endure until they expire, dying the pain of death every hour, in a night that pities neither wise man nor fool. What is more unsettling, to be wise is not to be provident. "Man may his fate foresee, but not prevent." And thus Webster's conclusion, in *The White Devil*: " 'Tis better to be fortunate than wise." Man is the natural fool of fortune. That is the title he is born with. It is the stars, and not our own endeavors, that govern. After all we are their tennis balls, struck and bandied which way please them. We do not get our deserts. The optimism is foolishness, to which we are prone.

> I would not take this from report. It is,
> And my heart breaks at it.   (4.6.143–44)

The wry conjunctions contrived by the playwright—who knows out of what bitterness or whimsy—attest to its folly. Edgar, in a sanguine mood, is sure that the worst returns to laughter. He is confronted at once with the bleeding visage of his father.

> The worst is not
> So long as we can say "This is the worst."   (4.1.26–27)

But Shakespeare is not done with him yet. "If ever I return to you again, I'll bring you comfort" (5.2.3–4). That is Edgar's promise to Gloucester before the battle. It is a rash promise, and poor comfort attends on it. A hiatus ensues, filled up with alarums and excursions. Then Edgar reenters and speaks again: "Away, old man. . . . King Lear hath lost" (5–6).

The optimism of Albany, as it is even more extravagant, is more sternly reproved.

> All friends shall taste
> The wages of their virtue, and all foes
> The cup of their deservings.   (5.3.305–06)

In that cheerful saying his philosophy is embodied. But the pentameter line, only three feet long, lacks its conclusion. Albany, rather cruelly, is made to supply the missing feet: "O, see, see!" It is the last agony of Lear to which his attention is directed.

Albany, as he presents the hopeful man who insists, a little too suavely, that God's in His Heaven, is Shakespeare's particular butt. It is he who cries, of Cordelia: "The gods defend her!" (258) The stage direction follows, enforcing the most monstrous conjunction in the play: "Enter Lear with Cordelia in his arms." The gods do not defend us. Perhaps they are unable to. "The gods reward your kindness," says Kent to Gloucester. That is the reading of the Folio, and surely it is the right reading. But the reading of the Quarto provokes speculation: "The gods deserve your kindness." It is as if the gods are weak, and require that humans collaborate with them in wielding the world. Lear, as his ardor for the right grows upon him, shakes the superflux to the wretched. His intent is, as he says, to show the heavens more just. It is at least tenable to interpret: his intent is to justify their feckless ways as he can.

Maybe the heavens are worse than insufficient. What is said of the King,

> If Fortune brag of two she loved and hated,
> One of them we behold,   (282–83)

suggests not merely a lack of capacity in the ordering of things, but a malevolent purpose, as if the gods had marked us down for their sport. On this reading, Lear's reference to himself and Cordelia as "God's spies" will mean, as an early commentator suggested, "spies placed over God Almighty, to watch his motions." Maybe there is need of surveillance, if

the human sacrifices on which the gods themselves throw incense are offered up for their pleasure; if the brand of fire that
parts the predestined victims is handed down, and with an antique malice, from Heaven. "Can so much wrath dwell in
heavenly spirits!" The Roman poet Virgil raised the question
first, and it is still a problem for Shakespeare. The chill that
invades us as, huddled with the others against the roaring
wind and rain, we await the advent of unaccommodated man:
"What art thou that dost grumble there i' th' straw?" is occa-
sioned by the wild surmise, so much more fearful because it
is involuntary, that the fiend is really walking up and down in
the earth, and with the sufferance and even the connivance of
Heaven. In the pitiless conclusion of *King Lear*,

> Thou'lt come no more,
> Never, never, never, never, never,   (309–10)

the dominion of the Prince of Darkness seems confirmed, and
his presence a substantial presence as, with his terrible vans,
he enshadows and overwhelms the just and the unjust alike.

That is, I daresay, only an apparition, the disnatured child
of night thoughts, and as such may be dispelled. But it needs
more than to rub one's eyes, or to mutter a pious ejaculation.
To such a degree is this true that even critics so tough-minded
as Dr. Johnson have averted their eyes rather than acquiesce
in the final horror with which the dramatist confronts them. It
is too literal, too realistic for "dramatick exhibition." And yet
it is remarkable that this play, in which Shakespeare's unremitting fidelity to fact is almost an occasion for scandal,
manifests in its beginning a studied and a deliberate indiffer-
ence to fact. If subsequent scenes are so realistic as hardly to
be endured, the opening scenes have not to do with realism
but with ritual and romance. Their abiding characteristic is a
niggling formality. They do not wear the aspect of life so
much as the aspect of art. Kent, lapsing into rude rhyme as he
takes his departure, catches and communicates that aspect.
His language is gnomic, admonitory, and simple—not
naïvely but consciously simple: "artificial." He is not, for the
moment, a real (an eccentric) man who displaces air like
Hamlet or Parolles. He is, and by design, a flat character,

highly conventionalized, who figures in an old-fashioned morality play. He would speak a prophecy before he goes.

The language of the other protagonists is of a piece with his. It does not evoke—not yet—the savage business of dragons of the prime (for all that the dragon is portentous in the threatening speeches of the King), so much as the ceremonious (the otherworldly!) business of proceedings at law and finance. Legal and fiscal metaphors reverberate. Gloucester, treating of his sons, asserts that the elder is no more dear than the younger, in his account. Lear, enacting his intention to abdicate the throne, renounces interest of territory, or possession. In lieu of Kent's insistence that he reserve his state, he stipulates his troop of knights as reservation, explicitly a legalism, in which the action of retaining a privilege is denoted. He would extend his largest bounty where nature challenges merit, or makes title to it. Regan, whose tenders of affection aim at that title, finds that Goneril has anticipated her very deed of love. The King, in whose simple-minded understanding love is a commodity, urges his youngest daughter to discover what portion her protestations can draw. But Cordelia loves only according to her bond. Failing to please, her price is fallen. Goneril pleases, in that she is taken as permitting to her father twice the retinue permitted by Regan. Her devotion may therefore be measured. She is precisely twice her sister's love.

Lear is not easily persuaded of his error, that devotion— in his psychology, a ponderable thing—is to be assessed and ought to be requited in ponderable ways. The inadmissible equation is there still, in the crass appeal to Regan when his agony is upon him:

> Thy half o' th' kingdom hast thou not forgot,
> Wherein I thee endowed.   (2.4.178–79)

He is appropriately answered, since that respects of fortune are his love:

> Good sir, to the purpose.   (180)

This veneer of the unreal and the ritualistic, overlaying the initial action of the play, is not peculiar to the love test. The characters themselves move in an air of unreality. There is about them a felt sense of contradiction, as between what they are and what they seem to be. Lear is not a king but the show of a king. It is an insubstantial pageant over which he presides, recalling, in its unreality, the specious parade with which an earlier tragedy of Shakespeare's commences, that of Richard II, the mockery king of snows. Kent's acumen is verified when, with a lack of respect that is intended to shock and thereby to quicken perception, he sees and salutes his master, not as a monarch but as an old man.

But if Lear is an unreal image, so are the wicked daughters. Their essential vacuity, echoing to the touch, announces itself as it issues in their exaggerated protestings of love. Kent points to it obliquely in his praise of Cordelia:

> Nor are those empty-hearted whose low sounds
> Reverb no hollowness.   (1.1.155–56)

Gloucester discerns it, magnified to cosmic proportions, in the disordered state of the macrocosm, riven by machinations, by the hollowness that is hypocrisy. All that glisters is taken for gold. The pretension of the hypocrite, who professes herself

> an enemy to all other joys
> Which the most precious square of sense professes,   (73–74)

weighs more than the practice of the candid and guileless retainer, who professes himself to be no less than he seems. The mere appearance is everything, and hence what is lifelike and vital is eclipsed. The characters are cut in alabaster, like monumental statues. The same metaphor describes the fool and the knave and the paragon of virtue, divesting each of human personality. Gloucester, who seems a good old man, is brazed by self-indulgence, become like hard metal. Regan, in whom nature appears tender-hefted, is hardened to insensibility, made of that self metal as her sister. Cordelia is, conversely, a little-seeming substance. But Cordelia is rendered also in nonhuman terms: her love, a precious metal, is more ponderous than her tongue.

Stylization of language and gesture is notable in such

a play as *The Tempest*, and for excellent and obvious reasons. Shakespeare's resort to it in *King Lear* seems, however, gratuitous, and even antipathetic to the spirit of the play. *Lear* is not masquelike nor, certainly, romantic, in the harrowing story it tells. But observe that *The Tempest* begins, not formally, but realistically, with the faithful depicting of a ship driving on the rocks, a wild and literal scene in which the blasphemy and execration of real and affrighted persons bass the throbbing of the storm. And then the scene shifts abruptly. The auditor or reader, whose belief is purchased at the outset by a terrific glimpse of the real world, is brought safe to shore: is induced to enter, and willingly, the world of enchantment and romance. The fact of the transition, and the implausibility attendant on it, elude him. The tempest is still dinning in his ears.

In *King Lear* the dramatic problem is exactly reversed. It is to ensure that those whose disenchantment the playwright is already preparing, who are to be compelled to look on the Gorgon-features, will not evince incredulity or petrifaction. The problem is resolved by emphasizing at the outset the elements of unreality and romance. The impelling action of *Lear* is made to resemble a fairy tale, which is, I suppose, its ultimate source. The auditor or reader is fooled. Before he is aware, he has become a participant in the fierce and excessively painful dispute between damnation and impassioned clay.

But there is more than craft to Shakespeare's design in thus introducing his drama. He makes his characters unreal initially because he means them, at least in part, to be symbolic. The stylized quality of the beginning, as of a charade, its legalistic and ceremonious nature, the exalting in it of appearance as against reality, all work to the fulfilling of that primary intention. And though *Lear* is essentially representational drama, though realism very quickly takes precedence over ritual, the element of the symbolic is never dissipated altogether but figures in important ways until the end. Just as in *Twelfth Night*, whose burden is mistaken identity and the hocus-pocus of identical twins, realism intrudes persistently to temper and give substance to romance—

In nature there's no blemish but the mind;
None can be called deformèd but the unkind.
Virtue is beauty; but the beauteous evil
Are empty trunks, o'erflourished by the devil.

                               (*Twelfth Night*, 3.4.379–82)

—so in *King Lear,* an anti-romantic play in that its burden is
a relentless anatomizing of evil, the symbolic declines to
yield entirely to the representational. It persists, not to give
substance to the real, which is substantial enough—

        Out, vile jelly!
   Where is thy luster now?   (3.7.84–85)

—but to order the real and make it meaningful, to avoid
a confounding of it with the merely sensational. Not to grasp
this ordering function is, necessarily, to run counter, to smell
a fault where no fault is. Thus the embarrassment of critics so
estimable as Goethe (for whom the action of the play was a
tissue of the improbable and absurd), and Coleridge (who
saw the first scene as dispensable), and A. C. Bradley (who
detected and enumerated in the whole, more and grosser in-
consistencies than in any other of the great tragedies).

Misconstruction of the role and character of Cordelia
typifies this failure to come to terms with the symbolic.
Cordelia is, of old, a deeply disquieting figure. Why does
she love, and yet remain silent? The question has en-
gendered a little galaxy of answers. It is a question not
to be asked. The first principle of good dramatic manners
is to concede to the dramatist his given, so long as he
is able to exploit it. Here, the given is the heroine's fatal
reserve. It is the lever that starts the play on its progress. As
such, it may not be queried, any more than the procedure
that governs in chess or in the writing of an Italian sonnet.

But "reserve" is after all the wrong word. It suggests the
wrong frame of reference. It leads to the rationalization of
conduct on realistic grounds. To make the horrid point, this
judgment of a contemporary critic may be cited, that
Cordelia loved her father "less than she loved her own way
and hated her sisters." That is a fair sample of the appeal to
realism. It is at all costs to be avoided. Cordelia does not

betray, what Coleridge thought to perceive, "some little faulty admixture of pride and sullenness." No stain of guilt or responsibility attaches to her. She is not imperious, like the King, not headstrong, not intractable. The appeal to heredity is a variation of the appeal to realism, and is, in this context, equally and altogether inapposite. Shakespeare's characters, unlike Eugene O'Neill's, have no antecedents. It is of no use to say that Cordelia is her father's daughter. The reason she will not speak is because she cannot speak; and she cannot because the heart of a fool is in his mouth but the mouth of the wise is in his heart.

This is to say that the muteness of Cordelia (like the fantastic credulity of Gloucester) is not so much a reflection of character as it is the embodiment of an idea. Less real than symbolic, her affinity is more to a creature of fairy tale like Cinderella than to a heroine of the realistic drama like Blanche DuBois in *A Streetcar Named Desire*. In delineating her behavior the playwright may be, psychologically, so penetrating and exact as really to catch the manners living as they rise: that is partly an extra, added attraction, over and above what we need. More important is his intention, not to portray a believable woman, but to dramatize the proposition that plainness is more than eloquence, that beauty is to be purchased by the weight, that meager lead, which rather threatens than promises aught, buys more than silver and gold. The agitation of those who worry the details of the love test in an attempt to make it credible, which means to make it conformable to the canons of the realistic theater, is founded on their misapprehension of symbolic action.

When Cordelia is depicted as the last and least, it is not her slightness of stature that the dramatist is glancing at— or not that, decisively. He is preparing an ironic and a pregnant echo, to amplify Kent's assertion, a little later:

> Thy youngest daughter does not love thee least.   (1.1.154)

But more than that, he is invoking the promise of Scripture, unspoken in the play, and yet close to the theme, which is the heart (but not the moral!) of the play: The first shall be

last and the last shall be first. When Cordelia herself exclaims, as she prepares to engage the British powers,

> O dear father,
> It is thy business that I go about,   (4.4.23–24)

it is not altogether the realistic business of an imminent battle to which she is adverting. (Certainly that business does
not much preoccupy Shakespeare.) And therefore we are
not to wonder why the King of France was, so inopportu-
nely, called back to his kingdom, nor whether Shakespeare's allegiance or circumspection dictated the victory of
the English. We want to catch in what is said an older saying, the sentence of the Evangelist, so much more than a literary reminiscence, and estimate accordingly the symbolic
role the speaker plays: "Knew ye not that I must go about
my father's business." It may be that Cordelia is that quin-
tessence of womanhood celebrated reverentially (and with
an appropriate silence as to particulars) by critics like A. W.
Schlegel: "Of Cordelia's heavenly beauty of soul, I do not
dare to speak." But it is not after all the literal woman to
whom Shakespeare is holding up the mirror. Compare Beat-
rice in *Much Ado*, or Rosalind in *As You Like It*.

It is a nice but an indispensable point to determine, just
when the dramatist intends that the canons of ordinary realism are to be set aside or, better, transcended. Pretty
clearly he wishes to transcend them when, in Act 2, Kent
is made to sleep in the stocks, and Edgar, unmindful of
him, to step forward and tell of his proposed transformation. Bradley is bemused: "One cannot help asking . . .
whether Edgar is mad that he should return from his
hollow tree . . . to his father's castle in order to solilo-
quize." But Shakespeare, in juxtaposing the two characters, is not concerned with motivation or, certainly, with
locale. No doubt the Bedlam is understood to remain on
the heath. But precisely where he is, is not a question that
ought to detain us. Neither are we to ask why he fails to
perceive that someone else is up there with him on
stage, in full view of the audience, and so, presumably, of
himself; nor how Kent, for all his travails, can sleep

undisturbed through twenty lines of blank verse. In the bringing together of the two good men, each of whom has been driven to the lowest and most dejected point of fortune, a dramatic emblem is achieved, a speaking picture, whose purport is not realistic but symbolic. What Shakespeare is after is this dark asssociation, or sequence:

> A good man's fortune may grow out at heels.   (2.2.160)

> Edgar I nothing am.   (2.3.21)

In the same way the symbolic overtops the conventionally real when, in the final act, Edgar issues his challenge to Edmund. One is not to belabor the improbability of Edmund's failure to recognize his brother, though, in point of fact, the failure is itself symbolic: the villain is indeed beguiled, and not because the plot demands this but because of his own willful behavior. But what is central to the scene is the intimation one hears, in the blast of the trumpet that announces the combat, of that final trump that vindicates the right and summons the perpetrator of wrong to the Judgment. When—another illustration—Edgar, opposing Oswald, assumes the character of a rustic, the clownish dialect he speaks is, realistically, absurd: what is its occasion? Symbolically, however, it is deeply congruous. The power of truth is attested to, however ludicrous its aspect, and the frailty which is falsehood exposed, in this meeting of the ragged fellow, whose West Country accent gives him out to be a bumpkin, but who intrinsically merits and possesses all honors, and the gilded courtier, whose extrinsic show and sophistication betoken all honors and are as paste and cover to none.

> The Prince of Darkness is a gentleman.   (3.4.146)

In Edgar's vanquishing of Oswald, which is the triumph of the lowly and the unprepossessing over the world of robes and furred gowns, Lear's great social speeches are enacted and answered.

A similar intention, to effect on stage a symbolic tableau, dictates the grouping of the protagonists at the end of the

play. All are there in the resolution, occupying, I think, the
same positions they assumed at first, and not least the
wicked sisters, whose dead bodies are brought on, no doubt
to exemplify this judgment of the heavens, but more, to direct the attention of the audience back and back, over all
the dreadful ground that has been traced, to the opening
scene. In their beginning is their ending. Perhaps the great
wheel of the play, now come full circle, is impelled in its
progress by something more than mechanical law.

What this other law may be is the central question Shakespeare poses and endeavors to answer. Lear, as is fitting, is
made to enunciate it: "Who is it that can tell me who I am?"
(1.4.236) But the question is not peculiar to Lear but is im-
plicit in the utterance and conduct of all those who inhabit the
darkness with him. Kent as Caius is interrogated by the King:

> What art thou?
> A man, sir.   (10–11)

But what is it, to be a man? What is man to profess?
To what law are his services bound? Gloucester interrogates
Edgar: "Now, good sir, what are you?" and is answered:

> A most poor man, made tame to fortune's blows,
> Who, by the art of known and feeling sorrows,
> Am pregnant to good pity.   (4.6.224–25)

Cornwall, whose disposition will not be rubbed or stopped,
does not manifest that pity. It is ascendant, though tardily,
in Gloucester, who, if he dies for it, must relieve his master. Why is that? And why had Kent rather break his own
heart than the King's? How does one construe that fitness
to which Albany appeals, in declining to let his hands
obey his blood; or that pleasure, a more intriguing word,
which inclines the Old Man to succor the blinded Gloucester, "Come on't what will"? What point inheres in Albany's characterization of Oswald, as Oswald reports it:

> he called me sot,
> And told me I had turned the wrong side out;   (4.2.8–9)

and in what manner does it comment on the Captain's decision to collaborate in the killing of the King and Cordelia:

> If it be man's work, I'll do it.   (5.3.40)

There ought here to ensue a brief though perceptible silence, in token of the irony and expectation with which these laconic words are charged. The dramatist is bidding us essay a definition of the nature of man's work and, concomitantly, of the nature of man. Edmund, with his customary coldbloodedness, addresses himself to the task:

> men
> Are as the time is.   (31–32)

Kent speaks to it, describing Oswald:

> A tailor made thee.   (2.2.55–56)

So in whimsical ways does the Fool, begging pardon of Goneril:

> Cry you mercy, I took you for a joint stool;   (3.6.51)

and also the King, whose confusion is at once real and assumed:

> Your name, fair gentlewoman?   (1.4.242)

and, in sterner ways, the Servant, drawing his sword against Cornwall:

> Nay, then, come on, and take the chance of anger.   (3.7.79–80)

To divine the way in which these lines reticulate is to resolve at least a corner of the mystery which is the play.

—RUSSELL FRASER
University of Michigan

The Tragedy of
KING LEAR

[DRAMATIS PERSONAE

Lear, King of Britain
King of France
Duke of Burgundy
Duke of Cornwall, husband to Regan
Duke of Albany, husband to Goneril
Earl of Kent
Earl of Gloucester
Edgar, son to Gloucester
Edmund, bastard son to Gloucester
Curan, a courtier
Oswald, steward to Goneril
Old Man, tenant to Gloucester
Doctor
Lear's Fool
A Captain, subordinate to Edmund
Gentlemen, attending on Cordelia
A Herald
Servants to Cornwall
Goneril ⎫
Regan ⎬ daughters to Lear
Cordelia ⎭
Knights attending on Lear, Officers,
    Messengers, Soldiers, Attendants

Scene: Britain]

The Tragedy of King Lear

ACT 1

Scene 1.   [*King Lear's palace.*]

Enter Kent, Gloucester, and Edmund.

Kent. I thought the King had more affected°¹ the Duke
of Albany° than Cornwall.

Gloucester. It did always seem so to us; but now, in
the division of the kingdom, it appears not which of
the dukes he values most, for equalities are so   5
weighed that curiosity in neither can make choice of
either's moiety.°

Kent. Is not this your son, my lord?

Gloucester. His breeding,° sir, hath been at my
charge. I have so often blushed to acknowledge   10
him that now I am brazed° to't.

Kent. I cannot conceive° you.

Gloucester. Sir, this young fellow's mother could;
whereupon she grew round-wombed, and had in-
deed, sir, a son for her cradle ere she had a hus-   15
band for her bed. Do you smell a fault?

¹ The degree sign (°) indicates a footnote, which is keyed to the text by line
number. Text references are printed in **boldface** type; the annotation follows in roman type.
1.1.1 **affected** loved   2 **Albany** Albanacte, whose domain extended "from
the river Humber to the point of Caithness" (Holinshed)   5-7 **equalities . . .
moiety** i.e., shares are so balanced against one another that careful examination by neither can make him wish the other's portion   9 **breeding** up-
bringing   11 **brazed** made brazen, hardened   12 **conceive** understand (pun
follows)

3

Kent. I cannot wish the fault undone, the issue° of it
  being so proper.°

Gloucester. But I have a son, sir, by order of law,
20 some year elder than this, who yet is no dearer
  in my account:° though this knave° came something saucily° to the world before he was sent for,
  yet was his mother fair, there was good sport at his
  making, and the whoreson° must be acknowl-
25 edged. Do you know this noble gentleman, Edmund?

Edmund. No, my lord.

Gloucester. My Lord of Kent. Remember him here-
  after as my honorable friend.

30 *Edmund.* My services to your lordship.

Kent. I must love you, and sue° to know you better.

Edmund. Sir, I shall study deserving.

Gloucester. He hath been out° nine years, and away he
  shall again. The King is coming.

  Sound a sennet.° Enter one bearing a coronet,°
  then King Lear, then the Dukes of Cornwall
  and Albany, next Goneril, Regan, Cordelia,
  and Attendants.

35 *Lear.* Attend the lords of France and Burgundy,
  Gloucester.

Gloucester. I shall, my lord.   *Exit [with Edmund].*

Lear. Meantime we shall express our darker purpose.°
  Give me the map there. Know that we have divided
40 In three our kingdom; and 'tis our fast° intent
  To shake all cares and business from our age,
  Conferring them on younger strengths, while we

---

17 **issue** result (child)   18 **proper** handsome   21 **account** estimation   21
knave fellow (without disapproval)   22 **saucily** (1) insolently (2) lasciviously
24 **whoreson** fellow (lit., son of a whore)   31 **sue** entreat   33 **out** away,
abroad   34 s.d. **sennet** set of notes played on a trumpet, signalizing the
entrance or departure of a procession   34 s.d. **coronet** small crown, intended
for Cordelia   38 **darker purpose** hidden intention   40 **fast** fixed

Unburthened crawl toward death. Our son of
   Cornwall,
And you our no less loving son of Albany,
We have this hour a constant will to publish°   45
Our daughters' several° dowers, that future strife
May be prevented° now. The Princes, France and
   Burgundy,
Great rivals in our youngest daughter's love,
Long in our court have made their amorous sojourn,
And here are to be answered. Tell me, my daughters 50
(Since now we will divest us both of rule,
Interest° of territory, cares of state),
Which of you shall we say doth love us most,
That we our largest bounty may extend
Where nature doth with merit challenge.° Goneril,   55
Our eldest-born, speak first.

Goneril. Sir, I love you more than word can wield°
   the matter;
Dearer than eyesight, space° and liberty;
Beyond what can be valued, rich or rare;
No less than life, with grace, health, beauty, honor;   60
As much as child e'er loved, or father found;
A love that makes breath° poor, and speech
   unable:°
Beyond all manner of so much° I love you.

Cordelia. [*Aside*] What shall Cordelia speak? Love,
   and be silent.

Lear. Of all these bounds, even from this line to this,   65
With shadowy forests, and with champains riched,°
With plenteous rivers, and wide-skirted meads,°
We make thee lady. To thine and Albany's issues°
Be this perpetual.° What says our second daughter,

45 **constant will to publish** fixed intention to proclaim 46 **several**
separate 47 **prevented** forestalled 52 **Interest** legal right 55 **nature …
challenge** i.e., natural affection contends with desert for (or lays claim to)
bounty 57 **wield** handle 58 **space** scope 62 **breath** language 62 **unable**
impotent 63 **Beyond … much** beyond all these comparisons 66 **champains riched** enriched plains 67 **wide-skirted meads** extensive grass-
lands 68 **issues** descendants 69 **perpetual** in perpetuity

70   Our dearest Regan, wife of Cornwall? Speak.

Regan. I am made of that self mettle° as my sister,
    And prize me at her worth.° In my true heart
    I find she names my very deed of love;°
    Only she comes too short, that° I profess
75   Myself an enemy to all other joys
    Which the most precious square of sense
       professes,°
    And find I am alone felicitate°
    In your dear Highness' love.

Cordelia.   [*Aside*] Then poor Cordelia!
    And yet not so, since I am sure my love's
80   More ponderous° than my tongue.

Lear. To thee and thine hereditary ever
    Remain this ample third of our fair kingdom,
    No less in space, validity,° and pleasure
    Than that conferred on Goneril. Now, our joy,
85   Although our last and least;° to whose young love
    The vines of France and milk° of Burgundy
    Strive to be interest;° what can you say to draw
    A third more opulent than your sisters? Speak.

Cordelia. Nothing, my lord.

90 *Lear.* Nothing?

Cordelia. Nothing.

Lear. Nothing will come of nothing. Speak again.

Cordelia. Unhappy that I am, I cannot heave
    My heart into my mouth. I love your Majesty
95   According to my bond,° no more nor less.

Lear. How, how, Cordelia? Mend your speech a little,
    Lest you may mar your fortunes.

---

71 **self mettle** same material or temperament   72 **prize ... worth** value me the same (imperative)   73 **my ... love** what my love really is (a legalism)   74 **that** in that   76 **Which ... professes** which the choicest estimate of sense avows   77 **felicitate** made happy   80 **ponderous** weighty 83 **validity** value   85 **least** youngest, smallest   86 **milk** i.e., pastures   87 **interest** closely connected, as interested parties   95 **bond** i.e., filial obligation

Cordelia.   Good my lord,
   You have begot me, bred me, loved me. I
   Return those duties back as are right fit,°
   Obey you, love you, and most honor you.   *100*
   Why have my sisters husbands, if they say
   They love you all? Haply,° when I shall wed,
   That lord whose hand must take my plight° shall
     carry
   Half my love with him, half my care and duty.
   Sure I shall never marry like my sisters,   *105*
   To love my father all.

Lear. But goes thy heart with this?

Cordelia.   Ay, my good lord.

Lear. So young, and so untender?

Cordelia. So young, my lord, and true.

Lear. Let it be so, thy truth then be thy dower!   *110*
   For, by the sacred radiance of the sun,
   The mysteries of Hecate° and the night,
   By all the operation of the orbs°
   From whom we do exist and cease to be,
   Here I disclaim all my paternal care,   *115*
   Propinquity and property of blood,°
   And as a stranger to my heart and me
   Hold thee from this for ever. The barbarous
     Scythian,°
   Or he that makes his generation messes°
   To gorge his appetite, shall to my bosom   *120*
   Be as well neighbored, pitied, and relieved,
   As thou my sometime° daughter.

Kent.   Good my liege——

Lear. Peace, Kent!

99 **Return ... fit** i.e., am correspondingly dutiful   102 **Haply** perhaps
103 **plight** troth plight   112 **mysteries of Hecate** secret rites of Hecate
(goddess of the infernal world, and of witchcraft)   113 **operation of
the orbs** astrological influence   116 **Propinquity and property of blood**
relationship and common blood   118 **Scythian** (type of the savage)   119
makes his generation messes eats his own offspring   122 **sometime**
former

Come not between the Dragon° and his wrath.
125 I loved her most, and thought to set my rest°
On her kind nursery.° Hence and avoid my sight!
So be my grave my peace, as here I give
Her father's heart from her! Call France. Who stirs?
Call Burgundy. Cornwall and Albany,
130 With my two daughters' dowers digest° the third;
Let pride, which she calls plainness, marry her.°
I do invest you jointly with my power,
Pre-eminence, and all the large effects
That troop with majesty.° Ourself,° by monthly
        course,
135 With reservation° of an hundred knights,
By you to be sustained, shall our abode
Make with you by due turn. Only we shall retain
The name, and all th' addition° to a king. The sway,
Revènue, execution of the rest,
140 Belovèd sons, be yours; which to confirm,
This coronet° part between you.

Kent.   Royal Lear,
Whom I have ever honored as my king,
Loved as my father, as my master followed,
As my great patron thought on in my prayers——

Lear. The bow is bent and drawn; make from the
145   shaft.°

Kent. Let it fall° rather, though the fork° invade
The region of my heart. Be Kent unmannerly
When Lear is mad. What wouldst thou do, old
        man?
Think'st thou that duty shall have dread to speak

---

124 **Dragon** (1) heraldic device of Britain (2) emblem of ferocity   125 **set
my rest** (1) stake my all (a term from the card game of primero) (2) find my
rest   126 **nursery** care, nursing   130 **digest** absorb   131 **Let . . . her** i.e.,
let her pride be her dowry and gain her a husband   134-35 **effects/That
troop with majesty** accompaniments that go with kingship   134 **Ourself**
(the royal "we")   135 **reservation** the action of reserving a privilege (a legalism)   138 **addition** titles and honors   141 **coronet** (the crown which
was to have been Cordelia's)   145 **make from the shaft** avoid the
arrow   146 **fall** strike   146 **fork** forked head of the arrow

When power to flattery bows? To plainness honor's
   bound   150
When majesty falls to folly. Reserve thy state,°
And in thy best consideration° check
This hideous rashness. Answer my life my
   judgment,°
Thy youngest daughter does not love thee least,
Nor are those empty-hearted whose low sounds   155
Reverb° no hollowness.°

Lear.   Kent, on thy life, no more!

Kent. My life I never held but as a pawn°
To wage° against thine enemies; nor fear to lose it,
Thy safety being motive.°

Lear.   Out of my sight!

Kent. See better, Lear, and let me still° remain   160
The true blank° of thine eye.

Lear. Now by Apollo——

Kent.   Now by Apollo, King,
Thou swear'st thy gods in vain.

Lear.   O vassal! Miscreant!°
                [*Laying his hand on his sword.*]

Albany, Cornwall. Dear sir, forbear!

Kent. Kill thy physician, and the fee bestow   165
Upon the foul disease. Revoke thy gift,
Or, whilst I can vent clamor° from my throat,
I'll tell thee thou dost evil.

Lear.   Hear me, recreant!°
On thine allegiance,° hear me!
That thou hast sought to make us break our vows,   170

---

151 **Reserve thy state** retain your kingly authority   152 **best consideration**
most careful reflection   153 **Answer . . . judgment** I will stake my life on
my opinion   156 **Reverb** reverberate   156 **hollowness** (1) emptiness (2) in-
sincerity   157 **pawn** stake in a wager   158 **wage** (1) wager (2) carry on
war   159 **motive** moving cause   160 **still** always   161 **blank** the white
spot in the center of the target (at which Lear should aim)   163 **vassal! Miscreant!** base wretch! Misbeliever!   167 **vent clamor** utter a cry   168 **recreant** traitor   169 **On thine allegiance** (to forswear, which is to commit high
treason)

Which we durst never yet, and with strained° pride
To come betwixt our sentence° and our power,
Which nor our nature nor our place can bear,
Our potency made good,° take thy reward.

175 Five days we do allot thee for provision°
To shield thee from diseases° of the world,
And on the sixth to turn thy hated back
Upon our kingdom. If, on the tenth day following,
Thy banished trunk° be found in our dominions,

180 The moment is thy death. Away! By Jupiter,
This shall not be revoked.

Kent. Fare thee well, King. Sith° thus thou wilt appear,
Freedom lives hence, and banishment is here.
[*To Cordelia*] The gods to their dear shelter take
      thee, maid,

185 That justly think'st, and hast most rightly said.
[*To Regan and Goneril*] And your large speeches
      may your deeds approve,°
That good effects° may spring from words of love.
Thus Kent, O Princes, bids you all adieu;
He'll shape his old course° in a country new. *Exit.*

*Flourish.° Enter Gloucester, with France and
      Burgundy; Attendants.*

190 *Gloucester.* Here's France and Burgundy, my noble
      lord.

Lear. My Lord of Burgundy,
We first address toward you, who with this king
Hath rivaled for our daughter. What in the least
Will you require in present° dower with her,
Or cease your quest of love?

195 *Burgundy.*   Most royal Majesty,
I crave no more than hath your Highness offered,

---

171 **strained** forced (and so excessive)   172 **sentence** judgment, decree
174 **Our potency made good** my royal authority being now asserted   175 **for
provision** for making preparation   176 **diseases** troubles   179 **trunk** body
182 **Sith** since   186 **approve** prove true   187 **effects** results   189 **shape . . .
course** pursue his customary way   189 s.d. **Flourish** trumpet fanfare
194 **present** immediate

Nor will you tender° less.

Lear.   Right noble Burgundy,
When she was dear° to us, we did hold her so;
But now her price is fallen. Sir, there she stands.
If aught within that little seeming substance,°   *200*
Or all of it, with our displeasure pieced,°
And nothing more, may fitly like° your Grace,
She's there, and she is yours.

Burgundy.   I know no answer.

Lear. Will you, with those infirmities she owes,°
Unfriended, new adopted to our hate,   *205*
Dow'red with our curse, and strangered° with our
      oath,
Take her, or leave her?

Burgundy.   Pardon me, royal sir.
Election makes not up° on such conditions.

Lear. Then leave her, sir; for, by the pow'r that made
      me,
I tell you all her wealth. [*To France.*] For you,
      great King,   *210*
I would not from your love make such a stray
To° match you where I hate; therefore beseech° you
T' avert your liking a more worthier way°
Than on a wretch whom nature is ashamed
Almost t' acknowledge hers.

France.   This is most strange,   *215*
That she whom even but now was your best object,°
The argument° of your praise, balm of your age,
The best, the dearest, should in this trice of time
Commit a thing so monstrous to dismantle°

---

197 **tender** offer   198 **dear** (1) beloved (2) valued at a high price   200 **little seeming substance** person who is (1) inconsiderable (2) outspoken
201 **pieced** added to it   202 **fitly like** please by its fitness   204 **owes** possesses   206 **strangered** made a stranger   208 **Election makes not up** no
one can choose   211-12 **make such a stray / To** stray so far as to
212 **beseech** I beseech   213 **avert . . . way** turn your affections from her
and bestow them on a better person   216 **best object** i.e., the one you loved
most   217 **argument** subject   219 **dismantle** strip off

220   So many folds of favor. Sure her offense
         Must be of such unnatural degree
         That monsters it,° or your fore-vouched° affection
         Fall into taint;° which to believe of her
         Must be a faith that reason without miracle
         Should never plant in me.°

225 *Cordelia.*   I yet beseech your Majesty,
         If for° I want that glib and oily art
         To speak and purpose not,° since what I well intend
         I'll do't before I speak, that you make known
         It is no vicious blot, murder, or foulness,
230   No unchaste action or dishonored step,
         That hath deprived me of your grace and favor;
         But even for want of that for which I am richer,
         A still-soliciting° eye, and such a tongue
         That I am glad I have not, though not to have it
         Hath lost° me in your liking.

235 *Lear.*   Better thou
         Hadst not been born than not t' have pleased me
         better.

France. Is it but this? A tardiness in nature°
         Which often leaves the history unspoke°
         That it intends to do. My Lord of Burgundy,
240   What say you° to the lady? Love's not love
         When it is mingled with regards° that stands
         Aloof from th' entire point.° Will you have her?
         She is herself a dowry.

Burgundy.   Royal King,
         Give but that portion which yourself proposed,
245   And here I take Cordelia by the hand,
         Duchess of Burgundy.

222 **That monsters it** as makes it monstrous, unnatural   222 **fore-vouched** previously sworn   223 **Fall into taint** must be taken as having been unjustified all along i.e., Cordelia was unworthy of your love from the first   224-25 **reason . . . me** my reason would have to be supported by a miracle to make me believe   226 **for** because   227 **purpose not** not mean to do what I promise   233 **still-soliciting** always begging   235 **lost** ruined   237 **tardiness in nature** natural reticence   238 **leaves the history unspoke** does not announce the action   240 **What say you** i.e., will you have   241 **regards** considerations (the dowry)   241-42 **stands . . . point** have nothing to do with the essential question (love)

Lear. Nothing. I have sworn. I am firm.

Burgundy. I am sorry then you have so lost a father
　　That you must lose a husband.

Cordelia.　　　　　　　　　　Peace be with Burgundy.
　　Since that respects of fortune° are his love,　　　　　250
　　I shall not be his wife.

France. Fairest Cordelia, that art most rich being
　　　　poor,
　　Most choice forsaken, and most loved despised,
　　Thee and thy virtues here I seize upon.
　　Be it lawful I take up what's cast away.　　　　　　255
　　Gods, gods! 'Tis strange that from their cold'st
　　　　neglect
　　My love should kindle to inflamed respect.°
　　Thy dow'rless daughter, King, thrown to my
　　　　chance,°
　　Is Queen of us, of ours, and our fair France.
　　Not all the dukes of wat'rish° Burgundy　　　　　260
　　Can buy this unprized precious° maid of me.
　　Bid them farewell, Cordelia, though unkind.
　　Thou losest here, a better where° to find.

Lear. Thou hast her, France; let her be thine, for we
　　Have no such daughter, nor shall ever see　　　　　265
　　That face of hers again. Therefore be gone,
　　Without our grace, our love, our benison.°
　　Come, noble Burgundy.

　　　　Flourish. Exeunt [*Lear, Burgundy, Cornwall,*
　　　　　Albany, Gloucester, and Attendants].

France. Bid farewell to your sisters.

Cordelia. The jewels of our father,° with washed°
　　　　eyes　　　　　　　　　　　　　　　　　270
　　Cordelia leaves you. I know you what you are,

250 **respects of fortune** mercenary considerations　257 **inflamed respect**
more ardent affection　258 **chance** lot　260 **wat'rish** (1) with many rivers
(2) weak, diluted　261 **unprized precious** unappreciated by others, and yet
precious　263 **here . . . where** in this place, in another place　267 **benison**
blessing　270 **The jewels of our father** you creatures prized by our father
270 **washed** (1) weeping (2) clear-sighted

And, like a sister,° am most loath to call
Your faults as they are named.° Love well our
    father.
To your professèd° bosoms I commit him.
275 But yet, alas, stood I within his grace,
I would prefer° him to a better place.
So farewell to you both.

Regan. Prescribe not us our duty.

Goneril.   Let your study
Be to content your lord, who hath received you
280 At Fortune's alms.° You have obedience scanted,°
And well are worth the want that you have wanted.°

Cordelia. Time shall unfold what plighted° cunning
    hides,
Who covers faults, at last shame them derides.°
Well may you prosper.

France.   Come, my fair Cordelia.
                         Exit France and Cordelia.

285 *Goneril.* Sister, it is not little I have to say of what
most nearly appertains to us both. I think our father
will hence tonight.

Regan. That's most certain, and with you; next month
with us.

290 *Goneril.* You see how full of changes his age is. The
observation we have made of it hath not been little.
He always loved our sister most, and with what
poor judgment he hath now cast her off appears
too grossly.°

295 *Regan.* 'Tis the infirmity of his age; yet he hath ever
but slenderly known himself.

---

272 **like a sister** because I am a sister i.e., loyal, affectionate   273 **as they
are named** i.e., by their right and ugly names   274 **professèd** pretending to
love   276 **prefer** recommend   280 **At Fortune's alms** as a charitable be-
quest from Fortune (and so, by extension, as one beggared or cast down by
Fortune)   280 **scanted** stinted   281 **worth . . . wanted** deserve to be denied,
even as you have denied   282 **plighted** pleated, enfolded   283 **Who . . . derides** those who hide their evil are finally exposed and shamed ("He that
hideth his sins, shall not prosper")   294 **grossly** obviously

Goneril. The best and soundest of his time° hath been but rash; then must we look from his age to receive not alone the imperfections of long-in-grafted° condition,° but therewithal° the unruly *300* waywardness that infirm and choleric years bring with them.

Regan. Such unconstant starts° are we like to have from him as this of Kent's banishment.

Goneril. There is further compliment° of leave-taking *305* between France and him. Pray you, let's hit° to-gether; if our father carry authority with such dispo-sition as he bears,° this last surrender° of his will but offend° us.

Regan. We shall further think of it.   *310*

Goneril. We must do something, and i' th' heat.°

Exeunt.

EDMUND , Rebelling against his
↗ father

Scene 2.   [*The Earl of Gloucester's castle.*]

Enter Edmund [*with a letter*].

Edmund. Thou, Nature,° art my goddess; to thy law
My services are bound. Wherefore should I
Stand in the plague of custom,° and permit
The curiosity° of nations to deprive me,
For that° I am some twelve or fourteen
    moonshines°   *5*

297 **of his time** period of his life up to now   299–300 **long-ingrafted** im-planted for a long time   300 **condition** disposition   300 **therewithal** with them   303 **unconstant starts** impulsive whims   305 **compliment** formal courtesy   306 **hit** agree   307–8 **carry . . . bears** continues, and in such frame of mind, to wield the sovereign power   308 **last surrender** recent abdication   309 **offend** vex   311 **i' th' heat** while the iron is hot   1.2.1 **Nature** (Ed-mund's conception of Nature accords with our description of a bastard as a nat-ural child)   3 **Stand . . . custom** respect hateful convention   4 **curiosity** nice distinctions   5 **For that** because   5 **moonshines** months

Lag of° a brother? Why bastard? Wherefore base?
When my dimensions are as well compact,°
My mind as generous,° and my shape as true,
As honest° madam's issue? Why brand they us
10   With base? With baseness? Bastardy? Base? Base?
Who, in the lusty stealth of nature, take
More composition° and fierce° quality
Than doth, within a dull, stale, tired bed,
Go to th' creating a whole tribe of fops°
15   Got° 'tween asleep and wake? Well then,
Legitimate Edgar, I must have your land.
Our father's love is to the bastard Edmund
As to th' legitimate. Fine word, "legitimate."
Well, my legitimate, if this letter speed,°
20   And my invention° thrive, Edmund the base
Shall top th' legitimate. I grow, I prosper.
Now, gods, stand up for bastards.

Enter Gloucester.

Gloucester. Kent banished thus? and France in choler
        parted?
    And the King gone tonight? prescribed° his pow'r?
25   Confined to exhibition?° All this done
    Upon the gad?° Edmund, how now? What news?

Edmund. So please your lordship, none.

Gloucester. Why so earnestly seek you to put up°
    that letter?

30   *Edmund.* I know no news, my lord.

Gloucester. What paper were you reading?

Edmund. Nothing, my lord.

Gloucester. No? What needed then that terrible dis-
    patch° of it into your pocket? The quality of noth-

6 **Lag of** short of being (in age)   7 **compact** framed   8 **generous** gallant
9 **honest** chaste   12 **composition** completeness   12 **fierce** energetic   14 **fops**
fools   15 **Got** begot   19 **speed** prosper   20 **invention** plan   24 **prescribed**
limited   25 **exhibition** an allowance or pension   26 **Upon the gad** on the spur
of the moment (as if pricked by a gad or goad)   28 **put up** put away, conceal
33–34 **terrible dispatch** hasty putting away

ing hath not such need to hide itself. Let's see. 35
Come, if it be nothing, I shall not need spectacles.

Edmund. I beseech you, sir, pardon me. It is a letter
from my brother that I have not all o'er-read; and
for so much as I have perused, I find it not fit
for your o'erlooking.° 40

Gloucester. Give me the letter, sir.

Edmund. I shall offend, either to detain or give it. The
contents, as in part I understand them, are to
blame.°

Gloucester. Let's see, let's see. 45

Edmund. I hope, for my brother's justification, he
wrote this but as an essay or taste° of my virtue.

Gloucester. (*Reads*) "This policy and reverence° of
age makes the world bitter to the best of our
times;° keeps our fortunes from us till our oldness 50
cannot relish° them. I begin to find an idle and
fond° bondage in the oppression of aged tyranny,
who sways, not as it hath power, but as it is suffered.° Come to me, that of this I may speak more.
If our father would sleep till I waked him, you 55
should enjoy half his revenue° for ever, and live
the beloved of your brother,　　　EDGAR."
Hum! Conspiracy? "Sleep till I waked him, you
should enjoy half his revenue." My son Edgar! Had
he a hand to write this? A heart and brain to 60
breed it in? When came you to this? Who brought
it?

Edmund. It was not brought me, my lord; there's the
cunning of it. I found it thrown in at the casement of
my closet.° 65

40 **o'erlooking** inspection　44 **to blame** blameworthy　47 **essay or taste**
test　48 **policy and reverence** policy of reverencing (hendiadys)
49–50 **best of our times** best years of our lives (i.e., our youth)　51
relish enjoy　51–52 **idle and fond** foolish　53–54 **who . . . suffered**
which rules, not from its own strength, but from our allowance　56 **revenue** income　64–65 **casement of my closet** window of my room

Gloucester. You know the character° to be your brother's?

Edmund. If the matter were good, my lord, I durst swear it were his; but in respect of that,° I would
70 fain° think it were not.

Gloucester. It is his.

Edmund. It is his hand, my lord; but I hope his heart is not in the contents.

Gloucester. Has he never before sounded° you in this
75 business?

Edmund. Never, my lord. But I have heard him oft maintain it to be fit that, sons at perfect° age, and fathers declined, the father should be as ward to the son, and the son manage his revenue.

80 *Gloucester.* O villain, villain! His very opinion in the letter. Abhorred villain, unnatural, detested,° brutish villain; worse than brutish! Go, sirrah,° seek him. I'll apprehend him. Abominable villain! Where is he?

85 *Edmund.* I do not well know, my lord. If it shall please you to suspend your indignation against my brother till you can derive from him better testimony of his intent, you should run a certain course;° where, if you violently proceed against
90 him, mistaking his purpose, it would make a great gap° in your own honor and shake in pieces the heart of his obedience. I dare pawn down° my life for him that he hath writ this to feel° my affection to your honor, and to no other pretense of
95 danger.°

Gloucester. Think you so?

66 **character** handwriting   69 **in respect of that** in view of what it is
70 **fain** prefer to   74 **sounded** sounded you out   77 **perfect** mature   81 **detested** detestable   82 **sirrah** sir (familiar form of address)   88–89 **run a certain course** i.e., proceed safely, know where you are going   91 **gap** breach   92 **pawn down** stake   93 **feel** test   94–95 **pretense of danger** dangerous purpose

Edmund. If your honor judge it meet,° I will place you where you shall hear us confer of this, and by an auricular assurance° have your satisfaction, and that without any further delay than this very *100* evening.

Gloucester. He cannot be such a monster.

Edmund. Nor is not, sure.

Gloucester. To his father, that so tenderly and entirely loves him. Heaven and earth! Edmund, seek *105* him out; wind me into him,° I pray you; frame° the business after your own wisdom. I would unstate myself to be in a due resolution.°

Edmund. I will seek him, sir, presently;° convey° the business as I shall find means, and acquaint you *110* withal.°

Gloucester. These late° eclipses in the sun and moon portend no good to us. Though the wisdom of Nature° can reason° it thus and thus, yet Nature finds itself scourged by the sequent effects.° Love *115* cools, friendship falls off,° brothers divide. In cities, mutinies;° in countries, discord; in palaces, treason; and the bond cracked 'twixt son and father. This villain of mine comes under the prediction,° there's son against father; the King falls *120* from bias of nature,° there's father against child. We have seen the best of our time.° Machinations, hollowness,° treachery, and all ruinous disorders follow us disquietly° to our graves. Find out this

¹²⁵ villain, Edmund; it shall lose thee nothing.° Do it
carefully. And the noble and true-hearted Kent
banished; his offense, honesty. 'Tis strange.

Exit.

Edmund. This is the excellent foppery° of the world,
that when we are sick in fortune, often the surfeits
¹³⁰ of our own behavior,° we make guilty of our dis-
asters the sun, the moon, and stars; as if we were
villains on° necessity; fools by heavenly compulsion; knaves, thieves, and treachers by spherical
predominance;° drunkards, liars, and adulterers by
¹³⁵ an enforced obedience of planetary influence;° and
all that we are evil in, by a divine thrusting on.°
An admirable evasion of whoremaster° man, to
lay his goatish° disposition on the charge of a
star. My father compounded° with my mother
¹⁴⁰ under the Dragon's Tail,° and my nativity° was
under Ursa Major,° so that it follows I am rough
and lecherous. Fut!° I should have been that° I
am, had the maidenliest star in the firmament twin-
kled on my bastardizing. Edgar——

Enter Edgar.

¹⁴⁵ and pat he comes, like the catastrophe° of the old
comedy. My cue is villainous melancholy, with a
sigh like Tom o' Bedlam.°—O, these eclipses do
portend these divisions. Fa, sol, la, mi.°

Edgar. How now, brother Edmund; what serious con-
¹⁵⁰ templation are you in?

125 **it ... nothing** you will not lose by it   128 **foppery** folly   129–30
often ... behavior often caused by our own excesses   132 **on** of
133–34 **treachers ... predominance** traitors because of the ascendancy of a
particular star at our birth   134–35 **by ... influence** because we had to submit
to the influence of our star   136 **divine thrusting on** supernatural compulsion
137 **whoremaster** lecherous   138 **goatish** scivious   139 **compounded** (1)
made terms (2) formed (a child)   140 **Dragon's Tail** the constellation Draco
140 **nativity** birthday   141 **Ursa Major** the Great Bear   142 **Fut!** 's foot
(an impatient oath)   142 **that** what   145 **catastrophe** conclusion   146–47
My ... Bedlam I must be doleful, like a lunatic beggar out of Bethlehem (Bedlam) Hospital, the London madhouse   148 **Fa, sol, la, mi** (Edmund's hum-
ming of the musical notes is perhaps prompted by his use of the word
"divisions," which describes a musical variation)

Edmund. I am thinking, brother, of a prediction I read
   this other day, what should follow these eclipses.

Edgar. Do you busy yourself with that?

Edmund. I promise you, the effects he writes of suc-   *155*
   ceed° unhappily: as of unnaturalness° between the
   child and the parent, death, dearth, dissolutions of
   ancient amities,° divisions in state, menaces and
   maledictions against King and nobles, needless diffidences,° banishment of friends, dissipation of co-   *160*
   horts,° nuptial breaches, and I know not what.

Edgar. How long have you been a sectary astronomical?°

Edmund. Come, come, when saw you my father last?

Edgar. Why, the night gone by.   *165*

Edmund. Spake you with him?

Edgar. Ay, two hours together.

Edmund. Parted you in good terms? Found you no
   displeasure in him by word nor countenance?°

Edgar. None at all.   *170*

Edmund. Bethink yourself wherein you may have offended him; and at my entreaty forbear his pres-
   ence° until some little time hath qualified° the heat
   of his displeasure, which at this instant so rageth
   in him that with the mischief of your person it   *175*
   would scarcely allay.°

Edgar. Some villain hath done me wrong.

Edmund. That's my fear, brother I pray you have a
   continent forbearance° till the speed of his rage
   goes slower; and, as I say, retire with me to my   *180*

155–56 **succeed** follow   157 **unnaturalness** unkindness   158 **amities** friend-
ships   159–60 **diffidences** distrusts   160–61 **dissipation of cohorts** falling
away of supporters   162–63 **sectary astronomical** believer in astrology
169 **countenance** expression   172–73 **forbear his presence** keep away from
him   173 **qualified** lessened   175–76 **with ... allay** even an injury to you
would not appease his anger   178–79 **have a continent forbearance** be restrained and keep yourself withdrawn

lodging, from whence I will fitly° bring you to hear
my lord speak. Pray ye, go; there's my key. If
you do stir abroad, go armed.

Edgar. Armed, brother?

185 *Edmund.* Brother, I advise you to the best. Go armed.
I am no honest man if there be any good meaning
toward you. I have told you what I have seen and
heard; but faintly, nothing like the image and hor-
ror° of it. Pray you, away.

190 *Edgar.* Shall I hear from you anon?°

Edmund. I do serve you in this business.

Exit Edgar.

A credulous father, and a brother noble,
Whose nature is so far from doing harms
That he suspects none; on whose foolish honesty
195 My practices° ride easy. I see the business.
Let me, if not by birth, have lands by wit.
All with me's meet° that I can fashion fit.°   *Exit.*

Scene 3.   [*The Duke of Albany's palace.*]

Enter Goneril, and [Oswald, her] Steward.

Goneril. Did my father strike my gentleman for chid-
ing of his Fool?°

Oswald. Ay, madam.

Goneril. By day and night he wrongs me. Every hour
5   He flashes into one gross crime° or other

---

181 **fitly** at a fit time   188–89 **image and horror** true horrible picture
190 **anon** in a little while   195 **practices** plots   197 **meet** proper   197 **fashion fit** shape to my purpose   1.3.2 **Fool** court jester   5 **crime** offense

That sets us all at odds. I'll not endure it.
His knights grow riotous,° and himself upbraids us
On every trifle. When he returns from hunting,
I will not speak with him. Say I am sick.
If you come slack of former services,°   10
You shall do well; the fault of it I'll answer.°

                              [*Horns within.*]

Oswald. He's coming, madam; I hear him.

Goneril. Put on what weary negligence you please,
You and your fellows. I'd have it come to question.°
If he distaste° it, let him to my sister,   15
Whose mind and mine I know in that are one,
Not to be overruled. Idle° old man,
That still would manage those authorities
That he hath given away. Now, by my life,
Old fools are babes again, and must be used   20
With checks as flatteries, when they are seen
    abused.°
Remember what I have said.

Oswald.   Well, madam.

Goneril. And let his knights have colder looks among
    you.
What grows of it, no matter; advise your fellows so.
I would breed from hence occasions, and I shall,   25
That I may speak.° I'll write straight° to my sister
To hold my course. Go, prepare for dinner.

                              Exeunt.

7 **riotous** dissolute   10 **come . . . services** are less serviceable to him than
formerly   11 **answer** answer for   14 **come to question** be discussed
openly   15 **distaste** dislike   17 **Idle** foolish   21 **With . . . abused** with re-
straints as well as soothing words when they are misguided   25–26 **breed . . .
speak** find in this opportunities for speaking out   26 **straight** at once

Scene 4.   [*A hall in the same.*]

Enter Kent [disguised].

Kent. If but as well I other accents borrow
    That can my speech defuse,° my good intent
    May carry through itself to that full issue°
    For which I razed my likeness.° Now, banished
      Kent,
    If thou canst serve where thou dost stand
5   condemned,
    So may it come,° thy master whom thou lov'st
    Shall find thee full of labors.

    Horns within.° Enter Lear, [Knights] and
              Attendants.

Lear. Let me not stay° a jot for dinner; go, get it
    ready. [*Exit an Attendant.*] How now, what art
10   thou?

Kent. A man, sir.

Lear. What dost thou profess?° What wouldst thou
    with us?

Kent. I do profess° to be no less than I seem, to
15   serve him truly that will put me in trust, to love
    him that is honest, to converse with him that is wise
    and says little, to fear judgment,° to fight when I
    cannot choose, and to eat no fish.°

1.4.2 **defuse** disguise   3 **full issue** perfect result   4 **razed my likeness**
shaved off, disguised my natural appearance   6 **So may it come** so may it
fall out   7 s.d. **within** offstage   8 **stay** wait   12 **What dost thou profess**
what do you do   14 **profess** claim   17 **judgment** (by a heavenly or earthly
judge)   18 **eat no fish** i.e., (1) I am no Catholic, but a loyal Protestant (2) I
am no weakling (3) I use no prostitutes

Lear. What art thou?

Kent. A very honest-hearted fellow, and as poor as   20
the King.

Lear. If thou be'st as poor for a subject as he's for a
king, thou art poor enough. What wouldst thou?

Kent. Service.

Lear. Who wouldst thou serve?   25

Kent. You.

Lear. Dost thou know me, fellow?

Kent. No, sir, but you have that in your countenance°
which I would fain° call master.

Lear. What's that?   30

Kent. Authority.

Lear. What services canst thou do?

Kent. I can keep honest counsel,° ride, run, mar a
curious tale in telling it,° and deliver a plain message bluntly. That which ordinary men are fit for, I   35
am qualified in, and the best of me is diligence.

Lear. How old art thou?

Kent. Not so young, sir, to love a woman for singing, nor so old to dote on her for anything. I have
years on my back forty-eight.   40

Lear. Follow me; thou shalt serve me. If I like thee no
worse after dinner, I will not part from thee yet.
Dinner, ho, dinner! Where's my knave?° my Fool?
Go you and call my Fool hither.

                 [*Exit an Attendant.*]

        Enter Oswald.

You, you, sirrah, where's my daughter?   45

Oswald. So please you——   *Exit.*

---

28 **countenance** bearing   29 **fain** like to   33 **honest counsel** honorable
secrets   33–34 **mar . . . it** i.e., I cannot speak like an affected courtier ("curious"="elaborate," as against "plain")   43 **knave** boy

Lear. What says the fellow there? Call the clotpoll°
back. [*Exit a Knight.*] Where's my Fool? Ho, I
think the world's asleep.

[*Re-enter Knight.*]

50   How now? Where's that mongrel?

Knight. He says, my lord, your daughter is not well.

Lear. Why came not the slave back to me when I
called him?

Knight. Sir, he answered me in the roundest° manner,
55   he would not.

Lear. He would not?

Knight. My lord, I know not what the matter is;
but to my judgment your Highness is not enter-
tained° with that ceremonious affection as you
60   were wont. There's a great abatement of kindness
appears as well in the general dependants° as in the
Duke himself also and your daughter.

Lear. Ha? Say'st thou so?

Knight. I beseech you pardon me, my lord, if I be
65   mistaken; for my duty cannot be silent when I
think your Highness wronged.

Lear. Thou but rememb'rest° me of mine own conception.° I have perceived a most faint neglect°
of late, which I have rather blamed as mine own
70   jealous curiosity° than as a very pretense° and
purpose of unkindness. I will look further into't.
But where's my Fool? I have not seen him this two
days.

Knight. Since my young lady's going into France, sir,
75   the Fool hath much pined away.

Lear. No more of that; I have noted it well. Go you

47 **clotpoll** clodpoll, blockhead   54 **roundest** rudest   58–59 **entertained**
treated   61 **dependants** servants   67 **rememb'rest** remindest   67–68 **conception** idea   68 **faint neglect** i.e., "weary negligence" (1.3.13)   69–70 **mine
own jealous curiosity** suspicious concern for my own dignity   70 **very
pretense** actual intention

and tell my daughter I would speak with her. Go
you, call hither my Fool.   [*Exit an Attendant.*]
                    Enter Oswald.
O, you, sir, you! Come you hither, sir. Who am I,
sir?   *80*

Oswald. My lady's father.

Lear. "My lady's father"? My lord's knave, you
   whoreson dog, you slave, you cur!

Oswald. I am none of these, my lord; I beseech your
   pardon.   *85*

Lear. Do you bandy° looks with me, you rascal?
                                      [*Striking him.*]

Oswald. I'll not be strucken,° my lord.

Kent. Nor tripped neither, you base football° player.
                                      [*Tripping up his heels.*]

Lear. I thank thee, fellow. Thou serv'st me, and I'll
   love thee.   *90*

Kent. Come, sir, arise, away. I'll teach you differences.° Away, away. If you will measure your lubber's° length again, tarry; but away. Go to!° Have
   you wisdom?° So.°   [*Pushes Oswald out.*]

Lear. Now, my friendly knave, I thank thee. There's *95*
   earnest° of thy service.   [*Giving Kent money.*]

                    Enter Fool.

Fool. Let me hire him too. Here's my coxcomb.°
                                      [*Offering Kent his cap.*]

Lear. How now, my pretty knave? How dost thou?

Fool. Sirrah, you were best° take my coxcomb.

Kent. Why, Fool?   *100*

86 **bandy** exchange insolently (metaphor from tennis)   87 **strucken** struck
88 **football** (a low game played by idle boys to the scandal of sensible men)
91–92 **differences** (of rank)   92–93 **lubber's** lout's   93 **Go to** (expression
of derisive incredulity)   93–94 **Have you wisdom** i.e., do you know what's
good for you   94 **So** good   96 **earnest** money for services rendered
97 **coxcomb** professional fool's cap, shaped like a coxcomb   99 **you were
best** you had better

Fool. Why? For taking one's part that's out of favor.
Nay, an° thou canst not smile as the wind sits,°
thou'lt catch cold shortly. There, take my coxcomb.
Why, this fellow has banished° two on's daughters,
105   and did the third a blessing against his will. If thou
follow him, thou must needs wear my coxcomb.
—How now, Nuncle?° Would I had two coxcombs
and two daughters.

Lear. Why, my boy?

110 *Fool.* If I gave them all my living,° I'd keep my coxcombs myself. There's mine; beg another of thy
daughters.

Lear. Take heed, sirrah—the whip.

Fool. Truth's a dog must to kennel; he must be
115   whipped out, when Lady the Brach° may stand by
th' fire and stink.

Lear. A pestilent gall° to me.

Fool. Sirrah, I'll teach thee a speech.

Lear. Do.

120 *Fool.* Mark it, Nuncle.
        Have more than thou showest,
        Speak less than thou knowest,
        Lend less than thou owest,°
        Ride more than thou goest,°
125   Learn more than thou trowest,°
        Set less than thou throwest,°
        Leave thy drink and thy whore,
        And keep in-a-door,
        And thou shalt have more
130   Than two tens to a score.°

Kent. This is nothing, Fool.

102 **an** if   102 **smile ... sits** ingratiate yourself with those in
power   104 **banished** alienated (by making them independent)   107 **Nuncle** (contraction of "mine uncle")   110 **living** property   115 **Brach**
bitch   117 **gall** sore   123 **owest** ownest   124 **goest** walkest   125 **trowest**
knowest   126 **Set ... throwest** bet less than you play for (get odds from
your opponent)   129–30 **have ... score** i.e., come away with more than
you had (two tens, or twenty shillings, make a score, or one pound)

Fool. Then 'tis like the breath of an unfeed° lawyer
—you gave me nothing for't. Can you make no use
of nothing, Nuncle?

Lear. Why, no, boy. Nothing can be made out of   *135*
nothing.

Fool. [*To Kent*] Prithee tell him, so much the
rent of his land comes to; he will not believe a
Fool.

Lear. A bitter° Fool.   *140*

Fool. Dost thou know the difference, my boy, between
a bitter Fool and a sweet one?

Lear. No, lad; teach me.

Fool.
      That lord that counseled thee
          To give away thy land,
      Come place him here by me,   *145*
          Do thou for him stand.
      The sweet and bitter fool
          Will presently appear;
      The one in motley° here,   *150*
          The other found out° there.°

Lear. Dost thou call me fool, boy?

Fool. All thy other titles thou hast given away; that
thou wast born with.

Kent. This is not altogether fool, my lord.   *155*

Fool. No, faith; lords and great men will not let me.°
If I had a monopoly° out, they would have part
on't. And ladies too, they will not let me have all
the fool to myself; they'll be snatching. Nuncle,
give me an egg, and I'll give thee two crowns.   *160*

---

132 **unfeed** unpaid for   140 **bitter** satirical   150 **motley** the drab costume
of the professional jester   151 **found out** revealed   151 **there** (the Fool
points at Lear, as a fool in the grain)   156 **let me** (have all the folly to myself)   157 **monopoly** (James I gave great scandal by granting to his "snatching" courtiers royal patents to deal exclusively in some commodity)

Lear. What two crowns shall they be?

Fool. Why, after I have cut the egg i' th' middle
and eat up the meat, the two crowns of the egg.
When thou clovest thy crown i' th' middle and
165 gav'st away both parts, thou bor'st thine ass on
thy back o'er the dirt.° Thou hadst little wit in thy
bald crown when thou gav'st thy golden one away.
If I speak like myself° in this, let him be whipped°
that first finds it so.

170 [*Singing*] Fools had ne'er less grace in a year,
        For wise men are grown foppish,
    And know not how their wits to wear,
        Their manners are so apish.°

Lear. When were you wont to be so full of songs,
175 sirrah?

Fool. I have used° it, Nuncle, e'er since thou mad'st
thy daughters thy mothers; for when thou gav'st
them the rod, and put'st down thine own breeches,
[*Singing*] Then they for sudden joy did weep,
180   And I for sorrow sung,
    That such a king should play bo-peep°
        And go the fools among.
Prithee, Nuncle, keep a schoolmaster that can teach
thy Fool to lie. I would fain learn to lie.

185 *Lear.* And° you lie, sirrah, we'll have you whipped.

Fool. I marvel what kin thou and thy daughters are.
They'll have me whipped for speaking true; thou'lt
have me whipped for lying; and sometimes I am
whipped for holding my peace. I had rather be any
190 kind o' thing than a Fool, and yet I would not be

165–66 **bor'st ... dirt** (like the foolish and unnatural countryman in Aesop's fable)   168 **like myself** like a Fool   168 **let him be whipped** i.e., let
the man be whipped for a Fool who thinks my true saying to be foolish
170–73 **Fools ... apish** i.e., fools were never in less favor than now, and
the reason is that wise men, turning foolish, and not knowing how to use
their intelligence, imitate the professional fools and so make them unnecessary   176 **used** practiced   181 **play bo-peep** (1) act like a child (2)
blind himself   185 **And** if

thee, Nuncle: thou hast pared thy wit o' both sides
and left nothing i' th' middle. Here comes one o'
the parings.

Enter Goneril.

Lear. How now, daughter? What makes that frontlet°
on? Methinks you are too much of late i' th'   *195*
frown.

Fool. Thou wast a pretty fellow when thou hadst no
need to care for her frowning. Now thou art an O
without a figure.° I am better than thou art now: I
am a Fool, thou art nothing. [*To Goneril.*] Yes,   *200*
forsooth, I will hold my tongue. So your face bids
me, though you say nothing. Mum, mum,
    He that keeps nor crust nor crum,°
    Weary of all, shall want° some.

[*Pointing to Lear*] That's a shealed peascod.°   *205*

Goneril. Not only, sir, this your all-licensed° Fool,
But other° of your insolent retinue
Do hourly carp and quarrel, breaking forth
In rank° and not-to-be-endurèd riots. Sir,
I had thought by making this well known unto you   *210*
To have found a safe° redress, but now grow
    fearful,
By what yourself too late° have spoke and done,
That you protect this course, and put it on
By your allowance;° which if you should, the fault
Would not 'scape censure, nor the redresses sleep,°   *215*
Which, in the tender of° a wholesome weal,°
Might in their working do you that offense,
Which else were shame, that then necessity
Will call discreet proceeding.°

194 **frontlet** frown (lit., ornamental band)   199 **figure** digit, to give value to
the cipher (Lear is a nought)   203 **crum** soft bread inside the loaf   204 **want**
lack   205 **shealed peascod** empty pea pod   206 **all-licensed** privileged
to take any liberties   207 **other** others   209 **rank** gross   211 **safe** sure
212 **too late** lately   213–14 **put . . . allowance** promote it by your approval
214 **allowance** approval   215 **redresses sleep** correction fail to follow
216 **tender of** desire for   216 **weal** state   217–19 **Might . . . proceeding** as I
apply it, the correction might humiliate you; but the need to take action can-
cels what would otherwise be unfilial conduct in me

220 *Fool.* For you know, Nuncle,
   The hedge-sparrow fed the cuckoo° so long
   That it had it head bit off by it° young.
  So out went the candle, and we were left darkling.°

Lear. Are you our daughter?

225 *Goneril.* Come, sir,
   I would you would make use of your good wisdom
   Whereof I know you are fraught° and put away
   These dispositions° which of late transport you
   From what you rightly are.

230 *Fool.* May not an ass know when the cart draws the
  horse? Whoop, Jug,° I love thee!

Lear. Does any here know me? This is not Lear.
  Does Lear walk thus? Speak thus? Where are his
   eyes?
  Either his notion° weakens, or his discernings°
235 Are lethargied°—Ha! Waking? 'Tis not so.
  Who is it that can tell me who I am?

Fool. Lear's shadow.

Lear. I would learn that; for, by the marks of sovereignty,° knowledge, and reason, I should be false°
240 persuaded I had daughters.

Fool. Which° they will make an obedient father.

Lear. Your name, fair gentlewoman?

Goneril. This admiration,° sir, is much o' th' savor°
   Of other your° new pranks. I do beseech you
245 To understand my purposes aright.
  As you are old and reverend, should be wise.
  Here do you keep a hundred knights and squires,

221 **cuckoo** (who lays its eggs in the nests of other birds)   222 **it** its
223 **darkling** in the dark   227 **fraught** endowed   228 **dispositions** moods
231 **Jug** Joan (? a quotation from a popular song)   234 **notion** understanding 234 **discernings** faculties   235 **lethargied** paralyzed   238–39 **marks
of sovereignty** i.e., tokens that Lear is king, and hence father to his daughters
239 **false** falsely   241 **Which** whom (Lear)   243 **admiration** (affected)
wonderment   243 **is much o' th' savor** smacks much   244 **other your** others of your

Men so disordered, so deboshed,° and bold,
That this our court, infected with their manners,
Shows° like a riotous inn. Epicurism° and lust   250
Makes it more like a tavern or a brothel
Than a graced° palace. The shame itself doth speak
For instant remedy. Be then desired°
By her, that else will take the thing she begs,
A little to disquantity your train,°   255
And the remainders° that shall still depend,°
To be such men as may besort° your age,
Which know themselves, and you.

Lear.   Darkness and devils!
Saddle my horses; call my train together.
Degenerate° bastard, I'll not trouble thee: 260
Yet have I left a daughter.

Goneril. You strike my people, and your disordered
    rabble
Make servants of their betters.

Enter Albany.

Lear. Woe, that too late repents. O, sir, are you
    come?
Is it your will? Speak, sir. Prepare my horses. 265
Ingratitude! thou marble-hearted fiend,
More hideous when thou show'st thee in a child
Than the sea-monster.

Albany.   Pray, sir, be patient.

Lear. Detested kite,° thou liest.
My train are men of choice and rarest parts,°   270
That all particulars of duty know,
And, in the most exact regard,° support
The worships° of their name. O most small fault,

248 **deboshed** debauched 250 **Shows** appears 250 **Epicurism** riotous living 252 **graced** dignified 253 **desired** requested 255 **disquantity your train** reduce the number of your dependents 256 **remainders** those who remain 256 **depend** attend on you 257 **besort** befit 260 **Degenerate** unnatural 269 **kite** scavenging bird of prey 270 **parts** accomplishments 272 **exact regard** strict attention to detail 273 **worships** honor

[handwritten: leal is Pissed @ Cordelia]

How ugly didst thou in Cordelia show!
Which, like an engine,° wrenched my frame of
275   nature
From the fixed place;° drew from my heart all love,
And added to the gall.° O Lear, Lear, Lear!
Beat at this gate that let thy folly in [*Striking
    his head.*]
And thy dear judgment out. Go, go, my people.

280 *Albany.* My lord, I am guiltless, as I am ignorant
Of what hath moved you.

[handwritten: Cursing her / Calling on Nature]

Lear.   It may be so, my lord.
Hear, Nature, hear; dear Goddess, hear:
Suspend thy purpose if thou didst intend
To make this creature fruitful.
285 Into her womb convey sterility,
Dry up in her the organs of increase,°
And from her derogate° body never spring
A babe to honor her. If she must teem,°
Create her child of spleen,° that it may live
290 And be a thwart disnatured° torment to her.
Let it stamp wrinkles in her brow of youth,
With cadent° tears fret° channels in her cheeks,
Turn all her mother's pains and benefits°
To laughter and contempt, that she may feel
295 How sharper than a serpent's tooth it is
To have a thankless child. Away, away!   *Exit.*

Albany. Now, gods that we adore, whereof comes
    this?

Goneril. Never afflict yourself to know the cause,
But let his disposition° have that scope
300 As° dotage gives it.

                    Enter Lear.

Lear. What, fifty of my followers at a clap?°

275 **engine** destructive contrivance   274–76 **wrenched ... place** i.e., disordered my natural self   277 **gall** bitterness   286 **increase** childbearing 287 **derogate** degraded   288 **teem** conceive   289 **spleen** ill humor   290 **thwart disnatured** perverse unnatural   292 **cadent** falling   292 **fret** wear 293 **benefits** the mother's beneficent care of her child   299 **disposition** mood 300 **As** that   *301* **at a clap** at one stroke

Within a fortnight?

Albany.   What's the matter, sir?

Lear. I'll tell thee. [*To Goneril*] Life and death,
   I am ashamed
   That thou hast power to shake my manhood°
      thus!
   That these hot tears, which break from me
      perforce,°   *305*
   Should make thee worth them. Blasts and fogs
      upon thee!
   Th' untented woundings° of a father's curse
   Pierce every sense about thee! Old fond° eyes,
   Beweep° this cause again, I'll pluck ye out
   And cast you, with the waters that you loose,°   *310*
   To temper° clay. Yea, is it come to this?
   Ha! Let it be so. I have another daughter,
   Who I am sure is kind and comfortable.°
   When she shall hear this of thee, with her nails
   She'll flay thy wolvish visage. Thou shalt find   *315*
   That I'll resume the shape° which thou dost think
   I have cast off for ever.
               Exit [*Lear with Kent and Attendants*].

Goneril.   Do you mark that?

Albany. I cannot be so partial, Goneril,
   To the great love I bear you°——

Goneril. Pray you, content. What, Oswald, ho!   *320*
   [*To the Fool*] You, sir, more knave than fool,
      after your master!

Fool. Nuncle Lear, Nuncle Lear, tarry. Take the Fool°
   with thee.

304 **shake my manhood** i.e., with tears   305 **perforce** involuntarily, against
my will   307 **untented woundings** wounds too deep to be probed with a
tent (a roll of lint)   308 **fond** foolish   309 **Beweep** if you weep over
310 **loose** (1) let loose (2) lose, as of no avail   311 **temper** mix with
and soften   313 **comfortable** ready to comfort   316 **shape** i.e., kingly role
318–19 **I cannot ... you** i.e., even though my love inclines me to
you, I must protest   322 **Fool** (1) the Fool himself (2) the epithet or
character of "fool"

    A fox, when one has caught her,
325   And such a daughter,
    Should sure to the slaughter,
    If my cap would buy a halter.°
    So the Fool follows after.°   *Exit.*

Goneril. This man hath had good counsel. A hundred
    knights!
330   'Tis politic° and safe to let him keep
    At point° a hundred knights: yes, that on every
      dream,
    Each buzz,° each fancy, each complaint, dislike,
    He may enguard° his dotage with their pow'rs
    And hold our lives in mercy.° Oswald, I say!

Albany. Well, you may fear too far.

335 *Goneril.*   Safer than trust too far.
    Let me still take away the harms I fear,
    Not fear still to be taken.° I know his heart.
    What he hath uttered I have writ my sister.
    If she sustain him and his hundred knights,
    When I have showed th' unfitness——
             Enter Oswald.
340   How now, Oswald?
    What, have you writ that letter to my sister?

Oswald. Ay, madam.

Goneril. Take you some company,° and away to
    horse.
    Inform her full of my particular° fear,
345   And thereto add such reasons of your own
    As may compact° it more. Get you gone,
    And hasten your return. [*Exit Oswald.*] No, no,
      my lord,
    This milky gentleness and course° of yours,
    Though I condemn not,° yet under pardon,

327–28 **halter, after** pronounced "hauter," "auter"   330 **politic** good policy
331 **At point** armed   332 **buzz** rumor   333 **enguard** protect   334 **in
mercy** at his mercy   337 **Not . . . taken** rather than remain fearful of being
overtaken by them   343 **company** escort   344 **particular** own   346 **compact** strengthen   348 **milky . . . course** mild and gentle way (hendiadys)   349 **condemn not** condemn it not

You are much more attasked° for want of wisdom   350
Than praised for harmful mildness.°

Albany. How far your eyes may pierce I cannot tell;
  Striving to better, oft we mar what's well.

Goneril. Nay then——

Albany. Well, well, th' event.°   *Exeunt.* 355

Scene 5. [*Court before the same.*]

Enter Lear, Kent, and Fool.

Lear. Go you before to Gloucester with these letters.
  Acquaint my daughter no further with anything
  you know than comes from her demand out of
  the letter.° If your diligence be not speedy, I shall
  be there afore you.   5

Kent. I will not sleep, my lord, till I have delivered
  your letter.   *Exit.*

Fool. If a man's brains were in's heels, were't° not in
  danger of kibes?°

Lear. Ay, boy.   10

Fool. Then I prithee be merry. Thy wit shall not go
  slipshod.°

Lear. Ha, ha, ha.

Fool. Shalt° see thy other daughter will use thee
  kindly;° for though she's as like this as a crab's°   15
  like an apple, yet I can tell what I can tell.

350 **attasked** taken to task, blamed   351 **harmful mildness** dangerous indulgence   355 **th' event** i.e., we'll see what happens   1.5.3–4 **than . . .
letter** than her reading of the letter brings her to ask   8 **were't** i.e., the
brains   9 **kibes** chilblains   11–12 **Thy . . . slipshod** your brains shall not
go in slippers (because you have no brains to be protected from chilblains)   14 **Shalt** thou shalt   15 **kindly** (1) affectionately (2) after her kind
or nature   15 **crab** crab apple

Lear. Why, what canst thou tell, my boy?

Fool. She will taste as like this as a crab does to a
crab. Thou canst tell why one's nose stands i' th'
middle on's° face?

Lear. No.

Fool. Why, to keep one's eyes of° either side's nose,
that what a man cannot smell out, he may spy
into.

Lear. I did her wrong.

Fool. Canst tell how an oyster makes his shell?

Lear. No.

Fool. Nor I neither; but I can tell why a snail has a
house.

Lear. Why?

Fool. Why, to put 's head in; not to give it away to
his daughters, and leave his horns° without a case.

Lear. I will forget my nature.° So kind a father! Be
my horses ready?

Fool. Thy asses are gone about 'em. The reason why
the seven stars° are no moe° than seven is a pretty°
reason.

Lear. Because they are not eight.

Fool. Yes indeed. Thou wouldst make a good Fool.

Lear. To take't again perforce!° Monster ingratitude!

Fool. If thou wert my Fool, Nuncle, I'd have thee
beaten for being old before thy time.

Lear. How's that?

Fool. Thou shouldst not have been old till thou hadst
been wise.

20 **on's** of his   22 **of** on   32 **horns** (1) snail's horns (2) cuckold's horns
33 **nature** paternal instincts   36 **seven stars** the Pleiades   36 **moe** more
36 **pretty** apt   40 **To ... perforce** (1) of Goneril, who has forcibly taken
away Lear's privileges; or (2) of Lear, who meditates a forcible resumption
of authority

Lear. O, let me not be mad, not mad, sweet heaven!
  Keep me in temper;° I would not be mad!

                [*Enter Gentleman.*]

  How now, are the horses ready?

Gentleman. Ready, my lord.

Lear. Come, boy.   50

Fool. She that's a maid now, and laughs at my
      departure,
  Shall not be a maid long, unless things be cut
      shorter.°   *Exeunt*

---

47 **in temper** sane   51–52 **She . . . shorter** the maid who laughs, missing
the tragic implications of this quarrel, will not have sense enough to preserve her virginity ("things" = penises)

ACT 2

Scene 1. [*The Earl of Gloucester's castle.*]

Enter Edmund and Curan, severally.°

Edmund. Save° thee, Curan.

Curan. And you, sir. I have been with your father,
and given him notice that the Duke of Cornwall
and Regan his duchess will be here with him this
5   night.

Edmund. How comes that?

Curan. Nay, I know not. You have heard of the news
abroad? I mean the whispered ones, for they are yet
but ear-kissing arguments.°

10 *Edmund.* Not I. Pray you, what are they?

Curan. Have you heard of no likely° wars toward,°
'twixt the Dukes of Cornwall and Albany?

Edmund. Not a word.

Curan. You may do, then, in time. Fare you well,
15   sir.   *Exit.*

Edmund. The Duke be here tonight? The better!°
    best!

2.1.1 s.d. **severally** separately (from different entrances on stage)   1 **Save**
God save   9 **ear-kissing arguments** subjects whispered in the ear   11 **likely**
probable   11 **toward** impending   16 **The better** so much the better

This weaves itself perforce° into my business.
My father hath set guard to take my brother,
And I have one thing of a queasy question°
Which I must act. Briefness° and Fortune, work!   20
Brother, a word; descend. Brother, I say!
                    Enter Edgar.
My father watches. O sir, fly this place.
Intelligence° is given where you are hid.
You have now the good advantage of the night.
Have you not spoken 'gainst the Duke of Cornwall?   25
He's coming hither, now i' th' night, i' th' haste,°
And Regan with him. Have you nothing said
Upon his party° 'gainst the Duke of Albany?
Advise yourself.°

Edgar.   I am sure on't,° not a word.

Edmund. I hear my father coming. Pardon me: 30
In cunning° I must draw my sword upon you.
Draw, seem to defend yourself; now quit you° well.
Yield! Come before my father! Light ho, here!
Fly, brother. Torches, torches!—So farewell.
                              Exit Edgar.
Some blood drawn on me would beget opinion°   35
                    [*Wounds his arm*]
Of my more fierce endeavor. I have seen drunkards
Do more than this in sport. Father, father!
Stop, stop! No help?
      Enter Gloucester, and Servants with torches.

Gloucester. Now, Edmund, where's the villain?

Edmund. Here stood he in the dark, his sharp sword
    out,   40
Mumbling of wicked charms, conjuring the moon
To stand auspicious mistress.

Gloucester.   But where is he?

---

17 **perforce** necessarily   19 **of a queasy question** that requires delicate handling (to be "queasy" is to be on the point of vomiting)   20 **Briefness** speed
23 **Intelligence** information   26 **i' th' haste** in great haste   28 **Upon his
party** censuring his enmity   29 **Advise yourself** reflect   29 **on't** of it
31 **In cunning** as a pretense   32 **quit you** acquit yourself   35 **beget opinion**
create the impression

Edmund. Look, sir, I bleed.

Gloucester.   Where is the villain, Edmund?

Edmund. Fled this way, sir, when by no means he
      could——

Gloucester. Pursue him, ho! Go after.

                              [*Exeunt some Servants.*]
45   By no means what?

Edmund. Persuade me to the murder of your lordship;
      But that I told him the revenging gods
      'Gainst parricides did all the thunder bend;°
      Spoke with how manifold and strong a bond
50   The child was bound to th' father. Sir, in fine,°
      Seeing how loathly opposite° I stood
      To his unnatural purpose, in fell° motion°
      With his preparèd sword he charges home
      My unprovided° body, latched° mine arm;
55   But when he saw my best alarumed° spirits
      Bold in the quarrel's right,° roused to th'
            encounter,
      Or whether gasted° by the noise I made,
      Full suddenly he fled.

Gloucester.   Let him fly far.
      Not in this land shall he remain uncaught;
60   And found—dispatch.° The noble Duke my master,
      My worthy arch° and patron, comes tonight.
      By his authority I will proclaim it,
      That he which finds him shall deserve our thanks,
      Bringing the murderous coward to the stake.
65   He that conceals him, death.°

Edmund. When I dissuaded him from his intent,
      And found him pight° to do it, with curst° speech
      I threatened to discover° him. He replied,

48 **bend** aim   50 **in fine** finally   51 **loathly opposite** bitterly opposed
52 **fell** deadly   52 **motion** thrust (a term from fencing)   54 **unprovided** un-
protected   54 **latched** wounded (lanced)   55 **best alarumed** wholly aroused
56 **Bold . . . right** confident in the rightness of my cause   57 **gasted** struck
aghast   60 **dispatch** i.e., he will be killed   61 **arch** chief   65 **death** (the
same elliptical form that characterizes "dispatch," l.60)   67 **pight** determined
67 **curst** angry   68 **discover** expose

"Thou unpossessing° bastard, dost thou think,
If I would stand against thee, would the reposal°   *70*
Of any trust, virtue, or worth in thee
Make thy words faithed?° No. What I should
      deny—
As this I would, ay, though thou didst produce
My very character°—I'd turn it all
To thy suggestion,° plot, and damnèd practice.°   *75*
And thou must make a dullard of the world,°
If they not thought° the profits of my death
Were very pregnant° and potential spirits°
To make thee seek it."

Gloucester.   O strange and fastened° villain!
Would he deny his letter, said he? I never got° him.   *80*
                              Tucket° within.

Hark, the Duke's trumpets. I know not why he
      comes.
All ports° I'll bar; the villain shall not 'scape;
The Duke must grant me that. Besides, his picture I
will send far and near, that all the kingdom
May have due note of him; and of my land,   *85*
Loyal and natural° boy, I'll work the means
To make thee capable.°

            Enter Cornwall, Regan, and Attendants.

Cornwall. How now, my noble friend! Since I came
      hither,
Which I can call but now, I have heard strange
      news.

Regan. If it be true, all vengeance comes too short   *90*
Which can pursue th' offender. How dost, my lord?

Gloucester. O madam, my old heart is cracked, it's
      cracked.

---

69 **unpossessing** beggarly (landless)   70 **reposal** placing   72 **faithed** believed   74 **character** handwriting   75 **suggestion** instigation   75 **practice** device   76 **make ... world** think everyone stupid   77 **not thought** did not think   78 **pregnant** teeming with incitement   78 **potential spirits** powerful evil spirits   79 **fastened** hardened   80 **got** begot   80 s.d. **Tucket** (Cornwall's special trumpet call)   82 **ports** exits, of whatever sort   86 **natural** (1) kind (filial) (2) illegitimate   87 **capable** able to inherit

Regan. What, did my father's godson seek your life?
He whom my father named, your Edgar?

95 *Gloucester.* O lady, lady, shame would have it hid.

Regan. Was he not companion with the riotous knights
That tended upon my father?

Gloucester. I know not, madam. 'Tis too bad, too bad.

Edmund. Yes, madam, he was of that consort.°

100 *Regan.* No marvel then, though he were ill affected.°
'Tis they have put° him on the old man's death,
To have th' expense and waste° of his revenues.
I have this present evening from my sister
Been well informed of them, and with such cautions
105 That, if they come to sojourn at my house,
I'll not be there.

Cornwall.   Nor I, assure thee, Regan.
Edmund, I hear that you have shown your father
A childlike° office.

Edmund. It was my duty, sir.

110 *Gloucester.* He did bewray his practice,° and received
This hurt you see, striving to apprehend him.

Cornwall. Is he pursued?

Gloucester.   Ay, my good lord.

Cornwall. If he be taken, he shall never more
Be feared of doing° harm. Make your own purpose,
115 How in my strength you please.° For you, Edmund,
Whose virtue and obedience° doth this instant
So much commend itself, you shall be ours.
Natures of such deep trust we shall much need;
You we first seize on.

Edmund.   I shall serve you, sir,
Truly, however else.

120 *Gloucester.*   For him I thank your Grace.

---

99 **consort** company   100 **ill affected** disposed to evil   101 **put** set   102 **expense and waste** squandering   108 **childlike** filial   110 **bewray his practice** disclose his plot   114 **of doing** because he might do   114–15 **Make ... please** use my power freely, in carrying out your plans for his capture   116 **virtue and obedience** virtuous obedience

Cornwall. You know not why we came to visit you?

Regan. Thus out of season, threading dark-eyed night.
   Occasions, noble Gloucester, of some prize,°
   Wherein we must have use of your advice.
   Our father he hath writ, so hath our sister,   *125*
   Of differences,° which° I best thought it fit
   To answer from° our home. The several
     messengers
   From hence attend dispatch.° Our good old friend,
   Lay comforts to your bosom,° and bestow
   Your needful° counsel to our businesses,   *130*
   Which craves the instant use.°

Gloucester.   I serve you, madam.
   Your Graces are right welcome.

                            Exeunt. Flourish.

      Scene 2.   [*Before Gloucester's castle.*]

      Enter Kent and Oswald, severally.

Oswald. Good dawning° to thee, friend. Art of this
   house?°

Kent. Ay.

Oswald. Where may we set our horses?

Kent. I' th' mire.   *5*

Oswald. Prithee, if thou lov'st me, tell me.

Kent. I love thee not.

122 **prize** importance   125 **differences** quarrels   125 **which** (referring not
to "differences," but to the letter Lear has written)   126 **from** away
from   127 **attend dispatch** are waiting to be sent off   128 **Lay ... bosom**
console yourself (about Edgar's supposed treason)   129 **needful** needed
131 **craves the instant use** demands immediate transaction   2.2.1 **dawn-
ing** (dawn is impending, but not yet arrived)   1–2 **Art of this house** i.e., do
you live here

Oswald. Why then, I care not for thee.

Kent. If I had thee in Lipsbury Pinfold,° I would make
thee care for me.

Oswald. Why dost thou use me thus? I know thee not.

Kent. Fellow, I know thee.

Oswald. What dost thou know me for?

Kent. A knave, a rascal, an eater of broken meats;°
a base, proud, shallow, beggarly, three-suited,°
hundred-pound,° filthy worsted-stocking° knave; a
lily-livered, action-taking,° whoreson, glass-gazing,° superserviceable,° finical° rogue; one-trunk-
inheriting° slave; one that wouldst be a bawd in
way of good service,° and art nothing but the com-
position° of a knave, beggar, coward, pander, and
the son and heir of a mongrel bitch; one whom I
will beat into clamorous whining if thou deniest the
least syllable of thy addition.°

Oswald. Why, what a monstrous fellow art thou, thus
to rail on one that is neither known of thee nor
knows thee!

Kent. What a brazen-faced varlet art thou to deny
thou knowest me! Is it two days since I
tripped up thy heels and beat thee before the
King? [*Drawing his sword*] Draw, you rogue,
for though it be night, yet the moon shines. I'll
make a sop o' th' moonshine° of you. You whoreson cullionly barbermonger,° draw!

9 **Lipsbury Pinfold** a pound or pen in which strayed animals are enclosed
("Lipsbury" may denote a particular place, or may be slang for "between my
teeth")   14 **broken meats** scraps of food   15 **three-suited** (the wardrobe permitted to a servant or "knave")   16 **hundred-pound** (the extent of Oswald's
wealth, and thus a sneer at his aspiring to gentility)   16 **worsted-stocking**
(worn by servants)   17 **action-taking** one who refuses a fight and goes to law
instead   17–18 **glass-gazing** conceited   18 **superserviceable** sycophantic,
serving without principle.   18 **finical** overfastidious   18–19 **one-trunk-
inheriting** possessing only a trunkful of goods   19–20 **bawd . . . service** pimp,
to please his master   20–21 **composition** compound   24 **addition** titles
33 **sop o' th' moonshine** i.e., Oswald will admit the moonlight, and so sop it
up, through the open wounds Kent is preparing to give him   34 **cullionly barbermonger** base patron of hairdressers (effeminate man)

Oswald. Away, I have nothing to do with thee. 35

Kent. Draw, you rascal. You come with letters against the King, and take Vanity the puppet's° part against the royalty of her father. Draw, you rogue, or I'll so carbonado° your shanks. Draw, you rascal. Come your ways!° 40

Oswald. Help, ho! Murder! Help!

Kent. Strike, you slave! Stand, rogue! Stand, you neat° slave! Strike! [*Beating him*]

Oswald. Help, ho! Murder, murder!

Enter Edmund, with his rapier drawn, Cornwall, Regan, Gloucester, Servants.

Edmund. How now? What's the matter? Part! 45

Kent. With you,° goodman boy,° if you please! Come, I'll flesh° ye, come on, young master.

Gloucester. Weapons? Arms? What's the matter here?

Cornwall. Keep peace, upon your lives.
He dies that strikes again. What is the matter? 50

Regan. The messengers from our sister and the King.

Cornwall. What is your difference?° Speak.

Oswald. I am scarce in breath, my lord.

Kent. No marvel, you have so bestirred° your valor. You cowardly rascal, nature disclaims in thee.° A 55 tailor made thee.°

Cornwall. Thou art a strange fellow. A tailor make a man?

Kent. A tailor, sir. A stonecutter or a painter could

37 **Vanity the puppet's** Goneril, here identified with one of the personified characters in the morality plays, which were sometimes put on as puppet shows 39 **carbonado** cut across, like a piece of meat before cooking 40 **Come your ways** get along 42 **neat** (1) foppish (2) unmixed, as in "neat wine" 46 **With you** i.e., the quarrel is with you 46 **goodman boy** young man (peasants are "goodmen"; "boy" is a term of contempt) 47 **flesh** introduce to blood (term from hunting) 52 **difference** quarrel 54 **bestirred** exercised 55 **nature disclaims in thee** nature renounces any part in you 55–56 **A tailor made thee** (from the proverb "The tailor makes the man")

60 not have made him so ill, though they had been
but two years o' th' trade.

Cornwall. Speak yet, how grew your quarrel?

Oswald. This ancient ruffian, sir, whose life I have
spared at suit of° his gray beard——

65 *Kent.* Thou whoreson zed,° thou unnecessary letter!
My lord, if you will give me leave, I will tread this
unbolted° villain into mortar and daub the wall of
a jakes° with him. Spare my gray beard, you wagtail!°

70 *Cornwall.* Peace, sirrah!
You beastly° knave, know you no reverence?

Kent. Yes, sir, but anger hath a privilege.

Cornwall. Why art thou angry?

Kent. That such a slave as this should wear a sword,
Who wears no honesty. Such smiling rogues as
75   these,
Like rats, oft bite the holy cords° atwain
Which are too intrince° t' unloose; smooth°
      every passion
That in the natures of their lords rebel,
Being oil to fire, snow to the colder moods;
80 Renege,° affirm, and turn their halcyon beaks°
With every gale and vary° of their masters,
Knowing naught, like dogs, but following.
A plague upon your epileptic° visage!
Smile you° my speeches, as I were a fool?

64 **at suit of** out of pity for   65 **zed** the letter Z, generally omitted in contemporary dictionaries   67 **unbolted** unsifted, i.e., altogether a villain
68 **jakes** privy   68–69 **wagtail** a bird that bobs its tail up and down, and
thus suggests obsequiousness   71 **beastly** irrational   76 **holy cords** sacred
bonds of affection (as between husbands and wives, parents and children)   77 **intrince** entangled, intricate   77 **smooth** appease   80 **Renege**
deny   80 **halcyon beaks** (the halcyon or kingfisher serves here as a type of
the opportunist because, when hung up by the tail or neck, it was supposed
to turn with the wind, like a weathervane)   81 **gale and vary** varying
gale (hendiadys)   83 **epileptic** distorted by grinning   84 **Smile you** do you
smile at

Goose, if I had you upon Sarum Plain,°   85
I'd drive ye cackling home to Camelot.°

Cornwall. What, art thou mad, old fellow?

Gloucester. How fell you out? Say that.

Kent. No contraries° hold more antipathy
Than I and such a knave.   90

Cornwall. Why dost thou call him knave? What is his
fault?

Kent. His countenance likes° me not.

Cornwall. No more perchance does mine, nor his, nor
hers.

Kent. Sir, 'tis my occupation to be plain:
I have seen better faces in my time   95
Than stands on any shoulder that I see
Before me at this instant.

Cornwall.   This is some fellow
Who, having been praised for bluntness, doth
affect
A saucy roughness, and constrains the garb
Quite from his nature.° He cannot flatter, he;   100
An honest mind and plain, he must speak truth.
And° they will take it, so; if not, he's plain.
These kind of knaves I know, which in this
plainness
Harbor more craft and more corrupter ends
Than twenty silly-ducking observants°   105
That stretch their duties nicely.°

Kent. Sir, in good faith, in sincere verity,
Under th' allowance° of your great aspect,°
Whose influence,° like the wreath of radiant fire

85 **Sarum Plain** Salisbury Plain   86 **Camelot** the residence of King Arthur
(presumably a particular point, now lost, is intended here)   89 **contraries** opposites   92 **likes** pleases   99–100 **constrains ... nature** forces the manner
of candid speech to be a cloak, not for candor but for craft   102 **And** if
105 **silly-ducking observants** ridiculously obsequious attendants   106 **nicely**
punctiliously   08 **allowance** approval   108 **aspect** (1) appearance (2) position of the heavenly bodies   109 **influence** astrological power

On flick'ring Phoebus' front°——

110 *Cornwall.*   What mean'st by this?

Kent. To go out of my dialect,° which you discommend
so much. I know, sir, I am no flatterer. He° that
beguiled you in a plain accent was a plain knave,
which, for my part, I will not be, though I should
115 win your displeasure to entreat me to't.°

Cornwall. What was th' offense you gave him?

Oswald. I never gave him any.
It pleased the King his master very late°
To strike at me, upon his misconstruction;°
120 When he, compact,° and flattering his displeasure,
Tripped me behind; being down, insulted, railed,
And put upon him such a deal of man°
That worthied him,° got praises of the King
For him attempting who was self-subdued;°
125 And, in the fleshment° of this dread exploit,
Drew on me here again.

Kent.   None of these rogues and cowards
But Ajax is their fool.°

Cornwall.   Fetch forth the stocks!
You stubborn° ancient knave, you reverent°
    braggart,
We'll teach you.

Kent.   Sir, I am too old to learn.

---

110 **Phoebus' front** forehead of the sun   111 **dialect** customary manner of
speaking   112 **He** i.e., the sort of candid-crafty man Cornwall has been describing   114–15 **though ... to't** even if I were to succeed in bringing
your graceless person ("displeasure" personified, and in lieu of the expected
form, "your grace") to beg me to be a plain knave   118 **very late** recently
119 **misconstruction** misunderstanding   120 **compact** in league with the
king   122 **put ... man** pretended such manly behavior   123 **worthied
him** made him seem heroic   124 **For ... self-subdued** for attacking a man
(Oswald) who offered no resistance   125 **fleshment** the bloodthirstiness
excited by his first success or "fleshing"   126–27 **None ... fool** i.e., cowardly rogues like Oswald always impose on fools like Cornwall (who is
likened to Ajax: [1] the braggart Greek warrior [2] a jakes or privy)
128 **stubborn** rude   128 **reverent** old

Call not your stocks for me, I serve the King,   *130*
On whose employment I was sent to you.
You shall do small respect, show too bold malice
Against the grace and person° of my master,
Stocking his messenger.

Cornwall. Fetch forth the stocks. As I have life and
   honor,   *135*
   There shall he sit till noon.

Regan. Till noon? Till night, my lord, and all night
   too.

Kent. Why, madam, if I were your father's dog,
   You should not use me so.

Regan.   Sir, being his knave, I will.

Cornwall. This is a fellow of the selfsame color°   *140*
   Our sister speaks of. Come, bring away° the stocks.
                   Stocks brought out.

Gloucester. Let me beseech your Grace not to do so.
   His fault is much, and the good King his master
   Will check° him for't. Your purposed° low
     correction
   Is such as basest and contemnèd'st° wretches   *145*
   For pilf'rings and most common trespasses
   Are punished with.
   The King his master needs must take it ill
   That he, so slightly valued in° his messenger,
   Should have him thus restrained.

Cornwall.   I'll answer° that.   *150*

Regan. My sister may receive it much more worse,
   To have her gentleman abused, assaulted,
   For following her affairs. Put in his legs.
               [Kent is put in the stocks.]
   Come, my good lord, away!
            [Exeunt all but Gloucester and Kent.]

---

133 **grace and person** i.e., Lear as sovereign and in his personal character
140 **color** kind   141 **away** out   144 **check** correct   144 **purposed** intended   145 **contemnèd'st** most despised   149 **slightly valued in** little honored in the person of   150 **answer** answer for

Gloucester. I am sorry for thee, friend. 'Tis the Duke's
155   pleasure,
          Whose disposition° all the world well knows
          Will not be rubbed° nor stopped. I'll entreat for
          thee.

Kent. Pray do not, sir. I have watched° and traveled
          hard.
          Some time I shall sleep out, the rest I'll whistle.
160   A good man's fortune may grow out at heels.°
          Give° you good morrow.

Gloucester. The Duke's to blame in this. 'Twill be
          ill taken.°   *Exit.*

Kent. Good King, that must approve° the common
          saw,°
          Thou out of Heaven's benediction com'st
165   To the warm sun.°
          Approach, thou beacon to this under globe,°
          That by thy comfortable° beams I may
          Peruse this letter. Nothing almost sees miracles
          But misery.° I know 'tis from Cordelia,
170   Who hath most fortunately been informed
          Of my obscurèd° course. And shall find time
          From this enormous state, seeking to give
          Losses their remedies.° All weary and o'erwatched,
          Take vantage,° heavy eyes, not to behold
175   This shameful lodging. Fortune, good night;
          Smile once more, turn thy wheel.°

                                                   Sleeps.

---

156 **disposition** inclination   157 **rubbed** diverted (metaphor from the game of bowls)   158 **watched** gone without sleep   160 **A ... heels** even a good man may have bad fortune   161 **Give** God give   162 **taken** received   163 **approve** confirm   163 **saw** proverb   164–65 **Thou ... sun** i.e., Lear goes from better to worse, from Heaven's blessing or shelter to lack of shelter   166 **beacon ... globe** i.e., the sun, whose rising Kent anticipates   167 **comfortable** comforting   168–69 **Nothing ... misery** i.e., true perception belongs only to the wretched   171 **obscurèd** disguised   171–73 **shall ... remedies** (a possible reading: Cordelia, away from this monstrous state of things, will find occasion to right the wrongs we suffer)   174 **vantage** advantage (of sleep)   176 **turn thy wheel** i.e., so that Kent, who is at the bottom, may climb upward

[Scene 3.   *A wood.*]

Enter Edgar.

Edgar. I heard myself proclaimed,
  And by the happy° hollow of a tree
  Escaped the hunt. No port is free, no place
  That guard and most unusual vigilance
  Does not attend my taking.° Whiles I may 'scape,   5
  I will preserve myself; and am bethought°
  To take the basest and most poorest shape
  That ever penury, in contempt of man,
  Brought near to beast;° my face I'll grime with filth,
  Blanket° my loins, elf° all my hairs in knots,   10
  And with presented° nakedness outface°
  The winds and persecutions of the sky.
  The country gives me proof° and precedent
  Of Bedlam° beggars, who, with roaring voices,
  Strike° in their numbed and mortified° bare arms   15
  Pins, wooden pricks,° nails, sprigs of rosemary;
  And with this horrible object,° from low° farms,
  Poor pelting° villages, sheepcotes, and mills,
  Sometimes with lunatic bans,° sometime with
    prayers,
  Enforce their charity. Poor Turlygod, Poor Tom,°   20
  That's something yet: Edgar I nothing am.°   *Exit.*

2.3.2 **happy** lucky   5 **attend my taking** watch to capture me   6 **am be-
thought** have decided   8–9 **penury . . . beast** poverty, to show how contemptible man is, reduced to the level of a beast   10 **Blanket** cover only
with a blanket   10 **elf** tangle (into "elflocks," supposed to be caused by
elves)   11 **presented** the show of   11 **outface** brave   13 **proof** example
14 **Bedlam** (see 1.2.r.   146–47)   15 **strike** stick   15 **mortified** not alive to
pain   16 **pricks** skewers   17 **object** spectacle   17 **low** humble   18 **pelting** paltry   19 **bans** curses   20 **Poor . . . Tom** (Edgar recites the names a
Bedlam beggar gives himself)   21 **That's . . . am** there's a chance for me in
that I am no longer known for myself

[Scene 4.   *Before Gloucester's castle. Kent in the stocks.*]

Enter Lear, Fool, and Gentleman.

Lear. 'Tis strange that they should so depart from home,
And not send back my messenger.

Gentleman.   As I learned,
The night before there was no purpose° in them
Of this remove.°

Kent.   Hail to thee, noble master.

5 *Lear.* Ha!
Mak'st thou this shame thy pastime?°

Kent.   No, my lord.

Fool. Ha, ha, he wears cruel° garters. Horses are tied
by the heads, dogs and bears by th' neck, monkeys
by th' loins, and men by th' legs. When a man's over-
10 lusty at legs,° then he wears wooden netherstocks.°

Lear. What's he that hath so much thy place mistook
To set thee here?

Kent.   It is both he and she,
Your son and daughter.

Lear. No.

15 *Kent.* Yes.

Lear. No, I say.

Kent. I say yea.

2.4.3 **purpose** intention   4 **remove** removal   6 **Mak'st ... pastime** i.e.,
are you doing this to amuse yourself   7 **cruel** (1) painful (2) "crewel," a
worsted yarn used in garters   9–10 **overlusty at legs** (1) a vagabond (2) ?
sexually promiscuous   10 **netherstocks** stockings (as opposed to knee
breeches or upperstocks)

Lear. No, no, they would not.

Kent. Yes, they have.

Lear. By Jupiter, I swear no!   20

Kent. By Juno, I swear ay!

Lear.   They durst not do't;
They could not, would not do't. 'Tis worse than
    murder
To do upon respect° such violent outrage.
Resolve° me with all modest° haste which way
Thou mightst deserve or they impose this usage,   25
Coming from us.

Kent.   My lord, when at their home
I did commend° your Highness' letters to them,
Ere I was risen from the place that showed
My duty kneeling, came there a reeking post,°
Stewed° in his haste, half breathless, panting forth   30
From Goneril his mistress salutations,
Delivered letters, spite of intermission,°
Which presently° they read; on° whose contents
They summoned up their meiny,° straight took
    horse,
Commanded me to follow and attend   35
The leisure of their answer, gave me cold looks,
And meeting here the other messenger,
Whose welcome I perceived had poisoned mine,
Being the very fellow which of late
Displayed° so saucily against your Highness,   40
Having more man than wit° about me, drew;
He raised° the house, with loud and coward cries.
Your son and daughter found this trespass worth°
The shame which here it suffers.

23 **upon respect** (1) on the respect due to the King (2) deliberately
24 **Resolve** inform   24 **modest** becoming   27 **commend** deliver   29 **reeking post** sweating messenger   30 **stewed** steaming   32 **spite of intermission**
in spite of the interrupting of my business   33 **presently** at once   33 **on** on the
strength of   34 **meiny** retinue   40 **Displayed** showed off   41 **more man
than wit** more manhood than sense   42 **raised** aroused   43 **worth** deserving

45 *Fool.* Winter's not gone yet, if the wild geese fly that
        way.°
                    Fathers that wear rags
                        Do make their children blind,°
                    But fathers that bear bags°
50   Shall see their children kind.
                    Fortune, that arrant whore,
                        Ne'er turns the key° to th' poor.
        But for all this, thou shalt have as many dolors° for
        thy daughters as thou canst tell° in a year.

55 *Lear.* O, how this mother° swells up toward my heart!
        Hysterica passio,° down, thou climbing sorrow,
        Thy element's° below. Where is this daughter?

    Kent. With the Earl, sir, here within.

    Lear.   Follow me not;
        Stay here.   *Exit.*

    Gentleman. Made you no more offense but what you
60   speak of?

    Kent. None.
        How chance° the King comes with so small a
            number?

    Fool. And° thou hadst been set i' th' stocks for that
        question, thou'dst well deserved it.

65 *Kent.* Why, Fool?

    Fool. We'll set thee to school to an ant, to teach thee
        there's no laboring i' th' winter.° All that follow

45–46 **Winter's . . . way** i.e., more trouble is to come, since Cornwall and
Regan act so ("geese" is used contemptuously, as in Kent's quarrel with
Oswald, 2.2. 85–6) 48 **blind** i.e., indifferent 49 **bags** moneybags
52 **turns the key** i.e., opens the door 53 **dolors** (1) sorrows (2) dollars
(English name for Spanish and German coins) 54 **tell** (1) tell about
(2) count 55–56 **mother . . . Hysterica passio** hysteria, causing suffocation or choking 57 **element** proper place 62 **How chance** how does it
happen that 63 **And** if 66–67 **We'll . . . winter** (in the popular fable the
ant, unlike the improvident grasshopper, anticipates the winter when none
can labor by laying up provisions in the summer. Lear, trusting foolishly to
summer days, finds himself unprovided for, and unable to provide, now that
"winter" has come)

their noses are led by their eyes but blind men,
and there's not a nose among twenty but can smell
him that's stinking.° Let go thy hold when a great   70
wheel runs down a hill, lest it break thy neck with
following. But the great one that goes upward,
let him draw thee after. When a wise man gives
thee better counsel, give me mine again. I would
have none but knaves follow it since a Fool gives   75
it.

That sir, which serves and seeks for gain,
    And follows but for form,°
Will pack,° when it begins to rain,
    And leave thee in the storm.   80
But I will tarry; the Fool will stay,
    And let the wise man fly.
The knave turns Fool that runs away,
    The Fool no knave,° perdy.°

Kent. Where learned you this, Fool?   85

Fool. Not i' th' stocks, fool.

                Enter Lear and Gloucester.

Lear. Deny° to speak with me? They are sick, they
    are weary,
They have traveled all the night? Mere fetches,°
The images° of revolt and flying off!°
Fetch me a better answer.

Gloucester.   My dear lord,   90
    You know the fiery quality° of the Duke,
    How unremovable and fixed he is
    In his own course.

Lear.   Vengeance, plague, death, confusion!
    Fiery? What quality? Why, Gloucester, Gloucester,
    I'd speak with the Duke of Cornwall and his wife.   95

67–70 **All ... stinking** i.e., all can smell out the decay of Lear's fortunes   78 **form** show   79 **pack** be off   83–84 **The ... knave** i.e., the faith-
less man is the true fool, for wisdom requires fidelity. Lear's Fool, who
remains faithful, is at least no knave   84 **perdy** by God (Fr. *par Dieu*)
87 **Deny** refuse   88 **fetches** subterfuges, acts of tacking (nautical metaphor)
89 **images** exact likenesses   89 **flying off** desertion   91 **quality** temperament.

Gloucester. Well, my good lord, I have informed them
          so.

Lear. Informed them? Dost thou understand me,
          man?

Gloucester. Ay, my good lord.

Lear. The King would speak with Cornwall. The dear
          father
          Would with his daughter speak, commands—tends°
100   —service.
          Are they informed of this? My breath and blood!
          Fiery? The fiery Duke, tell the hot Duke that—
          No, but not yet. May be he is not well.
          Infirmity doth still neglect all office
105   Whereto our health is bound.° We are not
               ourselves
          When nature, being oppressed, commands the
               mind
          To suffer with the body. I'll forbear;
          And am fallen out° with my more headier will°
          To take the indisposed and sickly fit
          For the sound man. [*Looking on Kent*] Death on
110   my state!° Wherefore
          Should he sit here? This act persuades me
          That this remotion° of the Duke and her
          Is practice° only. Give me my servant forth.°
          Go tell the Duke and's wife I'd speak with them!
          Now, presently!° Bid them come forth and hear
115   me,
          Or at their chamber door I'll beat the drum
          Till it cry sleep to death.°

Gloucester. I would have all well betwixt you.

                                        Exit.

---

100 **tends** attends (i.e., awaits); with, possibly, an ironic second meaning,
"tenders," or "offers"   105 **Whereto ... bound** duties which we are required to perform, when in health   108 **fallen out** angry   108 **headier will**
headlong inclination   110 **state** royal condition   112 **remotion** (1) removal
(2) remaining aloof   113 **practice** pretense   113 **forth** i.e., out of the
stocks   115 **presently** at once   117 **cry ... death** follow sleep, like a cry
or pack of hounds, until it kills it

Lear. O me, my heart, my rising heart! But down!

Fool. Cry to it, Nuncle, as the cockney° did to   *120*
the eels when she put 'em i' th' paste° alive. She
knapped° 'em o' th' coxcombs° with a stick and
cried, "Down, wantons,° down!" 'Twas her brother
that, in pure kindness to his horse, buttered his
hay.°   *125*

Enter Cornwall, Regan, Gloucester, Servants.

Lear. Good morrow to you both.

Cornwall.   Hail to your Grace.

                   Kent here set at liberty.

Regan. I am glad to see your Highness.

Lear. Regan, I think you are. I know what reason
I have to think so. If thou shouldst not be glad,
I would divorce me from thy mother's tomb,   *130*
Sepulchring an adultress.° [*To Kent*] O, are you
   free?
Some other time for that. Beloved Regan,
Thy sister's naught.° O Regan, she hath tied
Sharp-toothed unkindness, like a vulture, here.

                [*Points to his heart.*]

I can scarce speak to thee. Thou'lt not believe   *135*
With how depraved a quality°—O Regan!

Regan. I pray you, sir, take patience. I have hope
You less know how to value her desert
Than she to scant her duty.°

Lear.   Say? how is that?

120 **cockney** Londoner (ignorant city dweller) 121 **paste** pastry pie
122 **knapped** rapped 122 **coxcombs** heads 123 **wantons** i.e., playful
things (with a sexual implication) 125 **buttered his hay** i.e., the city
dweller does from ignorance what the dishonest ostler does from craft:
greases the hay the traveler has paid for, so that the horse will not eat
130–31 **divorce . . . adultress** i.e., repudiate your dead mother as having
conceived you by another man 133 **naught** wicked 136 **quality** nature
137–39 **I . . . duty** (despite the double negative, the passage means, "I believe
that you fail to give Goneril her due, rather than that she fails to fulfill her
duty")

140 *Regan.* I cannot think my sister in the least
     Would fail her obligation. If, sir, perchance
     She have restrained the riots of your followers,
     'Tis on such ground, and to such wholesome end,
     As clears her from all blame.

Lear. My curses on her!

145 *Regan.*   O, sir, you are old,
     Nature in you stands on the very verge
     Of his confine.° You should be ruled, and led
     By some discretion that discerns your state
     Better than you yourself.° Therefore I pray you
150   That to our sister you do make return,
     Say you have wronged her.

Lear.   Ask her forgiveness?
     Do you but mark how this becomes the house:°
     "Dear daughter, I confess that I am old.

                                [Kneeling.]

     Age is unnecessary. On my knees I beg
155   That you'll vouchsafe me raiment, bed, and food."

Regan. Good sir, no more. These are unsightly tricks.
     Return you to my sister.

Lear.   *[Rising]* Never, Regan.
     She hath abated° me of half my train,
     Looked black upon me, struck me with her tongue,
160   Most serpentlike, upon the very heart.
     All the stored vengeances of heaven fall
     On her ingrateful top!° Strike her young bones,°
     You taking° airs, with lameness.

Cornwall.   Fie, sir, fie!

Lear. You nimble lightnings, dart your blinding flames
165   Into her scornful eyes! Infect her beauty,

146–47 **Nature ... confine** i.e., you are nearing the end of your life
148–49 **some ... yourself** some discreet person who understands your condition more than you do   152 **becomes the house** suits my royal and paternal position   158 **abated** curtailed   162 **top** head   162 **young bones** (the reference may be to unborn children, rather than to Goneril herself) 163 **taking** infecting

You fen-sucked° fogs, drawn by the pow'rful sun,
To fall and blister° her pride.

Regan.   O the blest gods!
So will you wish on me when the rash mood is on.

Lear. No, Regan, thou shalt never have my curse.
Thy tender-hefted° nature shall not give   *170*
Thee o'er to harshness. Her eyes are fierce, but thine
Do comfort, and not burn. 'Tis not in thee
To grudge my pleasures, to cut off my train,
To bandy° hasty words, to scant my sizes,°
And, in conclusion, to oppose the bolt°   *175*
Against my coming in. Thou better know'st
The offices of nature, bond of childhood,°
Effects° of courtesy, dues of gratitude.
Thy half o' th' kingdom hast thou not forgot,
Wherein I thee endowed.

Regan.   Good sir, to th' purpose.°   *180*

                       Tucket within.

Lear. Who put my man i' th' stocks?

Cornwall.   What trumpet's that?

Regan. I know't—my sister's. This approves° her
    letter,
That she would soon be here.

                 Enter Oswald.

                 Is your lady come?

Lear. This is a slave, whose easy borrowed° pride
Dwells in the fickle grace° of her he follows.   *185*
Out, varlet,° from my sight.

Cornwall.   What means your Grace?

166 **fen-sucked** drawn up from swamps by the sun   167 **fall and blister** fall upon and raise blisters   170 **tender-hefted** gently framed   174 **bandy** volley (metaphor from tennis)   174 **scant my sizes** reduce my allowances   175 **oppose the bolt** i.e., bar the door   177 **offices ... childhood** natural duties, a child's duty to its parent   178 **Effects** manifestations 180 **to th' purpose** come to the point   182 **approves** confirms   184 **easy borrowed** (1) facile and taken from another (2) acquired without anything to back it up (like money borrowed without security)   185 **grace** favor 186 **varlet** base fellow

Lear. Who stocked my servant? Regan, I have good
      hope
Thou didst not know on't.

                    Enter Goneril.

                              Who comes here? O heavens!
If you do love old men, if your sweet sway
190   Allow° obedience, if you yourselves are old,
Make it° your cause. Send down, and take my part.
[*To Goneril*] Art not ashamed to look upon
      this beard?
O Regan, will you take her by the hand?

Goneril. Why not by th' hand, sir? How have I
      offended?
195   All's not offense that indiscretion finds°
And dotage terms so.

Lear.   O sides,° you are too tough!
Will you yet hold? How came my man i' th' stocks?

Cornwall. I set him there, sir; but his own disorders°
Deserved much less advancement.°

Lear.   You? Did you?

200   *Regan.* I pray you, father, being weak, seem so.°
If till the expiration of your month
You will return and sojourn with my sister,
Dismissing half your train, come then to me.
I am now from home, and out of that provision
205   Which shall be needful for your entertainment.°

Lear. Return to her, and fifty men dismissed?
No, rather I abjure all roofs, and choose
To wage° against the enmity o' th' air,
To be a comrade with the wolf and owl,
210   Necessity's sharp pinch.° Return with her?
Why, the hot-blooded° France, that dowerless
      took

190 **Allow** approve of   191 **it** i.e., my cause   195 **finds** judges   196 **sides**
breast   198 **disorders** misconduct   199 **advancement** promotion 200 **seem
so** i.e., act weak   205 **entertainment** maintenance   208 **wage** fight
210 **Necessity's sharp pinch** (a summing up of the hard choice he has just
announced)   211 **hot-blooded** passionate

Our youngest born, I could as well be brought
To knee° his throne, and, squirelike,° pension beg
To keep base life afoot. Return with her?
Persuade me rather to be slave and sumpter°   215
To this detested groom. [*Pointing at Oswald.*]

Goneril.   At your choice, sir.

Lear. I prithee, daughter, do not make me mad.
I will not trouble thee, my child; farewell.
We'll no more meet, no more see one another.
But yet thou art my flesh, my blood, my daughter,   220
Or rather a disease that's in my flesh,
Which I must needs call mine. Thou art a boil,
A plague-sore, or embossèd carbuncle°
In my corrupted blood. But I'll not chide thee.
Let shame come when it will, I do not call it.   225
I do not bid the Thunder-bearer° shoot,
Nor tell tales of thee to high-judging° Jove.
Mend when thou canst, be better at thy leisure,
I can be patient, I can stay with Regan,
I and my hundred knights.

Regan.   Not altogether so.   230
I looked not for you yet, nor am provided
For your fit welcome. Give ear, sir, to my sister,
For those that mingle reason with your passion°
Must be content to think you old, and so—
But she knows what she does.

Lear.   Is this well spoken?   235

Regan. I dare avouch° it, sir. What, fifty followers?
Is it not well? What should you need of more?
Yea, or so many, sith that° both charge° and
     danger
Speak 'gainst so great a number? How in one house

---

213 **knee** kneel before   213 **squirelike** like a retainer   215 **sumpter** pack
horse   223 **embossèd carbuncle** swollen boil   226 **Thunder-bearer** i.e.,
Jupiter   227 **high-judging** (1) supreme (2) judging from heaven   233 **mingle ... passion** i.e., consider your turbulent behavior coolly and reasonably
236 **avouch** swear by   238 **sith that** since   238 **charge** expense

240   Should many people, under two commands,
    Hold° amity? 'Tis hard, almost impossible.

Goneril. Why might not you, my lord, receive attendance
    From those that she calls servants, or from mine?

Regan. Why not, my lord? If then they chanced to slack° ye,
245   We could control them. If you will come to me
    (For now I spy a danger), I entreat you
    To bring but five-and-twenty. To no more
    Will I give place or notice.°

Lear. I gave you all. *himmecserins*

Regan. *by recognition*   And in good time you gave it.

250 *Lear.* Made you my guardians, my depositaries,°
    But kept a reservation° to be followed
    With such a number. What, must I come to you
    With five-and-twenty? Regan, said you so?

Regan. And speak't again, my lord. No more with me.

Lear. Those wicked creatures yet do look well-
255   favored°
    When others are more wicked; not being the worst
    Stands in some rank of praise.° [*To Goneril*] I'll go with thee.
    Thy fifty yet doth double five-and-twenty,
    And thou art twice her love.°

Goneril.   Hear me, my lord.
260   What need you five-and-twenty? ten? or five?
    To follow° in a house where twice so many
    Have a command to tend you?

Regan.   What need one?

Lear. O reason° not the need! Our basest beggars

---

241 **hold** preserve   244 **slack** neglect   248 **notice** recognition   250 **depositaries** trustees   251 **reservation** condition   255 **well-favored** handsome   256–57 **not . . . praise** i.e., that Goneril is not so bad as Regan is one thing in her favor   259 **her love** i.e., as loving as she   261 **follow** attend on you   263 **reason** scrutinize

hic's reasoned love

Are in the poorest thing superfluous.°
Allow not nature more than nature needs,°   265
Man's life is cheap as beast's. Thou art a lady:
If only to go warm were gorgeous,
Why, nature needs not what thou gorgeous wear'st,
Which scarcely keeps thee warm.° But, for true
    need—
You heavens, give me that patience, patience I
    need—   270
You see me here, you gods, a poor old man,
As full of grief as age, wretched in both.
If it be you that stirs these daughters' hearts
Against their father, fool° me not so much
To bear° it tamely; touch me with noble anger,   275
And let not women's weapons, water drops,
Stain my man's cheeks. No, you unnatural hags!
I will have such revenges on you both
That all the world shall—I will do such things—
What they are, yet I know not; but they shall be   280
The terrors of the earth. You think I'll weep.
No, I'll not weep.

                              Storm and tempest.

I have full cause of weeping, but this heart
Shall break into a hundred thousand flaws°
Or ere° I'll weep. O Fool, I shall go mad!   285

        Exeunt Lear, Gloucester, Kent, and Fool.

Cornwall. Let us withdraw, 'twill be a storm.

Regan. This house is little; the old man and's people
    Cannot be well bestowed.°

Goneril. 'Tis his own blame; hath° put himself from
    rest°
And must needs taste his folly.   290

264 **Are . . . superfluous** i.e., have some trifle not absolutely necessary
265 **needs** i.e., to sustain life   267–69 **If . . . warm** i.e., if to satisfy the
need for warmth were to be gorgeous, you would not need the clothing you
wear, which is worn more for beauty than warmth   274 **fool** humiliate
275 **To bear** as to make me bear   284 **flaws** (1) pieces (2) cracks (3) gusts
of passion   285 **Or ere** before   288 **bestowed** lodged   289 **hath** he hath
289 **rest** (1) place of residence (2) repose of mind

Regan. For his particular,° I'll receive him gladly,
But not one follower.

Goneril.   So am I purposed.°
Where is my Lord of Gloucester?

Cornwall. Followed the old man forth.

                    Enter Gloucester.

                              He is returned.

Gloucester. The King is in high rage.

295 *Cornwall.*   Whither is he going?

Gloucester. He calls to horse, but will I know not
whither.

Cornwall. 'Tis best to give him way, he leads himself.°

Goneril. My lord, entreat him by no means to stay.

Gloucester. Alack, the night comes on, and the high
winds
300   Do sorely ruffle.° For many miles about
There's scarce a bush.

Regan.   O, sir, to willful men
The injuries that they themselves procure
Must be their schoolmasters. Shut up your doors.
He is attended with a desperate train,
305   And what they may incense° him to, being apt
To have his ear abused,° wisdom bids fear.

Cornwall. Shut up your doors, my lord; 'tis a wild
night.
My Regan counsels well. Come out o' th' storm.

                                        Exeunt.

[handwritten marginal notes: "let em learn" beside Regan's lines; "like Lear done to Cord + Kent" at bottom]

---

291 **his   particular** himself   personally   292 **purposed** determined
297 **give . . . himself** let him go; he insists on his own way   300 **ruffle** rage
305 **incense** incite   305–06 **being . . . abused** he being inclined to harken
to bad counsel

ACT 3

Scene 1. [*A heath.*]

Storm still.° Enter Kent and a Gentleman
severally.

Kent. Who's there besides foul weather?

Gentleman. One minded like the weather most
    unquietly.°

Kent. I know you. Where's the King?

Gentleman. Contending with the fretful elements;
    Bids the wind blow the earth into the sea,   5
    Or swell the curlèd waters 'bove the main,°
    That things might change,° or cease; tears his white
        hair,
    Which the impetuous blasts, with eyeless° rage,
    Catch in their fury, and make nothing of;
    Strives in his little world of man° to outscorn   10
    The to-and-fro-conflicting wind and rain.
    This night, wherein the cub-drawn° bear would
        couch,°
    The lion, and the belly-pinchèd° wolf
    Keep their fur dry, unbonneted° he runs,

3.1. s.d. **still** continually   2 **minded . . . unquietly** disturbed in mind, like
the weather   6 **main** land   7 **change** (1) be destroyed (2) be exchanged
(i.e., turned upside down) (3) change for the better   8 **eyeless** (1) blind (2)
invisible   10 **little world of man** (the microcosm, as opposed to the universe or macrocosm, which it copies in little)   12 **cub-drawn** sucked dry
by her cubs, and so ravenously hungry   12 **couch** take shelter in its lair
18 **belly-pinchèd** starved   14 **unbonneted** hatless

And bids what will take all.°

15 *Kent.*   But who is with him?

Gentleman. None but the Fool, who labors to outjest
His heart-struck injuries.

Kent.   Sir, I do know you,
And dare upon the warrant of my note°
Commend a dear thing° to you. There is division,
20 Although as yet the face of it is covered
With mutual cunning, 'twixt Albany and Cornwall;
Who have—as who have not, that° their great
    stars
Throned° and set high?—servants, who seem no
    less,°
Which are to France the spies and speculations
25 Intelligent° of our state. What hath been seen,
Either in snuffs and packings° of the Dukes,
Or the hard rein which both of them hath borne°
Against the old kind King, or something deeper,
Whereof, perchance, these are but furnishings°—
30 But, true it is, from France there comes a power°
Into this scattered° kingdom, who already,
Wise in our negligence, have secret feet
In some of our best ports, and are at point°
To show their open banner. Now to you:
35 If on my credit you dare build° so far
To° make your speed to Dover, you shall find
Some that will thank you, making° just° report
Of how unnatural and bemadding° sorrow
The King hath cause to plain.°
40 I am a gentleman of blood and breeding,°

15 **take all** (like the reckless gambler, staking all he has left)   18 **warrant
of my note** strength of what I have taken note (of you)   19 **Commend . . .
thing** entrust important business   22 **that** whom · 22–23 **stars/Throned**
destinies have throned   23 **seem no less** seem to be so   24–25
speculations/Intelligent giving intelligence   26 **snuffs and packings**
quarrels and plots   27 **hard . . . borne** close and cruel control they have exercised   29 **furnishings** excuses   30 **power** army   31 **scattered** dis-
united   33 **at point** ready   35 **If . . . build** if you can trust me, proceed
36 **To** as to   37 **making** for making   37 **just** accurate   38 **bemadding**
maddening   39 **plain** complain of   40 **blood and breeding** noble family

And from some knowledge and assurance° offer
This office° to you.

Gentleman. I will talk further with you.

Kent.   No, do not.
For confirmation that I am much more
Than my out-wall,° open this purse and take   45
What it contains. If you shall see Cordelia,
As fear not but you shall, show her this ring,
And she will tell you who that fellow° is
That yet you do not know. Fie on this storm!
I will go seek the King.   50

Gentleman. Give me your hand. Have you no more to
    say?

Kent. Few words, but, to effect,° more than all yet:
That when we have found the King—in which your
    pain°
That way, I'll this—he that first lights on him,
Holla the other.   *Exeunt [severally].* 55

Scene 2.   [*Another part of the heath.*]

Storm still.

Enter Lear and Fool.

Lear. Blow, winds, and crack your cheeks. Rage, blow!
    You cataracts and hurricanoes,° spout
    Till you have drenched our steeples, drowned the
        cocks.°

41 **knowledge and assurance** sure and trustworthy information   42 **office**
service (i.e., the trip to Dover)   45 **out-wall** superficial appearance   48 **fellow** companion   52 **to effect** in their importance   53 **pain** labor 3.2.2 **hurri-
canoes** waterspouts   3 **cocks** weathercocks

You sulph'rous and thought-executing° fires,
5   Vaunt-couriers° of oak-cleaving thunderbolts,
Singe my white head. And thou, all-shaking thunder,
Strike flat the thick rotundity° o' th' world,
Crack Nature's molds,° all germains spill° at once,
That makes ingrateful° man.

10 *Fool.* O Nuncle, court holy-water° in a dry house is
better than this rain water out o' door. Good
Nuncle, in; ask thy daughters blessing. Here's a
night pities neither wise man nor fools.

Lear. Rumble thy bellyful. Spit, fire. Spout, rain!
15   Nor rain, wind, thunder, fire are my daughters.
I tax° not you, you elements, with unkindness.
I never gave you kingdom, called you children,
You owe me no subscription.° Then let fall
Your horrible pleasure.° Here I stand your slave,
20   A poor, infirm, weak, and despised old man.
But yet I call you servile ministers,°
That will with two pernicious daughters join   .
Your high-engendered battles° 'gainst a head
So old and white as this. O, ho! 'tis foul.

25 *Fool.* He that has a house to put 's head in has a good
headpiece.°
           The codpiece° that will house
           Before the head has any,
           The head and he° shall louse:
30   So beggars marry many.°
           The man that makes his toe

4 **thought-executing** (1) doing execution as quick as thought (2) executing
or carrying out the thought of him who hurls the lightning 5 **Vaunt-
couriers** heralds, scouts who range before the main body of the army 7 **ro-
tundity** i.e., not only the sphere of the globe, but the roundness of gestation
(Delius) 8 **Nature's molds** the molds or forms in which men are made
8 **all germains spill** destroy the basic seeds of life 9 **ingrateful** ungrateful
10 **court holy-water** flattery 16 **tax** accuse 18 **subscription** allegiance,
submission 9 **pleasure** will 21 **ministers** agents 23 **high-engendered
battles** armies formed in the heavens 26 **headpiece** (1) helmet (2) brain
27 **codpiece** penis (lit., padding worn at the crotch of a man's hose) 29 **he**
it 30 **many** i.e., lice 27–30 **The … many** i.e., the man who gratifies
his sexual appetites before he has a roof over his head will end up a lousy
beggar

What he his heart should make
    Shall of a corn cry woe,
        And turn his sleep to wake.°
For there was never yet fair woman but she made   35
mouths in a glass.°

Enter Kent.

Lear. No, I will be the pattern of all patience,
I will say nothing.

Kent. Who's there?

Fool. Marry,° here's grace and a codpiece; that's a   40
wise man and a fool.°

Kent. Alas, sir, are you here? Things that love night
Love not such nights as these. The wrathful skies
Gallow° the very wanderers of the dark
And make them keep° their caves. Since I was man   45
Such sheets of fire, such bursts of horrid° thunder,
Such groans of roaring wind and rain, I never
Remember to have heard. Man's nature cannot
    carry°
Th' affliction nor the fear.

Lear.   Let the great gods
That keep this dreadful pudder° o'er our heads   50
Find out their enemies now.° Tremble, thou wretch,
That hast within thee undivulgèd crimes
Unwhipped of justice. Hide thee, thou bloody hand,
Thou perjured,° and thou simular° of virtue

31–34 **The ... wake** i.e., the man who, ignoring the fit order of things,
elevates what is base above what is noble, will suffer for it as Lear has, in
banishing Cordelia and enriching her sisters   35–36 **made mouths in a
glass** posed before a mirror (irrelevant nonsense, except that it calls to mind
the general theme of vanity and folly)   40 **Marry** by the Virgin Mary
40–41 **here's ... fool** (Kent's question is answered: The King ["grace"]
is here, and the Fool—who customarily wears an exaggerated codpiece.
But which is which is left ambiguous, since Lear has previously
been called a codpiece)   44 **Gallow** frighten   45 **keep** remain inside
46 **horrid** horrible   48 **carry** endure   50 **pudder** turmoil   51 **Find ...
now** i.e., discover sinners by the terror they reveal   54 **perjured** perjurer
54 **simular** counterfeiter

55   That art incestuous. Caitiff,° to pieces shake,
        That under covert and convenient seeming°
        Has practiced on° man's life. Close° pent-up guilts,
        Rive° your concealing continents° and cry
        These dreadful summoners grace.° I am a man
        More sinned against than sinning.

60 *Kent.*   Alack, bareheaded?
        Gracious my lord,° hard by here is a hovel;
        Some friendship will it lend you 'gainst the
            tempest.
        Repose you there, while I to this hard house
        (More harder than the stones whereof 'tis raised,
65   Which even but now, demanding after° you,
        Denied me to come in) return, and force
        Their scanted° courtesy.

    Lear.   My wits begin to turn.
        Come on, my boy. How dost, my boy? Art cold?
        I am cold myself. Where is this straw, my fellow?
70   The art° of our necessities is strange,
        That can make vile things precious. Come, your
            hovel.
        Poor Fool and knave, I have one part in my heart
        That's sorry yet for thee.

    Fool. [*Singing*]
        He that has and a little tiny wit,
75   With heigh-ho, the wind and the rain,
        Must make content with his fortunes fit,°
            Though the rain it raineth every day.

    Lear. True, my good boy. Come, bring us to this hovel.
                                    Exit [*with Kent*].

55 **Caitiff** wretch   56 **seeming** hypocrisy   57 **practiced on** plotted against
57 **Close** hidden   58 **Rive** split open   58 **continents** containers   58–59 **cry
. . . grace** beg mercy from the vengeful gods (here figured as officers who
summoned a man charged with immorality before the ecclesiastical
court)   61 **Gracious my lord** my gracious lord   65 **demanding after** asking for   67 **scanted** stinted   70 **art** magic powers of the alchemists, who
sought to transmute base metals into precious   76 **Must . . . fit** must
be satisfied with a fortune as tiny as his wit

Fool. This is a brave° night to cool a courtesan. I'll
   speak a prophecy ere I go: 80

   When priests are more in word than matter;
   When brewers mar their malt with water;
   When nobles are their tailors' tutors,
   No heretics burned, but wenches' suitors;°
   When every case in law is right,   85
   No squire in debt nor no poor knight;
   When slanders do not live in tongues;
   Nor cutpurses come not to throngs;
   When usurers tell their gold i' th' field,°
   And bawds and whores do churches build,°   90
   Then shall the realm of Albion°
   Come to great confusion.
   Then comes the time, who lives to see't,
   That going shall be used with feet.°

This prophecy Merlin° shall make, for I live before   95
his time.   *Exit.*

Scene 3. [*Gloucester's castle.*]

Enter Gloucester and Edmund.

Gloucester. Alack, alack, Edmund, I like not this unnatural dealing. When I desired their leave that I
   might pity° him, they took from me the use of mine

79 **brave** fine   81–84 **When . . . suitors** (the first four prophecies are fulfilled already, and hence "confusion" has come to England. The priest does
not suit his action to his words. The brewer adulterates his beer. The noble-
man is subservient to his tailor [i.e., cares only for fashion]. Religious
heretics escape, and only those burn [i.e., suffer] who are afflicted with
venereal disease)   89 **tell . . . field** count their money in the open
85–90 **When . . . build** (the last six prophecies, as they are Utopian, are
meant ironically. They will never be fulfilled)   91 **Albion** England
94 **going . . . feet** people will walk on their feet   95 **Merlin** King Arthur's
great magician who, according to Holinshed's **Chronicles,** lived later than
Lear   3.3.3 **pity** show pity to

own house, charged me on pain of perpetual dis-
5   pleasure neither to speak of him, entreat for him,
or any way sustain° him.

Edmund. Most savage and unnatural.

Gloucester. Go to; say you nothing. There is division°
between the Dukes, and a worse° matter than that.
10   I have received a letter this night—'tis dangerous
to be spoken°—I have locked the letter in my
closet.° These injuries the King now bears will be
revenged home;° there is part of a power° already
footed;° we must incline to° the King. I will look°
15   him and privily° relieve him. Go you and maintain
talk with the Duke, that my charity be not of° him
perceived. If he ask for me, I am ill and gone to
bed. If I die for it, as no less is threatened me, the
King my old master must be relieved. There is
20   strange things toward,° Edmund; pray you be careful.   *Exit.*

Edmund. This courtesy forbid° thee shall the Duke
Instantly know, and of that letter too.
This seems a fair deserving,° and must draw me
25   That which my father loses—no less than all.
The younger rises when the old doth fall.

                                    Exit.

3.3.6 **sustain** care for   8 **division** falling out   9 **worse** more serious (i.e.,
the French invasion)   11 **spoken** spoken of   12 **closet** room   13 **home** to
the utmost   13 **power** army   14 **footed** landed   14 **incline to** take the
side of   14 **look** search for   15 **privily** secretly   16 **of** by   20 **toward**
impending   22 **courtesy forbid** kindness forbidden (i.e., to Lear)   24 **fair
deserving** an action deserving reward

Scene 4. [*The heath. Before a hovel.*]

Enter Lear, Kent, and Fool.

Kent. Here is the place, my lord. Good my lord,
     enter.
   The tyranny of the open night's too rough
   For nature to endure.

                              Storm still.

Lear.   Let me alone.

Kent. Good my lord, enter here.

Lear.   Wilt break my heart?°

Kent. I had rather break mine own. Good my lord,
     enter.   5

Lear. Thou think'st 'tis much that this contentious
     storm
   Invades us to the skin: so 'tis to thee;
   But where the greater malady is fixed,°
   The lesser is scarce felt. Thou'dst shun a bear;
   But if thy flight lay toward the roaring sea,   10
   Thou'dst meet the bear i' th' mouth.° When the
     mind's free,°
   The body's delicate. The tempest in my mind
   Doth from my senses take all feeling else,
   Save what beats there. Filial ingratitude,
   Is it not as° this mouth should tear this hand   15
   For lifting food to't? But I will punish home.°
   No, I will weep no more. In such a night
   To shut me out! Pour on, I will endure.

3.4.4 **break my heart** i.e., by shutting out the storm which distracts
me from thinking 8 **fixed** lodged (in the mind) 11 **i' th' mouth** in the
teeth 11 **free** i.e., from care 15 **as** as if 16 **home** to the utmost

In such a night as this! O Regan, Goneril,
Your old kind father, whose frank° heart gave
20   all—
O, that way madness lies; let me shun that.
No more of that.

Kent.   Good my lord, enter here.

Lear. Prithee go in thyself; seek thine own ease.
This tempest will not give me leave to ponder
25 On things would hurt me more, but I'll go in.
[*To the Fool*] In, boy; go first. You houseless
    poverty°—
Nay, get thee in. I'll pray, and then I'll sleep.

                          Exit [*Fool*].

Poor naked wretches, wheresoe'er you are,
That bide° the pelting of this pitiless storm,
30 How shall your houseless heads and unfed sides,
Your looped and windowed° raggedness, defend
    you
From seasons such as these? O, I have ta'en
Too little care of this! Take physic, pomp;°
Expose thyself to feel what wretches feel,
35 That thou mayst shake the superflux° to them,
And show the heavens more just.

Edgar. [*Within*] Fathom and half, fathom and half!°
    Poor Tom!

                  Enter Fool.

Fool. Come not in here, Nuncle, here's a spirit. Help
40 me, help me!

Kent. Give me thy hand. Who's there?

Fool. A spirit, a spirit. He says his name's Poor Tom.

Kent. What art thou that dost grumble there i' th'
    straw?
    Come forth.

---

20 **frank** liberal (magnanimous)   26 **houseless poverty** (the unsheltered poor, abstracted)   29 **bide** endure   31 **looped and windowed** full of holes 33 **Take physic, pomp** take medicine to cure yourselves, you great men   35 **superflux** superfluity   37 **Fathom and half** (Edgar, because of the downpour, pretends to take soundings)

Enter Edgar [disguised as a madman].

Edgar. Away! the foul fiend follows me. Through the   45
sharp hawthorn blows the cold wind.° Humh! Go to
thy cold bed, and warm thee.°

Lear. Didst thou give all to thy daughters? And art
thou come to this?

Edgar. Who gives anything to Poor Tom? Whom the   50
foul fiend hath led through fire and through flame,
through ford and whirlpool, o'er bog and quag-
mire; that hath laid knives under his pillow and
halters in his pew,° set ratsbane° by his porridge,°
made him proud of heart, to ride on a bay trotting   55
horse over four-inched bridges,° to course° his
own shadow for° a traitor. Bless thy five wits,°
Tom's a-cold. O, do, de, do, de, do, de. Bless thee
from whirlwinds, star-blasting,° and taking.° Do
Poor Tom some charity, whom the foul fiend vexes.   60
There could I have him now—and there—and there
again—and there.

Storm still.

Lear. What, has his daughters brought him to this
pass?°
Couldst thou save nothing? Wouldst thou give 'em
all?

Fool. Nay, he reserved a blanket,° else we had been   65
all shamed.

Lear. Now all the plagues that in the pendulous° air
Hang fated o'er° men's faults light on thy
daughters!

45–46 **Through . . . wind** (a line from the ballad of "The Friar of Orders
Gray")   46–47 **go . . . thee** (a reminiscence of *The Taming of the Shrew*,
Induction, 1.10)   53–54 **knives . . . halters . . . ratsbane** (the fiend tempts
Poor Tom to suicide)   54 **pew** gallery or balcony outside a window
54 **porridge** broth   55–56 **ride . . . bridges** i.e., risk his life   56 **course**
chase   57 **for** as   57 **five wits** i.e., common wit, imagination, fantasy, estimation, memory   59 **star-blasting** the evil caused by malignant stars
59 **taking** pernicious influences   63 **pass** wretched condition   65 **blanket**
i.e., to cover his nakedness   67 **pendulous** overhanging   68 **fated o'er**
destined to punish

Kent. He hath no daughters, sir.

Lear. Death, traitor; nothing could have subdued°
70   nature
      To such a lowness but his unkind daughters.
      Is it the fashion that discarded fathers
      Should have thus little mercy on° their flesh?
      Judicious punishment—'twas this flesh begot
75   Those pelican° daughters.

Edgar. Pillicock sat on Pillicock Hill.° Alow, alow,
      loo, loo!°

Fool. This cold night will turn us all to fools and mad-
      men.

80 *Edgar.* Take heed o' th' foul fiend; obey thy parents;
      keep thy word's justice;° swear not; commit not°
      with man's sworn spouse; set not thy sweet heart on
      proud array. Tom's a-cold.

Lear. What hast thou been?

85 *Edgar.* A servingman, proud in heart and mind; that
      curled my hair, wore gloves in my cap;° served the
      lust of my mistress' heart, and did the act of dark-
      ness with her; swore as many oaths as I spake
      words, and broke them in the sweet face of
90   heaven. One that slept in the contriving of lust,
      and waked to do it. Wine loved I deeply, dice
      dearly; and in woman out-paramoured the Turk.°
      False of heart, light of ear,° bloody of hand; hog
      in sloth, fox in stealth, wolf in greediness, dog in
95   madness, lion in prey.° Let not the creaking° of
      shoes nor the rustling of silks betray thy poor

70 **subdued** reduced   73 **on** i.e., shown to   75 **pelican** (supposed to feed on
its parent's blood)   76 **Pillicock ... Hill** (probably quoted from a nursery
rhyme, and suggested by "pelican." **Pillicock** is a term of endearment
and the phallus)   76–77 **Alow ... loo** (? a hunting call, or the refrain of
the song)   81 **keep ... justice** i.e., do not break thy word   81 **commit not**
i.e., adultery   86 **gloves in my cap** i.e., as a pledge from his mistress
92 **out-paramoured the Turk** had more concubines than the Sultan   93 **light
of ear** ready to hear flattery and slander   95 **prey** preying   95 **creaking**
(deliberately cultivated, as fashionable)

heart to woman. Keep thy foot out of brothels,
thy hand out of plackets,° thy pen from lenders'
books,° and defy the foul fiend. Still through the
hawthorn blows the cold wind; says suum, mun, *100*
nonny.° Dolphin° my boy, boy, sessa!° let him trot
by.

　　　　　　　　　　　　　　　　Storm still.

Lear. Thou wert better in a grave than to answer°
　with thy uncovered body this extremity° of the
　skies. Is man no more than this? Consider him *105*
　well. Thou ow'st° the worm no silk, the beast no
　hide, the sheep no wool, the cat° no perfume. Ha!
　here's three on's° are sophisticated.° Thou art the
　thing itself; unaccommodated° man is no more
　but such a poor, bare, forked° animal as thou art. *110*
　Off, off, you lendings!° Come, unbutton here.
　　　　　　　　　[*Tearing off his clothes.*]
Fool. Prithee, Nuncle, be contented, 'tis a naughty°
　night to swim in. Now a little fire in a wild° field
　were like an old lecher's heart—a small spark, all
　the rest on's body, cold. Look, here comes a walk- *115*
　ing fire.

　　　　　Enter Gloucester, with a torch.

Edgar. This is the foul fiend Flibbertigibbet.° He be-
　gins at curfew,° and walks till the first cock.° He
　gives the web and the pin,° squints° the eye, and
　makes the harelip; mildews the white° wheat, and *120*
　hurts the poor creature of earth.

98 **plackets** openings in skirts　98–99 **pen . . . books** i.e., do not enter your
name in the moneylender's account book　100–01 **suum, mun, nonny** the
noise of the wind　101 **Dolphin** the French Dauphin (identified by the English
with the devil. Poor Tom is presumably quoting from a ballad)　101 **sessa**
an interjection: "Go on!"　103 **answer** confront, bear the brunt of　104 **extremity** extreme severity　106 **ow'st** have taken from　107 **cat** civet cat,
whose glands yield perfume　108 **on's** of us　108 **sophisticated** adulterated,
made artificial　109 **unaccommodated** uncivilized　110 **forked** i.e., two-
legged　111 **lendings** borrowed garments　112 **naughty** wicked　113 **wild**
barren　117 **Flibbertigibbet** (a figure from Elizabethan demonology)　118
curfew: 9 P.M.　118 **first cock** midnight　119 **web and the pin** cataract
119 **squints** crosses　120 **white** ripening.

Swithold footed thrice the old;°
He met the nightmare,° and her nine fold;°
　Bid her alight°
125　　And her troth plight,°
And aroint° thee, witch, aroint thee!

Kent. How fares your Grace?

Lear. What's he?

Kent. Who's there? What is't you seek?

130 *Gloucester.* What are you there? Your names?

Edgar. Poor Tom, that eats the swimming frog, the
toad, the todpole, the wall-newt and the water;°
that in the fury of his heart, when the foul fiend
rages, eats cow-dung for sallets,° swallows the old
135　rat and the ditch-dog,° drinks the green mantle°
of the standing° pool; who is whipped from tithing°
to tithing, and stocked, punished, and imprisoned;
who hath had three suits to his back, six shirts to
his body,
140　　Horse to ride, and weapon to wear,
　　But mice and rats, and such small deer,°
　　Have been Tom's food for seven long year.°
Beware my follower!° Peace, Smulkin,° peace,
thou fiend!

Gloucester. What, hath your Grace no better com-
145　pany?

Edgar. The Prince of Darkness is a gentleman.
Modo° he's called, and Mahu.°

---

122 **Swithold . . . old** Withold (an Anglo-Saxon saint who subdued demons)
walked three times across the open country   123 **nightmare** demon
123 **fold** offspring   124 **alight** i.e., from the horse she had possessed
125 **her troth plight** pledge her word   126 **aroint** be gone   132 **todpole . . .
water** tadpole, wall lizard, water newt   134 **sallets** salads   135 **ditch-dog**
dead dog in a ditch   135 **mantle** scum   136 **standing** stagnant   136 **tithing**
a district comprising ten families   141–42 **But . . . year** (adapted from a popular romance, "Bevis of Hampton")   141 **deer** game   143 **follower** familiar
143, 147 **Smulkin, Modo, Mahu** (Elizabethan devils, from Samuel Harsnett's
Declaration of 1603)

Gloucester. Our flesh and blood, my Lord, is grown
     so vile
  That it doth hate what gets° it.

Edgar. Poor Tom's a-cold.   *150*

Gloucester. Go in with me. My duty cannot suffer°
  T' obey in all your daughters' hard commands.
  Though their injunction be to bar my doors
  And let this tyrannous night take hold upon you,
  Yet have I ventured to come seek you out   *155*
  And bring you where both fire and food is ready.

Lear. First let me talk with this philosopher.
  What is the cause of thunder?

Kent. Good my lord, take his offer; go into th' house.

Lear. I'll talk a word with this same learnèd Theban.°   *160*
  What is your study?°

Edgar. How to prevent° the fiend, and to kill vermin.

Lear. Let me ask you one word in private.

Kent. Importune him once more to go, my lord.
  His wits begin t' unsettle.

Gloucester.   Canst thou blame him?   *165*

                              Storm still.

  His daughters seek his death. Ah, that good Kent,
  He said it would be thus, poor banished man!
  Thou say'st the King grows mad—I'll tell thee,
     friend,
  I am almost mad myself. I had a son,
  Now outlawed from my blood;° he sought my life   *170*
  But lately, very late.° I loved him, friend,
  No father his son dearer. True to tell thee,
  The grief hath crazed my wits. What a night's this!

149 **gets** begets   151 **suffer** permit me   160 **Theban** i.e., Greek philosopher   161 **study** particular scientific study   162 **prevent** balk   170 **outlawed from my blood** disowned and tainted, like a carbuncle in the
corrupted blood   171 **late** recently

I do beseech your Grace——

Lear.   O, cry you mercy,° sir
175 Noble philosopher, your company.

Edgar. Tom's a-cold.

Gloucester. In, fellow, there, into th' hovel; keep thee
warm.

Lear. Come, let's in all.

Kent.   This way, my lord.

Lear.   With him
I will keep still with my philosopher.

Kent. Good my lord, soothe° him; let him take the
180 fellow.

Gloucester. Take him you on.°

Kent. Sirrah, come on; go along with us.

Lear. Come, good Athenian.°

Gloucester. No words, no words! Hush.

185 *Edgar.* Child Rowland to the dark tower came;°
His word was still,° "Fie, foh, and fum,
I smell the blood of a British man."°   *Exeunt.*

---

174 **cry you mercy** I beg your pardon   180 **soothe** humor   181 **you on**
with you   183 **Athenian** i.e., philosopher (like "Theban")   185 **Child . . .
came** (? from a lost ballad; "child"=a candidate for knighthood; **Rowland**
was Charlemagne's nephew, the hero of *The Song of Roland*)   186 **His . . .
still** his motto was always   186–87 **Fie . . . man** (a deliberately absurd link-
ing of the chivalric hero with the nursery tale of Jack the Giant-Killer)

Scene 5.   [*Gloucester's castle.*]

Enter Cornwall and Edmund.

Cornwall. I will have my revenge ere I depart his
house.

Edmund. How, my lord, I may be censured,° that
nature thus gives way to loyalty, something fears°
me to think of.   5

Cornwall. I now perceive it was not altogether your
brother's evil disposition made him seek his death;
but a provoking merit, set a-work by a reprovable
badness in himself.°

Edmund. How malicious is my fortune that I must   10
repent to be just! This is the letter which he spoke
of, which approves° him an intelligent party°
to the advantages° of France. O heavens, that his
treason were not! or not I the detector!

Cornwall. Go with me to the Duchess.   15

Edmund. If the matter of this paper be certain, you
have mighty business in hand.

Cornwall. True or false, it hath made thee Earl of
Gloucester. Seek out where thy father is, that he
may be ready for our apprehension.°   20

Edmund. [*Aside*] If I find him comforting° the
King, it will stuff his suspicion more fully.—I will
persever° in my course of loyalty, though the conflict be sore between that and my blood.°

3.5.8 **censured** judged   4 **something fears** somewhat frightens   8–9 **a
provoking . . . himself** a stimulating goodness in Edgar, brought into play by
a blamable badness in Gloucester   12 **approves** proves   12 **intelligent
party** (1) spy (2) well-informed person   13 **to the advantages** on behalf of
20 **apprehension** arrest   21 **comforting** supporting (a legalism)   23 **perse-
ver** persevere   24 **blood** natural feelings

25 *Cornwall.* I will lay trust upon° thee, and thou
shalt find a dearer father in my love.   *Exeunt.*

Scene 6.   *[A chamber in a farmhouse
adjoining the castle.]*

Enter Kent and Gloucester.

Gloucester. Here is better than the open air; take it
thankfully. I will piece out the comfort with what
addition I can. I will not be long from you.

Kent. All the power of his wits have given way to his
5   impatience.° The gods reward your kindness.

                         Exit [Gloucester].

Enter Lear, Edgar, and Fool.

Edgar. Frateretto° calls me, and tells me Nero° is
an angler in the lake of darkness. Pray, innocent,°
and beware the foul fiend.

Fool. Prithee, Nuncle, tell me whether a madman be a
10   gentleman or a yeoman.°

Lear. A king, a king.

Fool. No, he's a yeoman that has a gentleman to his
son; for he's a mad yeoman that sees his son a gentleman before him.

15 *Lear.* To have a thousand with red burning spits
     Come hizzing° in upon 'em——

---

25 **lay trust upon** (1) trust (2) advance 3.6.5 **impatience** raging
6 **Frateretto** Elizabethan devil, from Harsnett's *Declaration*   6 **Nero** (who
is mentioned by Harsnett, and whose angling is reported by Chaucer in
"The Monk's Tale")   7 **innocent** fool   10 **yeoman** farmer (just below a
gentleman in rank. The Fool asks what class of man has most indulged
his children, and thus been driven mad)   16 **hizzing** hissing

Edgar. The foul fiend bites my back.

Fool. He's mad that trusts in the tameness of a wolf,
a horse's health, a boy's love, or a whore's oath.

Lear. It shall be done; I will arraign° them straight.°   20
[*To Edgar*] Come, sit thou here, most learned
justice.°
[*To the Fool*] Thou, sapient° sir, sit here. Now,
you she-foxes——

Edgar. Look, where he° stands and glares. Want'st
thou eyes at trial, madam?°
Come o'er the bourn,° Bessy, to me.   25

Fool. Her boat hath a leak,
And she must not speak
Why she dares not come over to thee.°

Edgar. The foul fiend haunts Poor Tom in the voice
of a nightingale.° Hoppedance° cries in Tom's belly   30
for two white herring.° Croak° not, black angel; I
have no food for thee.

Kent. How do you, sir? Stand you not so amazed.°
Will you lie down and rest upon the cushions?

Lear. I'll see their trial first. Bring in their evidence.   35
[*To Edgar*] Thou, robèd man of justice, take
thy place.
[*To the Fool*] And thou, his yokefellow of equity,°
Bench° by his side. [*To Kent*] You are o' th'
commission;°
Sit you too.

Edgar. Let us deal justly.   40

---

20 **arraign** bring to trial   20 **straight** straightaway   21 **justice** justicer, judge   22 **sapient** wise   23 **he** i.e., a fiend   23–24 **Want'st ... madam** (to Goneril) i.e., do you want eyes to look at you during your trial? The fiend serves that purpose   25 **bourn** brook (Edgar quotes from a popular ballad)   26–28 **Her ... thee** (the Fool parodies the ballad)   30 **nightingale** i.e., the Fool's singing   30 **Hoppedance** Hoberdidance (another devil from Harsnett's *Declaration*)   31 **white herring** unsmoked (? as against the black and sulfurous devil)   31 **Croak** rumble (because his belly is empty)   33 **amazed** astonished   35 **evidence** the evidence of witnesses against them   37 **yokefellow of equity** partner in justice   38 **Bench** sit on the bench   38 **commission** those commissioned as king's justices

Sleepest or wakest thou, jolly shepherd?
    Thy sheep be in the corn;°
And for one blast of thy minikin° mouth
    Thy sheep shall take no harm.°
45 Purr, the cat is gray.°

Lear. Arraign her first. 'Tis Goneril, I here take my
    oath before this honorable assembly, she kicked
    the poor King her father.

Fool. Come hither, mistress. Is your name Goneril?

50 *Lear.* She cannot deny it.

Fool. Cry you mercy, I took you for a joint stool.°

Lear. And here's another, whose warped looks
    proclaim
    What store° her heart is made on. Stop her there!
    Arms, arms, sword, fire! Corruption in the place!°
55 False justicer, why hast thou let her 'scape?

Edgar. Bless thy five wits!

Kent. O pity! Sir, where is the patience now
    That you so oft have boasted to retain?

Edgar. [*Aside*] My tears begin to take his part so
    much
60 They mar my counterfeiting.°

Lear. The little dogs and all,
    Tray, Blanch, and Sweetheart—see, they bark at
    me.

Edgar. Tom will throw his head at them. Avaunt, you
    curs.
    Be thy mouth or black or° white,

41–44 **Sleepest . . . harm** (probably quoted or adapted from an Elizabethan song) 42 **corn** wheat 43 **minikin** shrill 45 **gray** (devils were thought to assume the shape of a gray cat) 51 **Cry . . . joint stool** (proverbial and deliberately impudent apology for overlooking a person. A joint stool was a low stool made by a joiner, perhaps here a stage property to represent Goneril and in line 52, Regan. "Joint stool" can also suggest the judicial bench; hence Goneril may be identified by the Fool, ironically, with those in power, who judge) 53 **store** stuff 54 **Corruption . . . place** bribery in the court 60 **counterfeiting** i.e., feigned madness 64 **or . . . or** either . . . or

Tooth that poisons if it bite;   65
Mastiff, greyhound, mongrel grim,
Hound or spaniel, brach° or lym,°
Or bobtail tike, or trundle-tail°—
Tom will make him weep and wail;
For, with throwing° thus my head,   70
Dogs leaped the hatch,° and all are fled.
Do, de, de, de. Sessa!° Come, march to wakes°
and fairs and market towns. Poor Tom, thy horn°
is dry.

Lear. Then let them anatomize Regan. See what breeds   75
about her heart.° Is there any cause in nature that
make° these hard hearts? [*To Edgar*] You, sir,
I entertain° for one of my hundred;° only I do not
like the fashion of your garments. You will say
they are Persian;° but let them be changed.   80

Kent. Now, good my lord, lie here and rest awhile.

Lear. Make no noise, make no noise; draw the
    curtains.°
So, so. We'll go to supper i' th' morning.

Fool. And I'll go to bed at noon.°

                    Enter Gloucester.

Gloucester. Come hither, friend. Where is the King
    my master?   85

Kent. Here, sir, but trouble him not; his wits are gone.

Gloucester. Good friend, I prithee take him in thy
    arms.

---

67 **brach** bitch   67 **lym** bloodhound (from the liam or leash with which
he was led)   68 **bobtail . . . trundle-tail** short-tailed or long-tailed cur
70 **throwing** jerking (as a hound lifts its head from the ground, the scent
having been lost)   71 **leaped the hatch** leaped over the lower half of a
divided door (i.e., left in a hurry)   72 **Sessa** be off   72 **wakes** feasts attending the dedication of a church   73 **horn** horn bottle which the Bedlam
used in begging a drink (Edgar is suggesting that he is unable to play his
role any longer)   75–76 **Then . . . heart** i.e., if the Bedlam's horn is dry, let
Regan, whose heart has become as hard as horn, be dissected   77 **make**
(subjunctive)   78 **entertain** engage   78 **hundred** i.e., Lear's hundred
knights   80 **Persian** gorgeous (ironically of Edgar's rags)   82 **curtains**
(Lear imagines himself in bed)   84 **And . . . noon** (the Fool's last words)

I have o'erheard a plot of death upon him.
There is a litter ready; lay him in't
And drive toward Dover, friend, where thou shalt
90   meet
Both welcome and protection. Take up thy master.
If thou shouldst dally half an hour, his life,
With thine and all that offer to defend him,
Stand in assurèd loss. Take up, take up,
95   And follow me, that will to some provision°
Give thee quick conduct.°

Kent.   Oppressèd nature sleeps.
This rest might yet have balmed thy broken
    sinews,°
Which, if convenience° will not allow,
Stand in hard cure.° [*To the Fool*] Come, help
    to bear thy master.
Thou must not stay behind.

100 *Gloucester.*   Come, come, away!
                Exeunt [*all but Edgar*].

Edgar. When we our betters see bearing our woes,
We scarcely think our miseries our foes.°
Who alone suffers suffers most i' th' mind,
Leaving free° things and happy shows° behind;
105   But then the mind much sufferance° doth o'erskip
When grief hath mates, and bearing fellowship.°
How light and portable° my pain seems now,
When that which makes me bend makes the
    King bow.
He childed as I fathered. Tom, away.
110   Mark the high noises,° and thyself bewray°
When false opinion, whose wrong thoughts° defile
    thee,

95 **provision** maintenance   96 **conduct** direction   97 **balmed thy broken sinews** soothed thy racked nerves 98 **convenience** fortunate occasion 99 **Stand . . . cure** will be hard to cure   102 **our foes** enemies peculiar to ourselves 104 **free** carefree 104 **shows** scenes 105 **sufferance** suffering 106 **bearing fellowship** suffering has company 107 **portable** able to be supported or endured 110 **Mark the high noises** observe the rumors of strife among those in power 110 **bewray** reveal 111 **wrong thoughts** misconceptions

In thy just proof repeals and reconciles thee.°
What will hap more° tonight, safe 'scape the King!
Lurk,° lurk.   [*Exit.*]

Scene 7.   [*Gloucester's castle.*]

*Enter Cornwall, Regan, Goneril, Edmund, and
Servants.*

Cornwall. [*To Goneril*] Post speedily to my Lord
your husband; show him this letter. The army of
France is landed. [*To Servants*] Seek out the
traitor Gloucester. [*Exeunt some of the Servants.*]

Regan. Hang him instantly.   5

Goneril. Pluck out his eyes.

Cornwall. Leave him to my displeasure. Edmund,
keep you our sister company. The revenges we are
bound° to take upon your traitorous father are not
fit for your beholding. Advise the Duke where you   10
are going, to a most festinate° preparation. We are
bound to the like. Our posts° shall be swift and
intelligent° betwixt us. Farewell, dear sister; farewell, my Lord of Gloucester.°

Enter Oswald.

How now? Where's the King?   15

Oswald. My Lord of Gloucester hath conveyed him
  hence.

112 **In ... thee** on the manifesting of your innocence recalls you from
outlawry and restores amity between you and your father   113 **What ...
more** whatever else happens   114 **Lurk** hide   3.7.9 **bound** (1) forced
(2) purposing to   11 **festinate** speedy   12 **posts** messengers   13 **intelligent**
full of information   14 **Lord of Gloucester** i.e., Edmund, now elevated
to the title

Some five or six and thirty of his knights,
Hot questrists° after him, met him at gate;
Who, with some other of the lords dependants,°
Are gone with him toward Dover, where they
    boast
20
To have well-armèd friends.

Cornwall.   Get horses for your mistress.
                              [Exit Oswald.]

Goneril. Farewell, sweet lord, and sister.

Cornwall. Edmund, farewell.
                    [Exeunt Goneril and Edmund.]

            Go seek the traitor Gloucester,
Pinion him like a thief, bring him before us.
            [Exeunt other Servants.]
25
Though well we may not pass upon° his life
Without the form of justice, yet our power
Shall do a court'sy to° our wrath, which men
May blame, but not control.

    Enter Gloucester, brought in by two or three.

                Who's there, the traitor?

Regan. Ingrateful fox, 'tis he.

30 *Cornwall.* Bind fast his corky° arms.

Gloucester. What means your Graces? Good my
    friends, consider
You are my guests. Do me no foul play, friends.

Cornwall. Bind him, I say.

                [Servants bind him.]

Regan.   Hard, hard! O filthy traitor.

Gloucester. Unmerciful lady as you are, I'm none.

Cornwall. To this chair bind him. Villain, thou shalt
35   find——

18 **questrists** searchers 19 **lords dependants** attendant lords (members of
Lear's retinue) 25 **pass upon** pass judgment on 27 **do a court'sy to**
indulge 30 **corky** sapless (because old)

[*Regan plucks his beard.*°]

Gloucester. By the kind gods, 'tis most ignobly done
　To pluck me by the beard.

Regan. So white, and such a traitor?

Gloucester.　　　　　　　　　　Naughty° lady,
　These hairs which thou dost ravish from my chin
　Will quicken° and accuse thee. I am your host.　　　40
　With robber's hands my hospitable favors°
　You should not ruffle° thus. What will you do?

Cornwall. Come, sir, what letters had you late° from
　France?

Regan. Be simple-answered,° for we know the truth.

Cornwall. And what confederacy have you with the
　traitors　　　　　　　　　　　　　　　　　　　45
　Late footed in the kingdom?

Regan. To whose hands you have sent the lunatic
　King:
　Speak.

Gloucester. I have a letter guessingly° set down,
　Which came from one that's of a neutral heart,
　And not from one opposed.

Cornwall.　　　　　　　　　Cunning.

Regan.　　　　　　　　　　　And false.　　　50

Cornwall. Where hast thou sent the King?

Gloucester. To Dover.

Regan. Wherefore to Dover? Wast thou not charged at
　peril°——

Cornwall. Wherefore to Dover? Let him answer that.

---

35 s.d. **plucks his beard** (a deadly insult)　38 **Naughty** wicked
40 **quicken** come to life　41 **hospitable favors** face of your host　42 **ruffle**
tear at violently　43 **late** recently　44 **simple-answered** straightforward in
answering　48 **guessingly** without certain knowledge　53 **charged at peril**
ordered under penalty

Gloucester. I am tied to th' stake, and I must stand
55 the course.°

Regan. Wherefore to Dover?

Gloucester. Because I would not see thy cruel nails
Pluck out his poor old eyes; nor thy fierce sister
In his anointed° flesh rash° boarish fangs.
60 The sea, with such a storm as his bare head
In hell-black night endured, would have buoyed° up
And quenched the stellèd° fires.
Yet, poor old heart, he holp° the heavens to rain.
If wolves had at thy gate howled that dearn° time,
Thou shouldst have said, "Good porter, turn the
65 key."°
All cruels else subscribe.° But I shall see
The wingèd° vengeance overtake such children.

Cornwall. See't shalt thou never. Fellows, hold the
chair.
Upon these eyes of thine I'll set my foot.

Gloucester. He that will think° to live till he be
70 old,
Give me some help. —O cruel! O you gods!

Regan. One side will mock° another. Th' other too.

Cornwall. If you see vengeance——

First Servant.   Hold your hand, my lord!
I have served you ever since I was a child;
75 But better service have I never done you
Than now to bid you hold.

Regan.   How now, you dog?

First Servant. If you did wear a beard upon your chin,

55 **course** coursing (in which a relay of dogs baits a bull or bear tied in
the pit) 59 **anointed** holy (because king) 59 **rash** strike with the tusk,
like a boar 61 **buoyed** risen 62 **stellèd** (1) fixed (as opposed to the planets
or wandering stars) (2) starry 63 **holp** helped 64 **dearn** dread 65 **turn
the key** i.e., unlock the gate 66 **All cruels else subscribe** all cruel creatures
but man are compassionate 67 **wingèd** (1) heavenly (2) swift 70 **will
think** expects 72 **mock** make ridiculous (because of the contrast)

I'd shake it° on this quarrel. What do you mean!°

Cornwall. My villain!°

　　　　　　　　　　　　　　　Draw and fight.

First Servant. Nay, then, come on, and take the
　　chance of anger.　　　　　　　　　　　　　　　80

Regan. Give me thy sword. A peasant stand up thus?

　　She takes a sword and runs at him behind,
　　　　　　　　kills him.

First Servant. O, I am slain! my lord, you have one
　　eye left
　　To see some mischief° on him. O!

Cornwall. Lest it see more, prevent it. Out, vile jelly.
　　Where is thy luster now?　　　　　　　　　　　85

Gloucester. All dark and comfortless. Where's my son
　　Edmund?
　　Edmund, enkindle all the sparks of nature°
　　To quit° this horrid act.

Regan. 　　　　　　　　Out, treacherous villain,
　　Thou call'st on him that hates thee. It was he
　　That made the overture° of thy treasons to us;　　90
　　Who is too good to pity thee.

Gloucester. O my follies! Then Edgar was abused.°
　　Kind gods, forgive me that, and prosper him.

Regan. Go thrust him out at gates, and let him smell
　　His way to Dover.　　　*Exit [one] with Gloucester.*
　　　　　　　How is't, my lord? How look you?°　　95

Cornwall. I have received a hurt. Follow me, lady.
　　Turn out that eyeless villain. Throw this slave
　　Upon the dunghill. Regan, I bleed apace.

---

78 **shake it** (an insult comparable to Regan's plucking of Gloucester's
beard)　78 **What ... mean** i.e., what terrible thing are you doing　79 **villain** serf (with a suggestion of the modern meaning)　83 **mischief** injury
87 **enkindle ... nature** fan your natural feeling into flame　88 **quit** requite
90 **overture** disclosure　92 **abused** wronged　95 **How look you** how
are you

Untimely comes this hurt. Give me your arm.
Exeunt.

100 *Second Servant.* I'll never care what wickedness I do,
If this man come to good.

Third Servant. If she live long,
And in the end meet the old course of death,°
Women will all turn monsters.

Second Servant. Let's follow the old Earl, and get the Bedlam
105 To lead him where he would. His roguish madness
Allows itself to anything.°

Third Servant. Go thou. I'll fetch some flax and whites of eggs
To apply to his bleeding face. Now heaven help him. [*Exeunt severally.*]

---

102 **meet ... death** die the customary death of old age 105–6 **His ... anything** his lack of all self-control leaves him open to any suggestion

ACT 4

Scene 1.   [*The heath.*]

Enter Edgar.

Edgar. Yet better thus, and known to be contemned,°
  Than still contemned and flattered. To be worst,
  The lowest and most dejected° thing of fortune,
  Stands still in esperance,° lives not in fear:
  The lamentable change is from the best,   5
  The worst returns to laughter.° Welcome then,
  Thou unsubstantial air that I embrace!
  The wretch that thou hast blown unto the worst
  Owes° nothing to thy blasts.

    Enter Gloucester, led by an Old Man.

                    But who comes here?
  My father, poorly led?° World, world, O world!   10
  But that thy strange mutations make us hate thee,
  Life would not yield to age.°

Old Man. O, my good lord, I have been your tenant,
  and your father's tenant, these fourscore years.

Gloucester. Away, get thee away; good friend, be
    gone: 15

4.1.1 **known to be contemned** conscious of being despised   **3 dejected**
abased   **4 esperance** hope   **6 returns to laughter** changes for the better
9 **Owes** is in debt for   10 **poorly led** (1) led like a poor man, with only one
attendant (2) led by a poor man   11–12 **But . . . age** we should not agree to
grow old and hence die, except for the hateful mutability of life

Thy comforts° can do me no good at all;
Thee they may hurt.°

Old Man.   You cannot see your way.

Gloucester. I have no way and therefore want° no
        eyes;
    I stumbled when I saw. Full oft 'tis seen,
20   Our means secure us, and our mere defects
    Prove our commodities.° Oh, dear son Edgar,
    The food° of thy abusèd° father's wrath!
    Might I but live to see thee in° my touch,
    I'd say I had eyes again!

Old Man.   How now! Who's there?

Edgar. [*Aside*] O Gods! Who is 't can say "I am at
25   the worst"?
    I am worse than e'er I was.

Old Man.   'Tis poor mad Tom.

Edgar. [*Aside*] And worse I may be yet: the worst
        is not
    So long as we can say "This is the worst."°

Old Man. Fellow, where goest?

Gloucester.   Is it a beggar-man?

30 *Old Man.* Madman and beggar too.

Gloucester. He has some reason,° else he could not
        beg.
    I' th' last night's storm I such a fellow saw,
    Which made me think a man a worm. My son
    Came then into my mind, and yet my mind
    Was then scarce friends with him. I have heard
35   more since.
    As flies to wanton° boys, are we to th' gods,

16 **comforts** ministrations   17 **hurt** injure   18 **want** require   20–21 **Our . . .
commodities** our resources make us overconfident, while our afflictions make
for our advantage   22 **food** i.e., the object on which Gloucester's anger
fed   22 **abusèd** deceived   23 **in** i.e., with, by means of   27–28 **the . . . worst**
so long as a man continues to suffer (i.e., is still alive), even greater suffering may await him   31 **reason** faculty of reasoning   36 **wanton** (1) playful
(2) reckless

They kill us for their sport.

Edgar. [*Aside*]   How should this be?°
   Bad is the trade that must play fool to sorrow,
   Ang'ring° itself and others. Bless thee, master!

Gloucester. Is that the naked fellow?

Old Man.   Ay, my lord.   40

Gloucester. Then, prithee, get thee gone: if for my
      sake
   Thou wilt o'ertake us hence a mile or twain
   I' th' way toward Dover, do it for ancient° love,
   And bring some covering for this naked soul,
   Which I'll entreat to lead me.

Old Man.   Alack, sir, he is mad.   45

Gloucester. 'Tis the times' plague,° when madmen
      lead the blind.
   Do as I bid thee, or rather do thy pleasure;°
   Above the rest,° be gone.

Old Man. I'll bring him the best 'parel° that I have,
   Come on 't what will.   *Exit.*   50

Gloucester. Sirrah, naked fellow——

Edgar. Poor Tom's a-cold. [*Aside*] I cannot daub
   it° further.

Gloucester. Come hither, fellow.

Edgar. [*Aside*] And yet I must. —Bless thy sweet
   eyes, they bleed.   55

Gloucester. Know'st thou the way to Dover?

Edgar. Both stile and gate, horse-way and footpath.
   Poor Tom hath been scared out of his good wits.
   Bless thee, good man's son, from the foul fiend!
   Five fiends have been in Poor Tom at once; of lust,   60

---

37 **How should this be** i.e., how can this horror be?   39 **Ang'ring** offending   43 **ancient** (1) the love the Old Man feels, by virtue of his long tenancy (2) the love that formerly obtained between master and man   46 **times' plague** characteristic disorder of this time   47 **thy pleasure** as you like   48 **the rest** all   49 **'parel** apparel   52–53 **daub it** lay it on (figure from plastering mortar)

as Obidicut;° Hobbididence, prince of dumbness;° Mahu, of stealing; Modo, of murder; Flibbertigibbet, of mopping and mowing:° who since
possesses chambermaids and waiting-women. So,
65   bless thee, master!

Gloucester. Here, take this purse, thou whom the
                heavens' plagues
Have humbled to all strokes:° that I am wretched
Makes thee the happier. Heavens, deal so still!
Let the superfluous° and lust-dieted° man,
70   That slaves° your ordinance,° that will not see
Because he does not feel, feel your pow'r quickly;
So distribution should undo excess,°
And each man have enough. Dost thou know
                Dover?

Edgar. Ay, master.

Gloucester. There is a cliff whose high and bending°
75   head
Looks fearfully° in the confinèd deep:°
Bring me but to the very brim of it,
And I'll repair the misery thou dost bear
With something rich about me: from that place
I shall no leading need.

80   *Edgar*.   *Give me thy arm:*
        Poor Tom shall lead thee.   *Exeunt.*

---

61 **Obidicut** Hoberdicut, a devil (like the four that follow, from Harsnett's
Declaration)   61–62 **dumbness** muteness (like the crimes and afflictions
in the next lines, the result of diabolic possession)   63 **mopping and mowing** grimacing and making faces   67 **humbled to all strokes** brought so
low as to bear anything humbly   69 **superfluous** possessed of super-
fluities   69 **lust-dieted** whose lust is gratified (like Gloucester's)   70 **slaves**
(1) tramples, spurns like a slave (2) ? tears, rends (Old English **slaefan**)
70 **ordinance** law   72 **So . . . excess** then the man with too much wealth
would distribute it among those with too little   75 **bending** overhanging
76 **fearfully** occasioning fear   76 **confinèd deep** the sea, hemmed in below

Scene 2.   [*Before the Duke of Albany's
palace.*]

Enter Goneril and Edmund.

Goneril. Welcome, my lord: I marvel our mild
husband
Not met° us on the way.

                    Enter Oswald.

                    Now, where's your master?

Oswald. Madam, within; but never man so changed.
I told him of the army that was landed:
He smiled at it. I told him you were coming;   5
His answer was, "The worse." Of Gloucester's
treachery,
And of the loyal service of his son
When I informed him, then he called me sot,°
And told me I had turned the wrong side out:
What most he should dislike seems pleasant to him;   10
What like,° offensive.

Goneril. [*To Edmund*] Then shall you go no
further.
It is the cowish° terror of his spirit,
That dares not undertake:° he'll not feel wrongs,
Which tie him to an answer.° Our wishes on the
way
May prove effects.° Back, Edmund, to my brother;   15
Hasten his musters° and conduct his pow'rs.°

4.2.2 **Not met** did not meet   8 **sot** fool   11 **What like** what he should like
12 **cowish** cowardly   13 **undertake** venture   14 **tie him to an answer**
oblige him to retaliate   14–15 **Our . . . effects** our desires (that you might
be my husband), as we journeyed here, may be fulfilled   16 **musters** col-
lecting of troops   16 **conduct his pow'rs** lead his army

I must change names° at home and give the
   distaff°
Into my husband's hands. This trusty servant
Shall pass between us: ere long you are like to hear,
20   If you dare venture in your own behalf,
A mistress's° command. Wear this; spare speech;

                      [*Giving a favor*]

Decline your head.° This kiss, if it durst speak,
Would stretch thy spirits up into the air:
Conceive,° and fare thee well.

Edmund. Yours in the ranks of death.

25 *Goneril.*   My most dear Gloucester!
                            Exit [*Edmund*].
O, the difference of man and man!
To thee a woman's services are due:
My fool usurps my body.°

Oswald.   Madam, here comes my lord.
                                  Exit.

                Enter Albany.

Goneril. I have been worth the whistle.°

Albany.   O Goneril!
30   You are not worth the dust which the rude wind
Blows in your face. I fear your disposition:°
That nature which contemns° its origin
Cannot be bordered certain in itself;°
She that herself will sliver and disbranch°

---

17 **change names** i.e., exchange the name of "mistress" for that of "master"
17 **distaff** spinning stick (wifely symbol) 21 **mistress's** lover's (and also, Albany having been disposed of, lady's or wife's) 22 **Decline your head** i.e., that Goneril may kiss him 24 **Conceive** understand (with a sexual implication, that includes "stretch thy spirits," l. 23; and "death," l. 25: "to die," meaning "to experience sexual intercourse") 28 **My fool usurps my body** my husband wrongfully enjoys me 29 **I . . . whistle** i.e., once you valued me (the proverb is implied, "It is a poor dog that is not worth the whistling")
31 **disposition** nature 32 **contemns** espises 33 **bordered . . . itself** kept within its normal bounds 34 **sliver and disbranch** cut off

From her material sap,° perforce must wither   35
And come to deadly use.°

Goneril. No more; the text° is foolish.

Albany. Wisdom and goodness to the vile seem vile:
Filths savor but themselves.° What have you done?
Tigers, not daughters, what have you performed?   40
A father, and a gracious agèd man,
Whose reverence even the head-lugged bear°
    would lick,
Most barbarous, most degenerate, have you
    madded.°
Could my good brother suffer you to do it?
A man, a prince, by him so benefited!   45
If that the heavens do not their visible spirits°
Send quickly down to tame these vile offenses,
It will come,
Humanity must perforce prey on itself,
Like monsters of the deep.

Goneril.   Milk-livered° man!   50
That bear'st a cheek for blows, a head for wrongs;
Who hast not in thy brows an eye discerning
Thine honor from thy suffering;° that not know'st
Fools do those villains pity who are punished
Ere they have done their mischief.° Where's thy
    drum?   55
France spreads his banners in our noiseless°
    land,
With plumèd helm° thy state begins to threat,°

---

35 **material sap** essential and life-giving sustenance   36 **come to deadly use** i.e., be as a dead branch for the burning   37 **text** i.e., on which your sermon is based   39 **Filths savor but themselves** the filthy relish only the taste of filth   42 **head-lugged bear** bear-baited by the dogs, and hence enraged   43 **madded** made mad   46 **visible spirits** avenging spirits in material form   50 **Milk-livered** lily-livered (hence cowardly, the liver being regarded as the seat of courage)   52–53 **discerning ... suffering** able to distinguish between insults that ought to be resented, and ordinary pain that is to be borne   54–55 **Fools ... mischief** only fools are sorry for criminals whose intended criminality is prevented by punishment   56 **noiseless** i.e., the drum, signifying preparation for war, is silent   57 **helm** helmet   7 **thy ... threat** France begins to threaten Albany's realm

Whilst thou, a moral° fool, sits still and cries
"Alack, why does he so?"

Albany.   See thyself, devil!
60 Proper° deformity seems not in the fiend
So horrid as in woman.

Goneril.   O vain fool!

Albany. Thou changèd and self-covered° thing,
    for shame,
Be-monster not thy feature.° Were 't my fitness°
To let these hands obey my blood,°
65 They are apt enough to dislocate and tear
Thy flesh and bones: howe'er° thou art a fiend,
A woman's shape doth shield thee.

Goneril. Marry,° your manhood mew°——

Enter a Messenger.

Albany. What news?

Messenger. O, my good lord, the Duke of Cornwall's
70   dead,
Slain by his servant, going to° put out
The other eye of Gloucester.

Albany.   Gloucester's eyes!

Messenger. A servant that he bred,° thrilled with
    remorse,°
Opposed against the act, bending his sword
75 To his great master, who thereat enraged
Flew on him, and amongst them felled° him dead,
But not without that harmful stroke which since

---

58 **moral** moralizing; but also with the implication that morality and folly are
one   60 **Proper** (1) natural (to a fiend) (2) fair-appearing   62 **changèd and
self-covered** i.e., transformed, by the contorting of her woman's face, on
which appears the fiendish behavior she has allowed herself. (Goneril has disguised nature by wickedness)   63 **Be-monster not thy feature** do not change
your appearance into a fiend's   63 **my fitness** appropriate for me   64 **blood**
passion   66 **howe'er** but even if   68 **Marry** by the Virgin Mary   68 **your
manhood mew** (1) coop up or confine your (pretended) manhood
(2) molt or shed it, if that is what is supposed to "shield" me from you   71 **going to** as he was about to   73 **bred** reared   73 **thrilled with remorse** pierced
by compassion   76 **amongst them felled** others assisting, they felled

` Hath plucked him after.°

Albany.   This shows you are above,
　You justicers,° that these our nether° crimes
　So speedily can venge.° But, O poor Gloucester!   80
　Lost he his other eye?

Messenger.   Both, both, my lord.
　This letter, madam, craves° a speedy answer;
　'Tis from your sister.

Goneril.   [*Aside*] One way I like this well;
　But being widow, and my Gloucester with her,
　May all the building in my fancy pluck   85
　Upon my hateful life.° Another way,°
　The news is not so tart.°—I'll read, and answer.
                                        Exit.

Albany. Where was his son when they did take his
　eyes?

Messenger. Come with my lady hither.

Albany.   He is not here.

Messenger. No, my good lord; I met him back° again.   90

Albany. Knows he the wickedness?

Messenger. Ay, my good lord; 'twas he informed
　against him,
　And quit the house on purpose, that their punish-
　ment
　Might have the freer course.

Albany.   Gloucester, I live
　To thank thee for the love thou showed'st the
　King,   95
　And to revenge thine eyes. Come hither, friend:
　Tell me what more thou know'st.   *Exeunt.*

78 **plucked him after** i.e., brought Cornwall to death with his servant
79 **justicers** judges   79 **nether** committed below (on earth)   80 **venge**
avenge   82 **craves** demands   85–86 **May ... life** these things (1.84) may
send my future hopes, my castles in air, crashing down upon the hateful (married) life I lead now   86 **Another way** looked at another way   87 **tart** sour
90 **back** going back

[Scene 3.   *The French camp near Dover.*]

Enter Kent and a Gentleman.

Kent. Why the King of France is so suddenly gone
   back, know you no reason?

Gentleman. Something he left imperfect in the
   state,° which since his coming forth is thought of,
5 which imports° to the kingdom so much fear and
   danger that his personal return was most required
   and necessary.

Kent. Who hath he left behind him general?

Gentleman. The Marshal of France, Monsieur La Far.

10 *Kent.* Did your letters pierce° the queen to any dem-
   onstration of grief?

Gentleman. Ay, sir; she took them, read them in my
      presence,
   And now and then an ample tear trilled° down
   Her delicate cheek: it seemed she was a queen
15 Over her passion, who most rebel-like
   Sought to be king o'er her.

Kent.   O, then it moved her.

Gentleman. Not to a rage: patience and sorrow
      strove
   Who should express her goodliest.° You have seen
   Sunshine and rain at once: her smiles and tears
20 Were like a better way:° those happy smilets°
   That played on her ripe lip seemed not to know
   What guests were in her eyes, which parted thence

4.3.3–4 **imperfect in the state** unsettled in his own kingdom   5 **imports** por-
tends   10 **pierce** impel   13 **trilled** trickled   18 **Who ... goodliest** which
should give her the most becoming expression   20 **Were like a better way**
i.e., improved on that spectacle   20 **smilets** little smiles

Patience
rectitude   *of Cordelia*
feeling

As pearls from diamonds dropped. In brief,
Sorrow would be a rarity most belovèd,
If all could so become it.°

Kent.   Made she no verbal question?   25

Gentleman. Faith, once or twice she heaved° the name
    of "father"
Pantingly forth, as if it pressed her heart;
Cried "Sisters! Sisters! Shame of ladies! Sisters!
Kent! Father! Sisters! What, i' th' storm? i' th'
    night?
Let pity not be believed!"° There she shook   30
The holy water from her heavenly eyes,
And clamor moistened:° then away she started
To deal with grief alone.

Kent.   It is the stars,
The stars above us, govern our conditions;°
Else one self mate and make could not beget   35
Such different issues.° You spoke not with her
    since?

Gentleman. No.

Kent. Was this before the King returned?

Gentleman.   No, since.

Kent. Well, sir, the poor distressèd Lear's i' th'
    town;
Who sometime in his better tune° remembers   40
What we are come about, and by no means
Will yield to see his daughter.

Gentleman.   Why, good sir?

Kent. A sovereign° shame so elbows° him: his own
    unkindness

24–25 **Sorrow . . . it** sorrow would be a coveted jewel if it became others as
it does her   26 **heaved** expressed with difficulty   30 **Let pity not be believed** let it not be believed for pity   32 **clamor moistened** moistened
clamor, i.e., mixed (and perhaps assuaged) her outcries with tears   34 **govern our conditions** determine what we are   35–36 **Else . . . issues** otherwise the same husband and wife could not produce such different children
40 **better tune** composed, less jangled intervals   43 **sovereign** overpower-
ing   43 **elbows** jogs his elbow i.e., reminds him

That stripped her from his benediction, turned her
45 To foreign casualties,° gave her dear rights
To his dog-hearted daughters: these things sting
His mind so venomously that burning shame
Detains him from Cordelia.

Gentleman.   Alack, poor gentleman!

Kent. Of Albany's and Cornwall's powers you heard
    not?

50 *Gentleman.* 'Tis so;° they are afoot.

Kent. Well, sir, I'll bring you to our master Lear,
And leave you to attend him: some dear cause°
Will in concealment wrap me up awhile;
When I am known aright, you shall not grieve
55 Lending me this acquaintance. I pray you, go
Along with me.   [*Exeunt.*]

[Scene 4.   *The same. A tent.*]

*Enter, with drum and colors, Cordelia, Doctor,
        and Soldiers.*

Cordelia. Alack, 'tis he: why, he was met even now
As mad as the vexed sea; singing aloud;
Crowned with rank femiter and furrow-weeds,
With hardocks, hemlock, nettles, cuckoo-flow'rs,
5 Darnel,° and all the idle weeds that grow
In our sustaining corn.° A century° send forth;
Search every acre in the high-grown field,

45 **casualties** chances   50 **'Tis so** i.e., I have heard of them   52 **dear cause**
important reason 4.4.3–5 **femiter ... Darnel: femiter** fumitory, whose
leaves and juice are bitter; **furrow-weeds** weeds that grow in the furrow;
or plowed land; **hardocks** ? hoar or white docks, burdocks, harlocks; **hemlock**
a poison; **nettles** plants which sting and burn; **cuckoo-flow'rs** identified with
a plant employed to remedy diseases of the brain; **Darnel** tares, noisome
weeds 6 **sustaining corn** life-maintaining wheat 6 **century** ? sentry;
troop of a hundred soldiers

And bring him to our eye [*Exit an Officer.*] What
   can man's wisdom°
In the restoring his bereavèd° sense?
He that helps him take all my outward° worth.　　　　10

Doctor. There is means, madam:
   Our foster-nurse° of nature is repose,
The which he lacks: that to provoke° in him,
Are many simples operative,° whose power
Will close the eye of anguish.

Cordelia.　　　　　　　　　　All blest secrets,　　　　15
All you unpublished virtues° of the earth,
Spring with my tears! be aidant and remediate°
In the good man's distress! Seek, seek for him,
Lest his ungoverned rage dissolve the life
That wants the means to lead it.°

          Enter Messenger.

Messenger.　　　　　　　　　News, madam;　　　　20
The Brittish pow'rs are marching hitherward.

Cordelia. 'Tis known before. Our preparation stands
In expectation of them. O dear father,
It is thy business that I go about;
Therefore° great France　　　　　　　　　　　　　25
My mourning and importuned° tears hath pitied.
No blown° ambition doth our arms incite,
But love, dear love, and our aged father's right:
Soon may I hear and see him!　　　　　　*Exeunt.*

---

8 **What can man's wisdom** what can science accomplish　9 **bereavèd**
impaired　10 **outward** material　12 **foster-nurse** fostering nurse　13 **provoke** induce　14 **simples operative** efficacious medicinal herbs　16 **unpublished virtues** i.e., secret remedial herbs　17 **remediate** remedial
20 **wants . . . it** i.e., lacks the reason to control the rage　25 **Therefore**
because of that　26 **importuned** importunate　27 **blown** puffed up

[Scene 5.   *Gloucester's castle.*]

Enter Regan and Oswald.

Regan. But are my brother's pow'rs set forth?

Oswald.   Ay, madam.

Regan. Himself in person there?

Oswald.   Madam, with much ado:°
Your sister is the better soldier.

Regan. Lord Edmund spake not with your lord at
home?

5   *Oswald.* No, madam.

Regan. What might import° my sister's letter to him?

Oswald. I know not, lady.

Regan. Faith, he is posted° hence on serious matter.
It was great ignorance,° Gloucester's eyes being
out,
10   To let him live. Where he arrives he moves
All hearts against us: Edmund, I think, is gone,
In pity of his misery, to dispatch
His nighted° life; moreover, to descry
The strength o' th' enemy.

Oswald. I must needs after him, madam, with my
15   letter.

Regan. Our troops set forth tomorrow: stay with us;
The ways are dangerous.

Oswald.   I may not, madam:
My lady charged my duty° in this business.

4.5.2 **ado** bother and persuasion   6 **import** purport, carry as its message
8 **is posted** has ridden speedily   9 **ignorance** folly   13 **nighted** (1) dark-
ened, because blinded (2) benighted   18 **charged my duty** ordered me as a
solemn duty

Regan. Why should she write to Edmund? Might not
  you
    Transport her purposes° by word? Belike,°   20
    Some things I know not what. I'll love thee much,
    Let me unseal the letter.

Oswald.   Madam, I had rather——

Regan. I know your lady does not love her husband;
    I am sure of that: and at her late° being here
    She gave strange eliads° and most speaking looks   25
    To noble Edmund. I know you are of her bosom.°

Oswald. I, madam?

Regan. I speak in understanding: y'are; I know 't:
    Therefore I do advise you, take this note:°
    My lord is dead; Edmund and I have talked;   30
    And more convenient° is he for my hand
    Than for your lady's: you may gather more.°
    If you do find him, pray you, give him this;°
    And when your mistress hears thus much from you,
    I pray, desire her call° her wisdom to her.   35
    So, fare you well.
    If you do chance to hear of that blind traitor,
    Perferment° falls on him that cuts him off.

Oswald. Would I could meet him, madam! I should
    show
    What party I do follow.

Regan.   Fare thee well.   40

                                        Exeunt.

---

20 **Transport her purposes** convey her intentions   20 **Belike** probably
24 **late** recently   25 **eliads** amorous looks   26 **of her bosom** in her confidence   29 **take this note** take note of this   31 **convenient** fitting
32 **gather more** surmise more yourself   33 **this** this advice   35 **call** recall
38 **Preferment** promotion

[Scene 6.   *Fields near Dover.*]

Enter Gloucester and Edgar.

Gloucester. When shall I come to th' top of that same
      hill?
Edgar. You do climb up it now. Look, how we labor.
Gloucester. Methinks the ground is even.
Edgar.   Horrible steep.
      Hark, do you hear the sea?
Gloucester.   No, truly.
5   *Edgar.* Why then your other senses grow imperfect
      By your eyes' anguish.°
Gloucester.   So may it be indeed.
      Methinks thy voice is altered, and thou speak'st
      In better phrase and matter than thou didst.
Edgar. Y'are much deceived: in nothing am I changed
      But in my garments.
10 *Gloucester.*   Methinks y'are better spoken.
      Edgar. Come on, sir; here's the place: stand still. How
          fearful
      And dizzy 'tis to cast one's eyes so low!
      The crows and choughs° that wing the midway air°
      Show scarce so gross° as beetles. Half way down
15   Hangs one that gathers sampire,° dreadful trade!
      Methinks he seems no bigger than his head.
      The fishermen that walk upon the beach
      Appear like mice; and yond tall anchoring° bark
      Diminished to her cock;° her cock, a buoy

4.6.6 **anguish** pain   13 **choughs** a kind of crow   13 **midway air** i.e.,
halfway down the cliff   14 **gross** large   15 **sampire** samphire, an aromatic
herb associated with Dover Cliffs   18 **anchoring** anchored   19 **cock** cock-
boat, a small boat usually towed behind the ship

Almost too small for sight. The murmuring surge   20
That on th' unnumb'red idle pebble° chafes
Cannot be heard so high. I'll look no more,
Lest my brain turn and the deficient sight
Topple° down headlong.

Gloucester.   Set me where you stand.

Edgar. Give me your hand: you are now within a foot   25
Of th' extreme verge: for all beneath the moon
Would I not leap upright.°

Gloucester.   Let go my hand.
Here, friend, 's another purse; in it a jewel
Well worth a poor man's taking. Fairies° and gods
Prosper it with thee! Go thou further off;   30
Bid me farewell, and let me hear thee going.

Edgar. Now fare ye well, good sir.

Gloucester.   With all my heart.

Edgar. [*Aside*] Why I do trifle thus with his despair
Is done to cure it.°

Gloucester.   O you mighty gods!

He kneels.

This world I do renounce, and in your sights   35
Shake patiently my great affliction off:
If I could bear it longer and not fall
To quarrel° with your great opposeless° wills,
My snuff° and loathèd part of nature should
Burn itself out. If Edgar live, O bless him!   40
Now, fellow, fare thee well.

He falls.

Edgar.   Gone, sir, farewell.

21 **unnumb'red idle pebble** innumerable pebbles, moved to and fro by
the waves to no purpose   23–24 **the deficient sight/Topple** my failing
sight topple me   27 **upright** i.e., even up in the air, to say nothing of forward, over the cliff   29 **Fairies** (who are supposed to guard and multiply
hidden treasure)   33–34 **Why . . . if** I play on his despair in order to cure it
37–38 **fall/To quarrel with** rebel against   38 **opposeless** not to be, and not
capable of being, opposed   39 **snuff** the guttering (and stinking) wick of a
burnt-out candle

[margin annotation: Suicide attempt. Gloucester is 'Suicidal' At this Point]

And yet I know not how° conceit° may rob
The treasury of life, when life itself
Yields to° the theft. Had he been where he thought,
45   By this had thought been past. Alive or dead?
Ho, you sir! friend! Hear you, sir! speak!
Thus might he pass° indeed: yet he revives.
What are you, sir?

Gloucester.   Away, and let me die.

Edgar. Hadst thou been aught but gossamer, feathers,
     air,
50   So many fathom down precipitating,°
Thou'dst shivered like an egg: but thou dost
     breathe;
Hast heavy substance; bleed'st not; speak'st; art
     sound.
Ten masts at each° make not the altitude
Which thou hast perpendicularly fell:
55   Thy life's° a miracle. Speak yet again.

Gloucester. <u>But have I fall'n, or no?</u>

Edgar. From the dread summit of this chalky bourn.°
Look up a-height;° the shrill-gorged° lark so far
Cannot be seen or heard: do but look up.

60 *Gloucester.* Alack, I have no eyes.
Is wretchedness deprived that benefit,
To end itself by death? 'Twas yet some comfort,
When misery could beguile° the tyrant's rage
And frustrate his proud will.

Edgar.   Give me your arm.
65   Up, so. How is 't? Feel you° your legs? You stand.

Gloucester. Too well, too well.

Edgar.   This is above all strangeness.
Upon the crown o' th' cliff, what thing was that

---

42 **how** but what   42 **conceit** imagination   44 **Yields to** allows   47 **pass**
die   50 **precipitating** falling   53 **at each** one on top of the other   55 **life's**
survival   57 **bourn** boundary   58 **a-height** on high   58 **gorged** throated,
voiced   63 **beguile** cheat (i.e., by suicide)   65 **Feel you** have you any feeling in

Which parted from you?

Gloucester.   A poor unfortunate beggar.

Edgar. As I stood here below, methought his eyes
    Were two full moons; he had a thousand noses,
    Horns whelked° and waved like the enridgèd° sea:
    It was some fiend; therefore, thou happy father,°
    Think that the clearest° gods, who make them
        honors
    Of men's impossibilities,° have preserved thee.

Gloucester. I do remember now: henceforth I'll bear   75
    Affliction till it do cry out itself
    "Enough, enough," and die. That thing you speak
        of,
    I took it for a man; often 'twould say
    "The fiend, the fiend"—he led me to that place.

Edgar. Bear free° and patient thoughts.
        *Enter Lear [fantastically dressed with wild
                flowers].*
                        But who comes here?   80
    The safer° sense will ne'er accommodate°
    His master thus.

Lear. No, they cannot touch me for coining;° I am
    the King himself.

Edgar. O thou side-piercing sight!   85

Lear. Nature's above art in that respect.° There's
    your press-money.° That fellow handles his bow

---

71 **whelked** twisted 71 **enridgèd** i.e., furrowed into waves 72 **happy father** fortunate old man 73 **clearest** purest 73–74 **who . . . impossibilities** who cause themselves to be honored and revered by performing miracles of which men are incapable 80 **free** i.e., emancipated from grief and despair, which fetter the soul 81 **safer** sounder, saner 81 **accommodate** dress, adorn 83 **touch me for coining** arrest me for minting coins (the king's prerogative) 86 **Nature's . . . respect** i.e., a born king is superior to legal (and hence artificial) inhibition. There is also a glance here at the popular Renaissance debate, concerning the relative importance of nature (inspiration) and art (training) 87 **press-money** (paid to conscripted soldiers)

like a crow-keeper;° draw me a clothier's yard.°
Look, look, a mouse! Peace, peace; this piece of
90   toasted cheese will do 't. There's my gauntlet;° I'll
prove it on° a giant. Bring up the brown bills.° O,
well flown,° bird! i' th' clout, i' th' clout:° hewgh!°
Give the word.°

Edgar. Sweet marjoram.°

95   *Lear.* Pass.

Gloucester. I know that voice.

Lear. Ha! Goneril, with a white beard! They flattered
me like a dog,° and told me I had white hairs
in my beard ere the black ones were there.° To
100   say "ay" and "no" to everything that I said! "Ay"
and "no" too was no good divinity.° When the
rain came to wet me once and the wind to make
me chatter; when the thunder would not peace at
my bidding; there I found 'em, there I smelt 'em
105   out. Go to, they are not men o' their words: they
told me I was everything; 'tis a lie, I am not ague-
proof.°

Gloucester. The trick° of that voice I do well remember: Is't not the king?

Lear.   Ay, every inch a king.
110   When I do stare, see how the subject quakes.
I pardon that man's life. What was thy cause?°

88 **crow-keeper** a farmer scaring away crows   88 **clothier's yard** (the
standard English arrow was a cloth-yard long. Here the injunction is to draw
the arrow back, like a powerful archer, a full yard to the ear)   90 **gauntlet**
armored glove, thrown down as a challenge   91 **prove it on** maintain my
challenge even against   91 **brown bills** halberds varnished to prevent rust
(here the reference is to the soldiers who carry them)   92 **well flown**
(falconer's cry; and perhaps a reference to the flight of the arrow)   92 **clout**
the target shot at   92 **hewgh** ? imitating the whizzing of the arrow
93 **word** password   94 **Sweet marjoram** herb, used as a remedy for brain
disease   96 **like a dog** as a dog flatters   98–99 **I . . . there** I was wise before I had even grown a beard   101 **no good divinity** (bad theology, because contrary to the Biblical saying [II Corinthians 1:18], "Our word
toward you was not yea and nay." See also James 5:12 "But let your yea be
yea, and your nay, nay; lest ye fall into condemnation"; and Matthew
5:36–37)   106–07 **ague-proof** secure against fever   108 **trick** intonation
111 **cause** offense

Adultery?
Thou shalt not die: die for adultery! No:
The wren goes to 't, and the small gilded fly
Does lecher° in my sight.   *115*
Let copulation thrive; for Gloucester's bastard son
Was kinder to his father than my daughters
Got° 'tween the lawful sheets.
To 't, luxury,° pell-mell! for I lack soldiers.°
Behold yond simp'ring dame,   *120*
Whose face between her forks presages snow,°
That minces° virtue and does shake the head
To hear of pleasure's name.°
The fitchew,° nor the soilèd° horse, goes to 't
With a more riotous appetite.   *125*
Down from the waist they are Centaurs,°
Though women all above:
But to the girdle° do the gods inherit,°
Beneath is all the fiend's.
There's hell, there's darkness, there is the
    sulphurous pit,   *130*
Burning, scalding, stench, consumption; fie, fie, fie!
pah, pah! Give me an ounce of civet;° good apothe-
cary, sweeten my imagination: there's money for thee.

Gloucester. O, let me kiss that hand!

Lear. Let me wipe it first; it smells of mortality.°   *135*

Gloucester. O ruined piece of nature! This great world
    Shall so wear out to nought.° Dost thou know me?

---

115 **lecher** copulate   118 **Got** begot   119 **luxury** lechery   119 **for . . . soldiers** i.e., ? (1) whom copulation will supply (2) and am therefore powerless
121 **Whose . . . snow** whose cold demeanor seems to promise chaste behavior ("forks": legs)   122 **minces** squeamishly pretends to   123 **pleasure's
name** the very name of sexual pleasure   124 **fitchew** polecat (and slang for
"prostitute")   124 **soilèd** put to pasture, and hence wanton with feeding
126 **Centaurs** lustful creatures, half man and half horse   128 **girdle** waist
128 **inherit** possess   132 **civet** perfume   135 **mortality** (1) death (2) existence   136–37 **This . . . nought** i.e., the universe (macrocosm) will decay to
nothing in the same way as the little world of man (microcosm)

Lear. I remember thine eyes well enough. Dost thou
squiny° at me? No, do thy worst, blind Cupid;° I'll
140   not love. Read thou this challenge;° mark but the
penning of it.

Gloucester. Were all thy letters suns, I could not see.

Edgar. I would not take° this from report: it is,
And my heart breaks at it.

145 *Lear.* Read.

Gloucester. What, with the case° of eyes?

Lear. O, ho, are you there with me?° No eyes in your
head, nor no money in your purse? Your eyes are
in a heavy case,° your purse in a light,° yet you
150   see how this world goes.

Gloucester. I see it feelingly.°

Lear. What, art mad? A man may see how this world
goes with no eyes. Look with thine ears: see how
yond justice rails upon yond simple° thief. Hark,
155   in thine ear: change places, and, handy-dandy,°
which is the justice, which is the thief? Thou hast
seen a farmer's dog bark at a beggar?

Gloucester. Ay, sir.

Lear. And the creature run from the cur? There thou
160   mightst behold the great image of authority:° a
dog's obeyed in office.°
Thou rascal beadle,° hold thy bloody hand!
Why dost thou lash that whore? Strip thy own
     back;
Thou hotly lusts to use her in that kind°

139 **squiny** squint, look sideways, like a prostitute   139 **blind Cupid** the
sign hung before a brothel   140 **challenge** a reminiscence of ll. 89–90
143 **take** believe   146 **case** empty sockets   147 **are ... me** is that what you
tell me   149 **heavy case** sad plight (pun on l. 146)   149 **light** i.e., empty
151 **feelingly** (1) by touch (2) by feeling pain (3) with emotion   154 **simple**
common, of low estate   155 **handy-dandy** i.e., choose, guess (after the children's game—"Handy-dandy, prickly prandy"—of choosing the right hand)
160 **image of authority** symbol revealing the true meaning of authority
160–61 **a ... office** i.e., whoever has power is obeyed   162 **beadle** parish
constable   164 **kind** i.e., sexual act

For which thou whip'st her. The usurer hangs the
  cozener.°   165
Through tattered clothes small vices do appear;
Robes and furred gowns° hide all. Plate sin with
  gold,
And the strong lance of justice hurtless° breaks;
Arm it in rags, a pygmy's straw does pierce it.
None does offend, none, I say, none; I'll able°
  'em: 170
Take that° of me, my friend, who have the power
To seal th' accuser's lips. Get thee glass eyes,°   *problematic*
And, like a scurvy politician,° seem   *of seeing*
To see the things thou dost not. Now, now, now,
  now.
Pull off my boots: harder, harder: so.   175

Edgar. O, matter and impertinency° mixed!
  Reason in madness!

Lear. If thou wilt weep my fortunes, take my eyes.
I know thee well enough; thy name is Gloucester:
Thou must be patient; we came crying hither: 180
Thou know'st, the first time that we smell the air
We wawl and cry. I will preach to thee: mark.

Gloucester. Alack, alack the day!

Lear. When we are born, we cry that we are come
To this great stage of fools. This'° a good block.°   185

164–65 **The usurer ... cozener** i.e., the powerful moneylender, in his
role as judge, puts to death the petty cheat   167 **Robes and furred
gowns** (worn by a judge)   168 **hurtless** i.e., without hurting the sinner
170 **able** vouch for   171 **that** (the immunity just conferred) (l. 170)
172 **glass eyes** spectacles   173 **scurvy politician** vile politic man
176 **matter and impertinency** sense and nonsense   185 **This'** this is
185 **block** (various meanings have been suggested, for example, the
stump of a tree, on which Lear is supposed to climb; a mounting-block,
which suggests "horse" l. 187; a hat [which Lear or another must be made
to wear], from the block on which a felt hat is molded, and which would
suggest a "felt" l. 187. The proposal here is that "block" be taken to denote
the quintain, whose function is to bear blows, "a mere lifeless block"
[*As You Like It,* 1.2.263], an object shaped like a man and used for tilting
practice. See also *Much Ado,* 2.1.246–7, "she misused me past the en-
durance of a block!" and, in the same passage, the associated reference,
"I stood like a man at a mark [target]" [1.253])

It were a delicate° stratagem, to shoe
A troop of horse with felt: I'll put 't in proof;°
And when I have stol'n upon these son-in-laws,
Then, kill, kill, kill, kill, kill, kill!
                    Enter a Gentleman [with Attendants].

190 *Gentleman.* O, here he is: lay hand upon him. Sir,
       Your most dear daughter—

Lear. No rescue? What, a prisoner? I am even
       The natural fool° of fortune. Use me well;
       You shall have ransom. Let me have surgeons;
       I am cut° to th' brains.

195 *Gentleman.*   You shall have anything.

Lear. No seconds?° all myself?
       Why, this would make a man a man of salt,°
       To use his eyes for garden water-pots,
       Ay, and laying autumn's dust.

200 *Gentleman.* Good sir—

Lear. I will die bravely,° like a smug° bridegroom.°
       What!
       I will be jovial: come, come; I am a king;
       Masters, know you that?

Gentleman. You are a royal one, and we obey you.

205 *Lear.* Then there's life in 't.° Come, and you get it,
       you shall get it by running. Sa, sa, sa, sa.°
                    Exit [running; Attendants follow].

Gentleman. A sight most pitiful in the meanest wretch,
       Past speaking of in a king! Thou hast one daughter
       Who redeems nature from the general curse
210   Which twain have brought her to.°

186 **delicate** subtle   187 **put 't in proof** test it   193 **natural fool** born sport
(with pun on "natural": "imbecile")   195 **cut** wounded   196 **seconds** supporters   197 **man of salt** i.e., all (salt) tears   201 **bravely** (1) smartly attired
(2) courageously   201 **smug** spick and span   201 **bridegroom** whose
"brave" sexual feats are picked up in the pun on "die"   205 **there's life in't**
there's still hope   206 **Sa . . . sa** hunting and rallying cry; also an interjection
of defiance   209–10 **general . . . to** (1) universal condemnation which Goneril
and Regan have made for (2) damnation incurred by the original sin of Adam
and Eve

Edgar. Hail, gentle° sir.

Gentleman.　　　　　Sir, speed° you: what's your will?

Edgar. Do you hear aught, sir, of a battle toward?°

Gentleman. Most sure and vulgar:° every one hears
　　　that,
　　Which can distinguish sound.

Edgar.　　　　　　　But, by your favor,
　　How near's the other army?　　　　　　　　　215

Gentleman. Near and on speedy foot; the main
　　　descry
　　Stands on the hourly thought.°

Edgar.　　　　　I thank you, sir: that's all.

Gentleman. Though that the Queen on special cause
　　　is here,
　　Her army is moved on.

Edgar.　　　　　I thank you, sir.

　　　　　　　　　　　Exit [*Gentleman*].

Gloucester. You ever-gentle gods, take my breath
　　　from me;　　　　　　　　　　　　　　　　220
　　Let not my worser spirit° tempt me again
　　To die before you please.

Edgar.　　　　　Well pray you, father.

Gloucester. Now, good sir, what are you?

Edgar. A most poor man, made tame° to fortune's
　　　blows;
　　Who, by the art of known and feeling sorrows,°　　225
　　Am pregnant° to good pity. Give me your hand,
　　I'll lead you to some biding.°

Gloucester.　　　　　Hearty thanks;

---

211 **gentle** noble　211 **speed** God speed　212 **toward** impending　213 **vulgar** common knowledge　216–17 **the . . . thought** we expect to see the main body of the army any hour　221 **worser spirit** bad angel, evil side of my nature　224 **tame** submissive　225 **art . . . sorrows** instruction of sorrows painfully experienced　226 **pregnant** disposed　227 **biding** place of refuge

The bounty and the benison° of heaven
To boot, and boot.°

Enter Oswald.

Oswald.   A proclaimed prize°! Most happy!°
230   That eyeless head of thine was first framed° flesh
To raise my fortunes. Thou old unhappy traitor,
Briefly thyself remember:° the sword is out
That must destroy thee.

Gloucester.   Now let thy friendly° hand
Put strength enough to 't.

[*Edgar interposes.*]

Oswald.   Wherefore, bold peasant,
235   Dar'st thou support a published° traitor? Hence!
Lest that th' infection of his fortune take
Like hold on thee. Let go his arm.

Edgar. Chill° not let go, zir, without vurther 'casion.°

Oswald. Let go, slave, or thou diest!

240 **Edgar.** Good gentleman, go your gait,° and let poor
volk° pass. And chud ha' bin zwaggered° out of my
life, 'twould not ha' bin zo long as 'tis by a vort-
night. Nay, come not near th' old man; keep out,
che vor' ye,° or I'se° try whether your costard°
245   or my ballow° be the harder: chill be plain with
you.

Oswald. Out, dunghill!

They fight.

228 **benison** blessing   229 **To boot, and boot** also, and in the highest degree
229 **proclaimed prize** i.e., one with a price on his head   229 **happy** fortunate (for Oswald)   230 **framed** created   232 **thyself remember** i.e., pray
think of your sins   233 **friendly** i.e., because it offers the death Gloucester
covets   235 **published** proclaimed   238 **Chill** . . . (Edgar speaks in rustic
dialect)   238 **Chill** I will   238 **vurther 'casion** further occasion   240 **gait**
way   241 **volk** folk   241 **And chud ha' bin zwaggered** if I could have
been swaggered   244 **Che vor' ye** I warrant you   244 **I'se** I shall
244 **costard** head (literally, "apple")   245 **ballow** cudgel

Edgar. Chill pick your teeth,° zir: come; no matter
    vor your foins.°

[*Oswald falls.*]

Oswald. Slave, thou hast slain me. Villain, take my
    purse: 250
If ever thou wilt thrive, bury my body,
And give the letters which thou find'st about° me
To Edmund Earl of Gloucester; seek him out
Upon the English party.° O, untimely death!
    Death!   255

He dies.

Edgar. I know thee well. A serviceable° villain,
As duteous° to the vices of thy mistress
As badness would desire.

Gloucester.   What, is he dead?

Edgar. Sit you down, father; rest you.
Let's see these pockets: the letters that he speaks
    of   260
May be my friends. He's dead; I am only sorry
He had no other deathsman.° Let us see:
Leave,° gentle wax;° and, manners, blame us not:
To know our enemies' minds, we rip their hearts;
Their papers° is more lawful.   265

Reads the letter.

"Let our reciprocal vows be remembered. You
have many opportunities to cut him off: if your
will want not,° time and place will be fruitfully
offered. There is nothing done, if he return the con-
queror: then am I the prisoner, and his bed my   270
jail; from the loathed warmth whereof deliver me,
and supply the place for your labor.
    "Your—wife, so I would° say—affectionate

248 **Chill pick your teeth** I will knock your teeth out   249 **foins** thrusts
252 **about** upon   254 **party** side   256 **serviceable** ready to be used
257 **duteous** obedient   262 **deathsman** executioner   263 **Leave** by your
leave   263 **wax** (with which the letter is sealed)   265 **Their papers** i.e., to
rip their papers   267–68 **if . . . not** if your desire (and lust) be not lacking
273 **would** would like to

servant, and for you her own for venture,°
275   'Goneril.' "
O indistinguished space of woman's will!°
A plot upon her virtuous husband's life;
And the exchange° my brother! Here in the sands
Thee I'll rake up,° the post unsanctified°
280   Of murderous lechers; and in the mature° time,
With this ungracious paper° strike° the sight
Of the death-practiced° Duke: for him 'tis well
That of thy death and business I can tell.

Gloucester. The King is mad: how stiff° is my vile
sense,°
285   That I stand up, and have ingenious° feeling
Of my huge sorrows! Better I were distract:°
So should my thoughts be severed from my griefs,
And woes by wrong imaginations° lose
The knowledge of themselves.
                                        Drum afar off.

Edgar.   Give me your hand:
290   Far off, methinks, I hear the beaten drum.
Come, father, I'll bestow° you with a friend.
                                        Exeunt.

Scene 7.   [*A tent in the French camp.*]

Enter Cordelia, Kent, Doctor, and Gentleman.

Cordelia. O thou good Kent, how shall I live and
work,

274 **and ... venture** i.e., and one who holds you her own for venturing (Edmund had earlier been promised union by Goneril, "If you dare venture in your own behalf," 4.2.20).   276 **indistinguished ... will** unlimited range of woman's lust   278 **exchange** substitute   279 **rake up** cover up, bury   279 **post unsanctified** unholy messenger   280 **mature** ripe   281 **ungracious paper** wicked letter   281 **strike** blast   282 **death-practiced** whose death is plotted   284 **stiff** unbending   284 **vile sense** hateful capacity for feeling   285 **ingenious** conscious   286 **distract** distracted, mad   288 **wrong imaginations** delusions   291 **bestow** lodge

To match thy goodness? My life will be too short,
And every measure fail me.　　*prophetic?*

Kent. To be acknowledged, madam, is o'erpaid.
All my reports go° with the modest truth,　　　　5
Nor more nor clipped,° but so.

Cordelia.　　　　　　　　Be better suited:°
These weeds° are memories° of those worser
　　hours:
I prithee, put them off.

Kent.　　　　　　　Pardon, dear madam;
Yet to be known shortens my made intent:°
My boon I make it,° that you know me not　　　10
Till time and I think meet.°

Cordelia. Then be 't so, my good lord. [*To the Doctor.*] How does the King?

Doctor. Madam, sleeps still.

Cordelia. O you kind gods!
Cure this great breach in his abusèd° nature.　　15
Th' untuned and jarring senses, O, wind up°
Of this child-changèd father.

Doctor.　　　　　　　So please your Majesty
That we may wake the King: he hath slept long.

Cordelia. Be governed by your knowledge, and
　　proceed
I' th' sway of° your own will. Is he arrayed?　　20

　　　Enter Lear in a chair carried by Servants.

4.7.5 **go** conform　6 **clipped** curtailed　6 **suited** attired　7 **weeds** clothes
7 **memories** reminders　9 **Yet . . . intent** to reveal myself just yet interferes
with the plan I have made　10 **My boon I make it** I ask this reward　11
meet fitting　15 **abusèd** disturbed　16 **wind up** tune　17 **child-changèd**
changed, deranged (and also, reduced to a child) by the cruelty of his children　20 **I' th' sway of** according to

Gentleman. Ay, madam; in the heaviness of sleep
   We put fresh garments on him.

Doctor. Be by, good madam, when we do awake him;
   I doubt not of his temperance.°

Cordelia.   Very well.

Doctor. Please you, draw near. Louder the music
25   there!

Cordelia. O my dear father, restoration hang
   Thy medicine on my lips, and let this kiss
   Repair those violent harms that my two sisters
   Have in thy reverence° made.

Kent.   Kind and dear Princess.

Cordelia. Had you not been their father, these white
30   flakes°
   Did challenge° pity of them. Was this a face
   To be opposed against the warring winds?
   To stand against the deep dread-bolted° thunder?
   In the most terrible and nimble stroke
   Of quick, cross° lightning to watch—poor
35   perdu!°—
   With this thin helm?° Mine enemy's dog,
   Though he had bit me, should have stood that night
   Against my fire; and wast thou fain,° poor father,
   To hovel thee with swine and rogues° forlorn,
40   In short° and musty straw? Alack, alack!
   'Tis wonder that thy life and wits at once
   Had not concluded all.° He wakes; speak to him.

Doctor. Madam, do you; 'tis fittest.

---

24 **temperance** sanity   29 **reverence** revered person   30 **flakes** hairs (in
long strands)   31 **challenge** claim   33 **deep dread-bolted** deep-voiced
and furnished with the dreadful thunderbolt   35 **cross** zigzag   35 **perdu**
(1) sentry in a forlorn position (2) lost one   36 **helm** helmet (his scanty
hair)   38 **fain** pleased   39 **rogues** vagabonds   40 **short** (when straw is
freshly cut, it is long, and suitable for bedding, given its flexibility and
crispness. As it is used, it becomes musty, shreds into pieces, is "short." In
contemporary Maine usage, "short manure" refers to dung mixed with straw
that has been broken up; "long manure" to dung mixed with coarse new
straw)   42 **concluded all** come to a complete end

Cordelia. How does my royal lord? How fares your
　　Majesty?

Lear. You do me wrong to take me out o' th' grave:　45
　　Thou art a soul in bliss; but I am bound
　　Upon a wheel of fire,° that mine own tears
　　Do scald like molten lead.

Cordelia.　　　　　　　Sir, do you know me?

Lear. You are a spirit, I know. Where did you die?

Cordelia. Still, still, far wide.°　　　　　　　50

Doctor. He's scarce awake: let him alone awhile.

Lear. Where have I been? Where am I? Fair daylight?
　　I am mightily abused.° I should ev'n die with pity,
　　To see another thus. I know not what to say.
　　I will not swear these are my hands: let's see;　55
　　I feel this pin prick. Would I were assured
　　Of my condition.

Cordelia.　　　　　　O, look upon me, sir,
　　And hold your hand in benediction o'er me.
　　You must not kneel.

Lear.　　　　　　Pray, do not mock me:
　　I am a very foolish fond° old man,　　　　60
　　Fourscore and upward, not an hour more nor less;
　　And, to deal plainly,
　　I fear I am not in my perfect mind.
　　Methinks I should know you and know this man,
　　Yet I am doubtful; for I am mainly° ignorant　65
　　What place this is, and all the skill I have
　　Remembers not these garments, nor I know not
　　Where I did lodge last night. Do not laugh at me,
　　For, as I am a man, I think this lady
　　To be my child Cordelia.

Cordelia.　　　　　　And so I am, I am.　70

Lear. Be your tears wet? Yes, faith. I pray, weep not.
　　If you have poison for me, I will drink it.

47 **wheel of fire** (torment associated by the Middle Ages with Hell, where
Lear thinks he is)　50 **wide** i.e., of the mark (of sanity)　53 **abused** deluded　60 **fond** in dotage　65 **mainly** entirely

I know you do not love me; for your sisters
Have, as I do remember, done me wrong.
You have some cause, they have not.

75 *Cordelia.*   No cause, no cause.

Lear. Am I in France?

Kent.   In your own kingdom, sir.

Lear. Do not abuse° me.

Doctor. Be comforted, good madam: the great rage,°
        You see, is killed in him: and yet it is danger
80   To make him even o'er° the time he has lost.
        Desire him to go in; trouble him no more
        Till further settling.°

Cordelia. Will 't please your Highness walk?°

Lear. You must bear with me. Pray you now, forget
85   and forgive. I am old and foolish.

> *Exeunt. Mane[n]t° Kent and Gentleman.*

Gentleman. Holds it true, sir, that the Duke of Corn-
        wall was so slain?

Kent. Most certain, sir.

Gentleman. Who is conductor of his people?

90 *Kent.* As 'tis said, the bastard son of Gloucester.

Gentleman. They say Edgar, his banished son, is with
        the Earl of Kent in Germany.

Kent. Report is changeable.° 'Tis time to look about;
        the powers° of the kingdom approach apace.

95 *Gentleman.* The arbitrement° is like to be bloody.
        Fare you well, sir.   [*Exit.*]

Kent. My point and period will be throughly
            wrought,°
        Or well or ill, as this day's battle's fought.

> *Exit.*

---

77 **abuse** deceive   78 **rage** frenzy   80 **even o'er** smooth over by filling in;
and hence, "recollect"   82 **settling** calming   83 **walk** (perhaps in the
sense of "withdraw")   85 s.d. **Mane[n]t** remain   93 **Report is changeable** rumors are unreliable   94 **powers** armies   95 **arbitrement** deciding
encounter   97 **My . . . wrought** the aim and end, the close of my life would
be completely worked out

ACT 5

Scene 1.   [*The British camp near Dover.*]

Enter, with drum and colors, Edmund, Regan,
Gentlemen, and Soldiers.

Edmund. Know° of the Duke if his last purpose hold,°
  Or whether since he is advised° by aught
  To change the course: he's full of alteration
  And self-reproving: bring his constant pleasure.°

                [*To a Gentleman, who goes out.*]

Regan. Our sister's man is certainly miscarried.°   5

Edmund. 'Tis to be doubted,° madam.

Regan.   Now, sweet lord,
  You know the goodness I intend upon you:
  Tell me, but truly, but then speak the truth,
  Do you not love my sister?

Edmund.   In honored° love.

Regan. But have you never found my brother's way   10
  To the forfended° place?

Edmund.   That thought abuses° you.

___

5.1.1 **Know** learn   1 **last purpose hold** most recent intention (to fight) be
maintained   2 **advised** induced   4 **constant pleasure** fixed (final) decision
5 **miscarried** come to grief   6 **doubted** feared   9 **honored** honorable
11 **forfended** forbidden   11 **abuses** (1) deceives (2) demeans, is unworthy of

127

Regan. I am doubtful that you have been conjunct
  And bosomed with her, as far as we call hers.°

Edmund. No, by mine honor, madam.

15 *Regan.* I shall never endure her: dear my lord,
  Be not familiar with her.

Edmund.   Fear° me not.—
  She and the Duke her husband!

*Enter, with drum and colors, Albany, Goneril
  [and] Soldiers.*

Goneril. [*Aside*] I had rather lose the battle than
  that sister
  Should loosen° him and me.

20 *Albany.* Our very loving sister, well be-met.°
  Sir, this I heard, the King is come to his daughter,
  With others whom the rigor of our state°
  Forced to cry out. Where I could not be honest,°
  I never yet was valiant: for this business,
25 It touches us, as° France invades our land,
  Not bolds the King, with others, whom, I fear,
  Most just and heavy causes make oppose.°

Edmund. Sir, you speak nobly.

Regan.   Why is this reasoned?°

Goneril. Combine together 'gainst the enemy;
30 For these domestic and particular broils°
  Are not the question° here.

Albany.   Let's then determine
  With th' ancient of war° on our proceeding.

Edmund. I shall attend you presently at your tent.

12–13 **I . . . hers** I fear that you have united with her intimately, in the
fullest possible way   16 **Fear** distrust   19 **loosen** separate   20 **be-met**
met   22 **rigor . . . state** tyranny of our government   23 **honest** honorable
25 **touches us, as** concerns me, only in that   26–27 **Not . . . oppose** and not
in that France emboldens the King and others, who have been led, by real
and serious grievances, to take up arms against us   28 **reasoned** argued
30 **particular broils** private quarrels   31 **question** issue   32 **th' ancient
of war** experienced commanders

Regan. Sister, you'll go with us?°

Goneril. No.   35

Regan. 'Tis most convenient;° pray you, go with us.

Goneril. [*Aside*] O, ho, I know the riddle.°—I
    will go.
    Exeunt both the Armies. Enter Edgar [*disguised*].

Edgar. If e'er your Grace had speech with man so
        poor,
    Hear me one word.

Albany. [*To those going out*] I'll overtake you. [*To
        Edgar*] Speak.

                    Exeunt [*all but Albany and Edgar*].

Edgar. Before you fight the battle, ope this letter.   40
    If you have victory, let the trumpet sound
    For° him that brought it: wretched though I seem,
    I can produce a champion that will prove°
    What is avouchèd° there. If you miscarry,
    Your business of° the world hath so an end,   45
    And machination° ceases. Fortune love you.

Albany. Stay till I have read the letter.

Edgar.   I was forbid it.
    When time shall serve, let but the herald cry,
    And I'll appear again.

Albany. Why, fare thee well: I will o'erlook° thy
        paper.   *Exit* [*Edgar*].   50
            Enter Edmund.

Edmund. The enemy's in view: draw up your powers.
    Here is the guess° of their true strength and
        forces
    By diligent discovery;° but your haste

---

34 **us** me (rather than Edmund)   36 **convenient** fitting, desirable   37 **rid-dle** real reason (for Regan's curious request)   41–42 **sound/For** summon   43 **prove** i.e., by trial of combat   44 **avouchèd** maintained   45 **of** in   46 **machination** plotting   50 **o'erlook** read over   52 **guess** estimate   53 **By diligent discovery** obtained by careful reconnoitering

Is now urged on you.

Albany.   We will greet° the time. *Exit.*

55   *Edmund.* To both these sisters have I sworn my love;
        Each jealous° of the other, as the stung
        Are of the adder. Which of them shall I take?
        Both? One? Or neither? Neither can be enjoyed,
        If both remain alive: to take the widow
60   Exasperates, makes mad her sister Goneril;
        And hardly° shall I carry out my side,°
        Her husband being alive. Now then, we'll use
        His countenance° for the battle; which being done,
        Let her who would be rid of him devise
65   His speedy taking off. As for the mercy
        Which he intends to Lear and to Cordelia,
        The battle done, and they within our power,
        Shall never see his pardon; for my state
        Stands on me to defend, not to debate.°   *Exit.*

Scene 2.   [*A field between the two camps.*]

        *Alarum° within. Enter, with drum and colors,
        Lear, Cordelia, and Soldiers, over the stage; and
        exeunt.*
                Enter Edgar and Gloucester.
    Edgar. Here, father,° take the shadow of this tree
        For your good host; pray that the right may thrive.
        If ever I return to you again,
        I'll bring you comfort.
    Gloucester.   Grace go with you, sir.
                                        Exit [*Edgar*].

54 **greet** i.e., meet the demands of   56 **jealous** suspicious   61 **hardly** with
difficulty   61 **carry ... side** (1) satisfy my ambition (2) fulfill my bargain
(with Goneril)   63 **countenance** authority   68–69 **for ... debate** my position requires me to act, not to reason about right and wrong 5.2. s.d.
Alarum a trumpet call to battle   1 **father** i.e., venerable old man (Edgar
has not yet revealed his identity)

Alarum and retreat° within. [Re-]enter Edgar.

Edgar. Away, old man; give me thy hand; away!   5
   King Lear hath lost, he and his daughter ta'en:°
   Give me thy hand; come on.

Gloucester. No further, sir; a man may rot even here.

Edgar. What, in ill thoughts again? Men must endure
   Their going hence, even as their coming hither: 10
   Ripeness° is all. Come on.

Gloucester.   And that's true too.
                                          Exeunt.

   Scene 3.   [*The British camp near Dover.*]

      Enter, in conquest, with drum and colors, Ed-
      mund; Lear and Cordelia, as prisoners; Soldiers,
      Captain.

Edmund. Some officers take them away: good guard,°
   Until their greater pleasures° first be known
   That are to censure° them.

Cordelia.   We are <u>not the first</u>
   Who with <u>best meaning° have incurred the worst</u>.
   For thee, oppressèd King, I am cast down;   5
   Myself could else out-frown false fortune's frown.
   Shall we not see these daughters and these sisters?

Lear. No, no, no, no! Come, let's away to prison:
   We two alone will sing like birds i' th' cage:
   When thou dost ask me blessing, I'll kneel down   10
   And ask of thee forgiveness: so we'll live,
   And pray, and sing, and tell old tales, and laugh

4 s.d. **retreat** (signaled by a trumpet)   6 **ta'en** captured   11 **Ripeness** maturity, as of fruit that is ready to fall 5.3.1 **good guard** let there be good
guard   2 **their greater pleasures** the will of those in command, the great
ones   3 **censure** pass judgment on   4 **meaning** intentions

At gilded butterflies,° and hear poor rogues
Talk of court news; and we'll talk with them too,
15 Who loses and who wins, who's in, who's out;
And take upon's the mystery of things,
As if we were God's spies:° and we'll wear out,°
In a walled prison, packs and sects of great ones
That ebb and flow by th' moon.°

Edmund.   Take them away.

20 *Lear.* Upon such sacrifices, my Cordelia,
The gods themselves throw incense.° Have I caught
thee?
He that parts us shall bring a brand from heaven,
And fire us hence like foxes.° Wipe thine eyes;
The good years° shall devour them,° flesh and fell,°
Ere they shall make us weep. We'll see 'em starved
25 first.
Come.   [*Exeunt Lear and Cordelia, guarded.*]

Edmund. Come hither, captain; hark.
Take thou this note: go follow them to prison:
One step I have advanced thee; if thou dost
30 As this instructs thee, thou dost make thy way
To noble fortunes: know thou this, that men
Are as the time is:° to be tender-minded
Does not become a sword:° thy great employment
Will not bear question;° either say thou'lt do 't,
Or thrive by other means.

35 *Captain.*   I'll do 't, my lord.

---

13 **gilded butterflies** i.e., gorgeously attired courtiers, fluttering after nothing   16–17 **take ... spies** profess to read the riddle of existence, as if endowed with divine omniscience   17 **wear out** outlast   18–19 **packs ... moon** intriguing and partisan cliques of those in high station, whose fortunes change every month   20–21 **Upon... incense** i.e., the gods approve our renunciation of the world   22–23 **He ... foxes** no human agency can separate us, but only divine interposition, as of a heavenly torch parting us like foxes who are driven from their place of refuge by fire and smoke   24 **good years** plague and pestilence ("undefined malefic power or agency," *N.E.D.*)   24 **them** i.e., the enemies of Lear and Cordelia   24 **fell** skin   32 **as the time is** i.e., absolutely determined by the exigencies of the moment   33 **become a sword** befit a soldier   34 **bear question** admit of discussion

Edmund. About it; and write happy° when th' hast
　done.
　Mark; I say, instantly, and carry it so°
　As I have set it down.

Captain. I cannot draw a cart, nor eat dried oats;
　If it be man's work, I'll do 't.　　　*Exit Captain.*　40

　　Flourish. Enter Albany, Goneril, Regan [another
　　　　　Captain, and] Soldiers.

Albany. Sir, you have showed today your valiant
　strain,°
　And fortune led you well: you have the captives
　Who were the opposites of° this day's strife:
　I do require them of you, so to use them
　As we shall find their merits° and our safety　　　45
　May equally determine.

Edmund.　　　　　　　　Sir, I thought it fit
　To send the old and miserable King
　To some retention and appointed guard;°
　Whose° age had charms in it, whose title more,
　To pluck the common bosom on his side,°　　　50
　And turn our impressed lances in our eyes°
　Which do command them. With him I sent the
　　Queen:
　My reason all the same; and they are ready
　Tomorrow, or at further space,° t' appear
　Where you shall hold your session.° At this time　55
　We sweat and bleed: the friend hath lost his friend;
　And the best quarrels, in the heat, are cursed
　By those that feel their sharpness.°
　The question of Cordelia and her father

36 **write happy** style yourself fortunate　37 **carry it so** manage the affair
in exactly that manner (as if Cordelia had taken her own life)　41 **strain**
(1) stock (2) character　43 **opposites of** opponents in　45 **merits** deserts
48 **retention … guard** confinement under duly appointed guard
49 **Whose** i.e., Lear's　50 **pluck … side** win the sympathy of the people to
himself　51 **turn … eyes** turn our conscripted lancers against us　54 **further space** a later time　55 **session** trial　57–58 **the … sharpness** the
worthiest causes may be judged badly by those who have been affected
painfully by them, and whose passion has not yet cooled

Requires a fitter place.

60 *Albany.*   Sir, by your patience,
I hold you but a subject of° this war,
Not as a brother.

Regan.   That's as we list to grace° him.
Methinks our pleasure might have been demanded,
Ere you had spoke so far. He led our powers,
65 Bore the commission of my place and person;
The which immediacy may well stand up
And call itself your brother.°

Goneril.   Not so hot:
In his own grace he doth exalt himself
More than in your addition.°

Regan.   In my rights,
70 By me invested, he compeers° the best.

Goneril. That were the most,° if he should husband
you.°

Regan. Jesters do oft prove prophets.

Goneril.   Holla, holla!
That eye that told you so looked but a-squint.°

Regan. Lady, I am not well; else I should answer
75 From a full-flowing stomach.° General,
Take thou my soldiers, prisoners, patrimony;°
Dispose of them, of me; the walls is thine:°
Witness the world, that I create thee here
My lord, and master.

Goneril.   Mean you to enjoy him?

80 *Albany.* The let-alone° lies not in your good will.

---

61 **subject of** subordinate in   62 **list to grace** wish to honor   65–67 **Bore . . .
brother** was authorized, as my deputy, to take command; his present status, as
my immediate representative, entitles him to be considered your equal
69 **your addition** honors you have bestowed on him   70 **compeers** equals
71 **most** most complete investing in your rights   71 **husband you** become your husband   73 **a-squint** cross-eyed   75 **From . . . stomach** angrily
76 **patrimony** inheritance   77 **walls is thine** i.e., Regan's person, which Edmund has stormed and won   80 **let-alone** power to prevent

Edmund. Nor in thine, lord.

Albany.   Half-blooded° fellow, yes.

Regan. [*To Edmund*] Let the drum strike, and prove
     my title thine.°

Albany. Stay yet; hear reason. Edmund, I arrest thee
     On capital treason; and in thy attaint°
     This gilded serpent [*pointing to Goneril*]. For
     your claim, fair sister,   85
     I bar it in the interest of my wife.
     'Tis she is subcontracted° to this lord,
     And I, her husband, contradict your banes.°
     If you will marry, make your loves° to me;
     My Lady is bespoke.°

Goneril.   An interlude!°   90

Albany. Thou art armed, Gloucester: let the trumpet
     sound:
     If none appear to prove upon thy person
     Thy heinous, manifest, and many treasons,
     There is my pledge° [*throwing down a glove*]:
        I'll make° it on thy heart,
     Ere I taste bread, thou art in nothing less   95
     Than I have here proclaimed thee.

Regan.   Sick, O, sick!

Goneril. [*Aside*] If not, I'll ne'er trust medicine.°

Edmund. [*Throwing down a glove*] There's my
     exchange:° what in the world he is
     That names me traitor, villain-like he lies:°
     Call by the trumpet:° he that dares approach,   100

81 **Half-blooded** bastard, and so only half noble   82 **prove . . . thine** prove
by combat your entitlement to my rights   84 **in thy attaint** as a sharer in the
treason for which you are impeached   87 **subcontracted** pledged by a contract which is called into question by the existence of a previous contract
(Goneril's marriage)   88 **contradict your banes** forbid your announced
intention to marry (by citing the precontract)   89 **loves** love-suits   90 **be-
spoke** already pledged   90 **interlude** play   94 **pledge** gage 94 **make** prove
97 **medicine** poison   98 **exchange** (technical term, denoting the glove Edmund throws down)   99 **villain-like he lies** (the lie direct, a challenge to
mortal combat)   100 **trumpet** trumpeter

On him, on you—who not?—I will maintain
My truth and honor firmly.

Albany. A herald, ho!

Edmund.   A herald, ho, a herald!

Albany. Trust to thy single virtue;° for thy soldiers,
105 All levied in my name, have in my name
Took their discharge.

Regan.   My sickness grows upon me.

Albany. She is not well; convey her to my tent.

                              [*Exit Regan, led.*]

              Enter a Herald.

Come hither, herald. Let the trumpet sound—
And read out this.

110 *Captain.* Sound, trumpet!

              A trumpet sounds.

Herald. (*Reads.*) "If any man of quality or degree°
within the lists° of the army will maintain upon Edmund, supposed Earl of Gloucester, that he is a
manifold traitor, let him appear by the third sound
115 of the trumpet: he is bold in his defense."

Edmund. Sound!

              First trumpet.

Herald. Again!

              Second trumpet.

Herald. Again!

              Third trumpet.

*Trumpet answers within. Enter Edgar, at the
third sound, armed, a trumpet before him.*°

Albany. Ask him his purposes, why he appears
Upon this call o' th' trumpet.

120 *Herald.*   What are you?

---

104 **single virtue** unaided valor   111 **quality or degree** rank or position
112 **lists** rolls   118 s.d. **trumpet before him** trumpeter preceding him

Your name, your quality,° and why you answer
This present summons?

Edgar.   Know, my name is lost;
By treason's tooth bare-gnawn and canker-bit:°
Yet am I noble as the adversary
I come to cope.°

Albany.   Which is that adversary?   125

Edgar. What's he that speaks for Edmund, Earl of
Gloucester?

Edmund. Himself: what say'st thou to him?

Edgar.   Draw thy sword,
That if my speech offend a noble heart,
Thy arm may do thee justice: here is mine.
Behold it is my privilege,   130
The privilege of mine honors,
My oath, and my profession.° I protest,
Maugre° thy strength, place, youth, and eminence,
Despite thy victor sword and fire-new° fortune,
Thy valor and thy heart,° thou art a traitor,   135
False to thy gods, thy brother, and thy father,
Conspirant° 'gainst this high illustrious prince,
And from th' extremest upward° of thy head
To the descent and dust below thy foot,°
A most toad-spotted traitor.° Say thou "No,"   140
This sword, this arm and my best spirits are bent°
To prove upon thy heart, whereto I speak,°
Thou liest.

Edmund.   In wisdom° I should ask thy name,
But since thy outside looks so fair and warlike,

121 **quality** rank   123 **canker-bit** eaten by the caterpillar   125 **cope** encounter   130–32 **it . . . profession** my knighthood entitles me to challenge
you, and to have my challenge accepted   133 **Maugre** despite   134 **fire-
new** fresh from the forge or mint   135 **heart** courage   137 **Conspirant** con-
spiring, a conspirator   138 **extremest upward** the very top   139 **the . . .
foot** your lowest part (sole) and the dust beneath it   140 **toad-spotted traitor**
spotted with treason (and hence venomous, as the toad is allegedly marked
with spots that exude venom)   141 **bent** directed   142 **whereto I speak**
(Edgar speaks from the heart, and speaks to the heart of Edmund)   143 **wisdom** prudence (since he is not obliged to fight with one of lesser rank)

And that thy tongue some say° of breeding
145   breathes,
What safe and nicely° I might well delay°
By rule of knighthood, I disdain and spurn:
Back do I toss these treasons° to thy head;
With the hell-hated° lie o'erwhelm thy heart;
150 Which for they yet glance by and scarcely bruise,
This sword of mine shall give them instant way,
Where they shall rest for ever.° Trumpets, speak!
    Alarums. [They] fight. [Edmund falls.]

Albany. Save° him, save him!

Goneril.   This is practice,° Gloucester:
By th' law of war thou wast not bound to answer
155 An unknown opposite;° thou are not vanquished,
But cozened and beguiled.

Albany.   Shut your mouth, dame,
Or with this paper shall I stop it. Hold, sir;°
Thou° worse than any name, read thine own evil.
No tearing, lady; I perceive you know it.

160 *Goneril.* Say, if I do, the laws are mine, not thine:
Who can arraign me for 't?

Albany.   Most monstrous! O!
Know'st thou this paper?

Goneril.   Ask me not what I know.
                          Exit.

Albany. Go after her; she's desperate; govern° her.

Edmund. What you have charged me with, that have
    I done;
165 And more, much more; the time will bring it out.
'Tis past, and so am I. But what art thou

145 **say** assay (i.e., touch, sign)   146 **safe and nicely** cautiously and punctiliously   146 **delay** i.e., avoid   148 **treasons** accusations of treason
149 **hell-hated** hated like hell   150–52 **Which . . . ever** which accusations
of treason, since as yet they do no harm, even though I have hurled them
back, I now thrust upon you still more forcibly, with my sword, so that they
may remain with you permanently   153 **Save** spare   153 **practice** trickery
155 **opposite** opponent   157 **Hold, sir** (to Edmund: "Just a moment!")
158 **Thou** (probably Goneril)   163 **govern** control

That hast this fortune on° me? If thou 'rt noble,
I do forgive thee.
Edgar.   Let's exchange charity.°
I am no less in blood° than thou art, Edmund;
If more,° the more th' hast wronged me.   *170*
My name is Edgar, and thy father's son.
The gods are just, and of our pleasant° vices
Make instruments to plague us:
The dark and vicious place° where thee he got°
Cost him his eyes.
Edmund.   Th' hast spoken right, 'tis true; *175*
The wheel is come full circle; I am here.°
Albany. Methought thy very gait did prophesy°
A royal nobleness: I must embrace thee:
Let sorrow split my heart, if ever I
Did hate thee or thy father!
Edgar.   Worthy° Prince, I know 't. *180*
Albany. Where have you hid yourself?
How have you known the miseries of your father?
Edgar. By nursing them, my lord. List a brief tale;
And when 'tis told, O, that my heart would burst!
The bloody proclamation to escape°   *185*
That followed me so near—O, our lives' sweetness,
That we the pain of death would hourly die
Rather than die at once!°—taught me to shift
Into a madman's rags, t' assume a semblance
That very dogs disdained: and in this habit°   *190*
Met I my father with his bleeding rings,°
Their precious stones new lost; became his guide,
Led him, begged for him, saved him from despair;

---

167 **fortune on** victory over   168 **charity** forgiveness and love   169 **blood**
lineage   170 **If more** if I am more noble (since legitimate)   172 **of our**
pleasant out of our pleasurable   174 **place** i.e., the adulterous bed   174 **got**
begot   176 **Wheel . . . here** i.e., Fortune's wheel, on which Edmund as-
cended, has now, in its downward turning, deposited him at the bottom,
whence he began   177 **gait did prophesy** carriage did promise   180 **Wor-**
thy honorable   185 **to escape** (my wish) to escape the sentence of death
186–88 **O . . . once** how sweet is life, that we choose to suffer death every
hour rather than make an end at once   190 **habit** attire   191 **rings** sockets

Never—O fault!—revealed myself unto him,
195   Until some half-hour past, when I was armed,
Not sure, though hoping, of this good success,
I asked his blessing, and from first to last
Told him our pilgrimage.° But his flawed° heart—
Alack, too weak the conflict to support—
200   'Twixt two extremes of passion, joy and grief,
Burst smilingly.

Edmund.   This speech of yours hath moved me,
And shall perchance do good: but speak you on;
You look as you had something more to say.

Albany. If there be more, more woeful, hold it in;
205   For I am almost ready to dissolve,°
Hearing of this.

Edgar.   This would have seemed a period°
To such as love not sorrow; but another,
To amplify too much, would make much more,
And top extremity.°
210   Whilst I was big in clamor,° came there in a man,
Who, having seen me in my worst estate,°
Shunned my abhorred° society; but then, finding
Who 'twas that so endured, with his strong arms
He fastened on my neck, and bellowed out
215   As he'd burst heaven; threw him on my father;
Told the most piteous tale of Lear and him
That ever ear received: which in recounting
His grief grew puissant,° and the strings of life
Began to crack: twice then the trumpets sounded,
And there I left him tranced.°

220 *Albany.*   But who was this?

Edgar. Kent, sir, the banished Kent; who in disguise
Followed his enemy° king, and did him service
Improper for a slave.

---

198 **our pilgrimage** of our (purgatorial) journey   198 **flawed** cracked   05 **dissolve** i.e., into tears   206 **period** limit   207–09 **but . . . extremity** just one woe
more, described too fully, would go beyond the extreme limit   210 **big in
clamor** loud in lamentation   211 **estate** condition   212 **abhorred** abhorrent
218 **puissant** overmastering   220 **tranced** insensible   222 **enemy** hostile

Enter a Gentleman, with a bloody knife.

Gentleman. Help, help, O, help!

Edgar. 　　　　　　　　What kind of help?

Albany. 　　　　　　　　　　Speak, man.

Edgar. What means this bloody knife?

Gentleman. 　　　　　　　'Tis hot, it smokes;°　225
　It came even from the heart of—O, she's dead!

Albany. Who dead? Speak, man.

Gentleman. Your lady, sir, your lady: and her
　　sister
　By her is poisoned; she confesses it.

Edmund. I was contracted° to them both: all three　230
　Now marry° in an instant.

Edgar. 　　　　　　　Here comes Kent.

Albany. Produce the bodies, be they alive or dead.

　　　　　　　　　　　　[Exit Gentleman.]

　This judgment of the heavens, that makes us
　　tremble,
　Touches us not with pity.

　　　　　　　　　Enter Kent.

　　　　　　　　　　O, is this he?
　The time will not allow the compliment°　235
　Which very manners° urges.

Kent. 　　　　　　　　I am come
　To bid my king and master aye° good night:
　Is he not here?

Albany. 　　　Great thing of° us forgot!
　Speak, Edmund, where's the King? and where's
　　Cordelia?
　Seest thou this object,° Kent?　240

The bodies of Goneril and Regan are brought in.

Kent. Alack, why thus?

225 **smokes** steams　230 **contracted** betrothed　231 **marry** i.e., unite in
death　235 **compliment** ceremony　236 **very manners** ordinary civility
237 **aye** forever　238 **thing of** matter by　240 **object** sight (the bodies of
Goneril and Regan)

Is Edmund trying to redeem himself?

Edmund.   Yet° Edmund was beloved:
  The one the other poisoned for my sake,
  And after slew herself.

Albany. Even so. Cover their faces.

245 *Edmund.* I pant for life:° some good I mean to do,
  Despite of mine own nature. Quickly send,
  Be brief in it, to th' castle; for my writ°
  Is on the life of Lear and on Cordelia:
  Nay, send in time.

Albany.   Run, run, O, run!

250 *Edgar.* To who, my lord? Who has the office?° Send
  Thy token of reprieve.°

Edmund. Well thought on: take my sword,
  Give it the captain.

Edgar.   Haste thee, for thy life.
                    [*Exit Messenger.*]

Edmund. He hath commission from thy wife and me
255   To hang Cordelia in the prison, and
  To lay the blame upon her own despair,
  That she fordid° herself.

Albany. The gods defend her! Bear him hence awhile.
                [*Edmund is borne off.*]

*Enter Lear, with Cordelia in his arms [Gentle-
    man, and others following].*

Lear. Howl, howl, howl, howl! O, you are men of
  stones:
260   Had I your tongues and eyes, I'd use them so
  That heaven's vault should crack. She's gone for
    ever.
  I know when one is dead and when one lives;
  She's dead as earth. Lend me a looking-glass;
  If that her breath will mist or stain the stone,°
  Why, then she lives.

241 **Yet** in spite of all   245 **pant for life** gasp for breath   247 **writ** command (ordering the execution)   250 **office** commission   251 **token of reprieve** sign that they are reprieved   257 **fordid** destroyed   264 **stone** i.e.,
the surface of the crystal looking glass

Kent.   Is this the promised end?°   265

Edgar. Or image° of that horror?

Albany.   Fall and cease.°

Lear. This feather stirs; she lives. If it be so,
   It is a chance which does redeem° all sorrows
   That ever I have felt.

Kent.   O my good master.

Lear. Prithee, away.

Edgar.   'Tis noble Kent, your friend.   270

Lear. A plague upon you, murderers, traitors all!
   I might have saved her; now she's gone for ever.
   Cordelia, Cordelia, stay a little. Ha,
   What is 't thou say'st? Her voice was ever soft,
   Gentle and low, an excellent thing in woman.   275
   I killed the slave that was a-hanging thee.

Gentleman: 'Tis true, my lords, he did.

Lear.   Did I not, fellow?
   I have seen the day, with my good biting falchion°
   I would have made them skip: I am old now,
   And these same crosses° spoil me.° Who are you?   280
   Mine eyes are not o' th' best: I'll tell you straight.°

Kent. If Fortune brag of two° she loved and hated,
   One of them we behold.

Lear. This is a dull sight.° Are you not Kent?

Kent.   The same,
   Your servant Kent. Where is your servant Caius?°   285

Lear. He's a good fellow, I can tell you that;
   He'll strike, and quickly too: he's dead and rotten.

Kent. No, my good lord; I am the very man.

265 **promised end** Doomsday   266 **image** exact likeness   266 **Fall and cease** i.e., let the heavens fall, and all things finish   268 **redeem** make good   278 **falchion** small curved sword   280 **crosses** troubles   280 **spoil me** i.e., my prowess as a swordsman   281 **tell you straight** recognize you straightway   282 **two** i.e., Lear, and some hypothetical second, who is also a prime example of Fortune's inconstancy ("loved and hated")   284 **dull sight** (1) melancholy spectacle (2) faulty eyesight (Lear's own, clouded by weeping)   285 **Caius** (Kent's name, in disguise)

    Lear. I'll see that straight.°

290 *Kent.* That from your first of difference and decay°
    Have followed your sad steps.

    Lear.   You are welcome hither.

    Kent. <u>Nor no man else:° all's cheerless, dark and
        deadly</u>
        <u>Your eldest daughters have fordone° themselves,
    And desperately° are dead.</u>

    Lear.   Ay, so I think.

295 *Albany.* He knows not what he says, and vain is it
    That we present us to him.

    Edgar.   Very bootless.°

             Enter a Messenger.

    Messenger. Edmund is dead, my lord.

    Albany.   That's but a trifle here.
    You lords and noble friends, know our intent.
    What comfort to this great decay may come°
300 Shall be applied. For us, we° will resign,
    During the life of this old majesty,
    To him our absolute power: [*To Edgar and Kent*]
        you, to your rights;
    With boot,° and such addition° as your honors
    Have more than merited. All friends shall taste
305 The wages of their virtue, and all foes
    The cup of their deservings. O, see, see!

    Lear. And my poor fool° is hanged: no, no, no
        life?
    Why should a dog, a horse, a rat, have life,

---

289 **see that straight** attend to that in a moment   290 **your . . . decay** beginning of your decline in fortune   292 **Nor no man else** no, I am not welcome, nor is anyone else   293 **fordone** destroyed   294 **desperately** in
despair   296 **bootless** fruitless   299 **What . . . come** whatever aid may
present itself to this great ruined man   300 **us, we** (the royal "we")
303 **boot** good measure   303 **addition** additional titles and rights
307 **fool** Cordelia ("fool" being a term of endearment. But it is perfectly
possible to take the word as referring also to the Fool)

And thou no breath at all? Thou'lt come no more,
Never, never, never, never, never.   310
Pray you, undo this button.° Thank you, sir.
Do you see this? Look on her. Look, her lips,
Look there, look there.

                                              He dies.

Edgar.   He faints. My lord, my lord!

Kent. Break, heart; I prithee, break.

Edgar.   Look up, my lord.

Kent. Vex not his ghost:° O, let him pass! He hates
    him   315
    That would upon the rack° of this tough world
    Stretch him out longer.°

Edgar.   He is gone indeed.

Kent. The wonder is he hath endured so long:
    He but usurped° his life.

Albany. Bear them from hence. Our present business   320
    Is general woe. [*To Kent and Edgar*] Friends of
        my soul, you twain,
    Rule in this realm and the gored state sustain.

Kent. I have a journey, sir, shortly to go;
    My master calls me, I must not say no.

Edgar. The weight of this sad time we must obey,°   325
    Speak what we feel, not what we ought to say.
    The oldest hath borne most: we that are young
    Shall never see so much, nor live so long.
                              Exeunt, with a dead march.

                        FINIS

311 **undo this button** i.e., to ease the suffocation Lear feels   315 **Vex ...
ghost** do not trouble his departing spirit   316 **rack** instrument of torture,
stretching the victim's joints to dislocation   317 **longer** (1) in time (2) in bodily
length   319 **usurped** possessed beyond the allotted term   325 **obey** submit to

Textual Note

The earliest extant version of Shakespeare's *King Lear* is the First Quarto of 1608. This premier edition is known as the Pied Bull Quarto, after the sign which hung before the establishment of the printer. The title page reads as follows: "M. William Shak-speare: / HIS / True Chronicle Historie of the life and / death of King Lear and his three / Daughters. / *With the vnfortunate life of* Edgar, *sonne* / and heire to the Earle of Gloster, and his / sullen and assumed humor of / Tom of Bedlam: / *As it was played before the Kings Maiestie at Whitehall vpon* / S. Stephans *night in Christmas Hollidayes.* / By his Maiesties seruants playing vsually at the Gloabe / on the Bancke-side. / LONDON, / Printed for *Nathaniel Butter,* and are to be sold at his shop in *Pauls* / Church-yard at the signe of the Pide Bull neere / S^t. *Austin's* Gate. 1608." Twelve copies of the First Quarto survive. They are, however, in ten different states, because proofreading, and hence correcting, took place as the play was being printed. The instances (167 in all) in which these copies of Q1 differ from one another have been enumerated by contemporary scholarship.[1] Various theories account for the origin of Q1. Perhaps it is a "reported" text, depending on memorial reconstruction by actors who had performed it, or on a shorthand transcription, or on a conventional but poor transcription of Shakespeare's "foul papers" (rough draft). In *Shakespeare's Revision of "King*

---

[1] W. W. Greg, *The Variants in the First Quarto of "King Lear,"* London, 1940 (for 1939).

Lear" (1980), Steven Urkowitz, disputing suggestions of memorial contaminating, concluded that Q was printed directly from the foul papers, not from a transcript of them.

In 1619 appeared the Second Quarto, known as the N. Butter Quarto, and falsely dated in the same year as the first (the title page reads: "Printed for Nathaniel Butter. 1608"). Actually Q2 was printed by William Jaggard as part of an intended collection of plays by or ascribed to Shakespeare, to be published by Jaggard's friend Thomas Pavier. The source of Q2 was apparently a copy of Q1 in which a number of sheets had been corrected.

Four years later *King Lear* was reprinted once more, this time in the first collection of Shakespeare's works, the First Folio of 1623. The source of the Folio text has been much debated. Some propose a corrected copy of Q1, perhaps collated with the theater's promptbook, a shorter, acting version of the play. Comparative study indicates that Q2 with its corrections was also important for the printing of F, and may have been its principal source. Gary Taylor, analyzing the work of the compositors who set the Folio text, suggested this; others suggested that F's compositors used an MS copy, probably derived from the promptbook, plus a version of Q2. Between the Q and F texts, variations, both accidental and substantive, are frequent. Accidental changes, those of orthography and punctuation, mean little for a modernized edition like this one. Substantive changes, those of words, may alter the sense. F lacks 285 lines that appear in Q1, and adds 115 lines not in Q1, also supplying many different readings and different punctuation and lineation.

Here are some examples of the way the texts differ. In Q's version of Act 1, Scene 2, Gloucester thinks his son Edgar cannot be the monster suggested by Edmund's forged letter. This follows:

> *Edmund.* Nor is not, sure.
> *Gloucester.* To his father, that so tenderly and entirely loves him.
>   Heaven and earth!

(103–5)

F cuts these two brief speeches, speeding up the pace but losing aspects of devious, credulous, and paternal behavior. A little earlier (Act 1, Scene 1), Lear enters for the first time, and Q has him expressing his purpose to divide the kingdom, transferring its ruler's obligations to younger hands. F's version of this passage is more circumstantial. Lear's age is emphasized, also his unbecoming self-indulgence. He will "Unburdened crawl toward death." Highlighting a filial relationship, he addresses "Our son of Cornwall" and "our no less loving son of Albany." Still vigorous, hardly the doting old man of some productions, he stresses his "constant will," and is provident in publicizing his daughters' dowries in order "that future strife may be prevented now." All this Q omits. To the present editor it seems reasonable to conflate the lines omitted in one text and added by the other text, a practice followed by all editors until recently, beginning with Alexander Pope in his edition of 1723–25.

The F text is seldom abridged simply to shorten the play. Its cuts are likely to change our sense of things, and this is true also of its amplifications. To many scholars, that looks like evidence of authorial intervention. Some propose two different versions of the play, each with its own integrity. They think the First Quarto of 1608 represents Shakespeare's initial version, satisfactory to him when he wrote it. He didn't remain satisfied, however, and before his death in 1616 revised this version substantially. His revision is preserved in the First Folio. Editors who think this, like the new *Oxford Shakespeare*'s (Stanley Wells and Gary Taylor, 1986), will offer separate texts of the play. The most forceful statement that *Lear* exists in two separate but equal versions is presented in *The Division of the Kingdom: Shakespeare's Two Versions of "King Lear"* (1983), edited by Gary Taylor and Michael Warren. This collection of essays by eleven scholars argues that Q is more or less the play as Shakespeare wrote it in 1605-06, and that F—with its additions and reassignment of some speeches—is based on a promptbook which represents Shakespeare's own reshaping of the play, perhaps around 1610–11. There is, however, at least one great difficulty with this theory: Even if we grant that F represents a revision, how can we be certain that Shakespeare was the reviser? When the Globe burned in 1613, presumably the promptbook was lost, and the company had to construct a new one, probably without Shakespeare's help, since he had retired to Stratford around 1611. The authors of *The Division of the Kingdom* argue that the omissions in F improve the play, but it is hard, for instance, to see F's omission of the mock trial scene in 3.6 as an improvement, even though one writer in the book assures us that this omission "strengthens the dramatic structure."

John Russell Brown, whose theater criticism is fortified by long experience as a director, is useful on the matter of textual priority. Arguing that the later date of F is no guarantee of Shakespeare's approval, he points out that playwrights, "even the most willful and the most gentle," are often bullied into making expedient changes by the theater people who put the play on stage. When the American poet-turned-playwright Archibald MacLeish gave the director Elia Kazan the text of his new drama, *J.B.*, he thought, said Kazan with amusement, that he had written a play. The director, knowing better, went on to stamp it with his own ideas. Sometimes the actor, especially a star actor, takes over the play, forcing the playwright to build up his part. Sir Henry Irving wouldn't have cared for a bit part. References to France and the French king's invasion of England drop from F, perhaps reflecting the censor's disapproval of allusions to state business in the reign of King James (beginning 1603). Other cuts, though they may be editorial, may as plausibly come from the scribe, or the book-keeper seeking to clarify performance, or may represent a compositor's error. And so on.

There seems no reason, accordingly, to deprive readers of anything Shakespeare wrote at any time. The present text of *King Lear* is therefore an amalgamation of Q and F. It relies chiefly on the Folio, but it turns to the Quarto when the Folio is guilty of an obvious misprinting, or when it omits pertinent material found in the Quarto, or when its version seems to the editor so inferior to the Quarto version as to demand precedence for the latter, or when an emendation, even though perhaps unnecessary (like Edwards' "top th' legitimate"), has been canonized by use and wont.

In the preparation of this text, the spelling of Folio and Quarto has been modernized; punctuation and capitalization have been altered, when alteration seemed suitable; character designations have been expanded or clarified (F "Cor." becomes "Cordelia," F "Bastard" and "Steward" become "Edmund" and "Oswald"); contractions not affecting pronunciation have been eliminated (F "banish'd" becomes "banished"); necessary quotation marks (as in the reading of a letter) have been supplied; as have diacritical marks whenever a syllable that is normally unemphasized must be stressed (as in "oppressèd"). These changes are not recorded.

All other departures from the Folio appearing in this text are recorded here in italic type. Unless specifically noted, these departures derive in every case from the First Quarto [Q]. If some other source is levied on, such as the Second Quarto [Q2] or Second Folio [F2] or the conjecture of an editor (for example, [Theobald]), that source is given, within brackets, immediately after the reading. There follows next, in roman type, the Folio reading which has been superseded. If an editor's emendation has been preferred to both Folio and Quarto readings, the emendation, with its provenance, is followed by the Folio and Quarto readings it replaces.

Stage directions are not given lineation. Reference to them in these notes is determined, therefore, by the line of text they follow. If a stage direction occurs at the beginning of a scene, reference is to the line of text it precedes. On occasion, the stage direction in the present text represents a conflation of Folio and Quarto. In that case, both Folio and Quarto readings are set down in the notes. Stage directions and notations of place, printed within brackets, are, unless otherwise noted, substantially from the Globe edition. The list of Dramatis Personae, first given by Rowe, is taken also from the Globe edition.

1.1. *Act 1 Scene 1* Actus Primus. Scena Prima   5 *equalities* qualities   34 s.d.   *Sound . . . Attendants* Sennet. Enter King Lear, Corn-

wall, Albany, Gonerill, Regan, Cordelia, and attendants [F] Sound
a Sennet, Enter one bearing a Coronet, then Lear, then the Dukes of
Albany, and Cornwall, next Gonerill, Regan, Cordelia, with
followers [Q]   70 *speak* [F omits]   98 *loved me. I* loved me
99 *Return* I return   106 *To love my father all* [F omits]   112 *mysteries* [F2] miseries [F] mistress [Q]   157 *as a pawn* as pawn
158 *nor* nere [i.e., "ne'er"]   165 *the* thy   172 *sentencs* sentences
176 *diseases* disasters   190 *Gloucester* Cor[delia]   208 *on* in
216 *best object* object   227 *well* will   235 *Better thou* Better thou
hadst   250 *respects of fortune* respect and Fortunes   268 s.d.
Lear . . . Attendants [Capell] Exit Lear and Burgundy [Q]
283 *shame them derides* with shame derides   291 *hath not been*
hath been   299–300 *ingrafted* ingraffed   306 *let's hit* let us sit

1.2. *Scene 2* Scena Secunda   21 *top th'* [Edwards] to' th' [F] tooth'
[Q]   103–05 *Edmund . . . earth* [F omits]   142 *Fut* [F omits]
144 *Edgar* [F omits]   145 *and pat* [Steevens] Pat [F] and out
[Q]   156–64 *as . . . come* [F omits]   165 *Why, the* The   178 *brother*
[F omits]   185 *Go armed* [F omits]   191 s.d. *Exit Edgar* Exit

1.3. *Scene 3* Scena Tertia   17–21 *Not . . . abused* [F omits]
25–26 *I would . . . speak* [F omits]   27 *Go, prepare* prepare

1.4. *Scene 4* Scena Quarta   1 *well* will   51 *daughter* Daughters   100 *Fool* my Boy   115 *Lady the Brach* [Steevens] the Lady
Brach [F] Ladie oth'e brach [Q]   144–59 *That . . . snatching* [F
omits]   158 *on't* [Q2] [F omits] an't [Q]   158 *ladies* [Q cor-
rected] [F omits] lodes [Q uncorrected]   167 *crown* Crownes
182 *fools* Foole   195 *Methinks* [F omits]   222 *it had* it's
had   225 *Come, Sir* [F omits]   234 *or his* his   237–41 *I . . . father* [F omits]   264 *O . . . come* [F omits]   298 *the cause* more of
it   311 *Yea . . . this* [F omits]   350 *You are* [F2] Your are [F]
Y'are [Q]   350 *attasked for* [Q corrected: "attaskt"] at task for [F]
alapt [Q uncorrected]

1.5. *Scene 5* Scena Quinta   1 s.d. *Enter . . . Fool* [Q2] Enter Lear,
Kent, Gentleman, and Foole   17 *Why . . . boy* What can'st tell Boy

2.1. *Act 2. Scene 1* Actus Secundus. Scena Prima   21 s.d. *Enter
Edgar* [placed by Theobald] [F prints after l. 20]   55 *But*
And   72 *I should* should I   73 *ay* [F omits]   80 *I . . . him*
[F omits]   80 s.d. *Tucket within* [placed by Malone] [F prints af-
ter l. 79]   81 *why* wher   89 *strange news* strangenesse

2.2. *Scene 2* Scena Secunda   23 *clamorous* [Q corrected] clamours
[F] clamarous [Q uncorrected]   44 s.d. *Enter . . . drawn*
Enter Bastard, Cornewall, Regan, Gloster, Servants [F] Enter Ed-
mund with his rapier drawne, Gloster the Duke and Dutchesse
[Q]   77 *too* t'   80 *Renege* Revenge   81 *gale* gall   110 *flick'ring*
[Pope: "flickering"] flicking [F] flitkering [Q]   125 *dread*

dead   132 *respect* respects   141 s.d. *Stocks brought out* [placed by Dyce] [F prints after l. 139] [Q omits]   143–47 *His . . . with* [F omits]   145 *contemnèd'st* [Capell] [F omits] contaned [Q uncorrected] temnest [Q corrected]   153 *For . . . legs* [F omits] 154 *Come . . . away* [F assigns to Cornwall]   154 *my good Lord* my Lord   154 s.d. *Exeunt . . . Kent* Exit [F] [Q omits] 155 *Duke's* Duke   176 s.d. *Sleeps* [F omits]

2.3. *Scene 3* [Steevens] [F, Q omit]   4 *unusual* unusall   15 *mortified bare arms* mortified Armes   18 *sheepcotes* Sheeps-Cotes

2.4.1 s.d. *Scene 4* [Steevens] [F, Q omit]   2 *messenger* Messengers   6 *thy* ahy   9 *man's* man   18–19 *No . . . have* [F omits] 30 *panting* painting   33 *whose* those   61 *the* the the   75 *have* hause   86 s.d. *Enter . . . Gloucester* [F prints after l. 84] 130 *mother's* Mother   167 *her pride* [F omits]   183 s.d. *Enter Oswald* [placed by Dyce] [F and Q print after l. 181]   185 *fickle* fickly   188 s.d. *Enter Goneril* [placed by Johnson] [F and Q print after l. 186]   282 s.d. *Storm and tempest* [F prints after l. 283] [Q omits]   285 s.d. *Exeunt . . . Fool* [Q2] Exeunt [F] Exeunt Lear, Leister, Kent, and Foole [Q]   294 s.d. *Enter Gloucester* [F and Q print after l. 293]

3.1. *Act 3. Scene 1* Actus Tertius. Scena Prima   7–14 *tears . . . all* [F omits]   30–42 *But . . . you* [F omits]

3.2. *Scene 2* Scena Secunda   3 *drowned* drown   71 *That* And   78 *True . . . boy* True boy

3.3. *Scene 3* Scaena Tertia

3.4. *Scene 4* Scena Quarta   7 *skin: so* [Rowe] skinso [F] skin, so [Q]   10 *thy* they   27 s.d. *Exit* [placed by Johnson] [F prints after l. 26] [Q omits]   38 s.d. *Enter Fool* [Duthie] Enter Edgar, and Foole [F, which prints after l. 36] [Q omits]   44 s.d. *Enter Edgar* Enter Edgar, and Foole [F, which prints after l. 36] [Q omits] 46 *blows . . . wind* blow the windes   47 *thy cold bed* thy bed   52 *ford* Sword   57 *Bless* Blisse   58 *Bless* blisse   63 *What, has* Ha's   91 *deeply* deerely   101 *sessa* [Malone] Sesey [F] caese [Q] cease [Q2]   116 s.d. *Enter . . . torch* [F prints after l. 111] Enter Gloster [Q, which prints after l. 116]   117 *foul fiend Flibbertigibbet* foule Flibbertigibbet   118 *till . . . cock* at first Cocke   138 *hath* had hath

3.5. *Scene 5* Scena Quinta   13 *his* this   25 *dearer* deere

3.6. *Scene 6* Scena Sexta   5 s.d. *Exit* [placed by Capell] [F prints after l. 3]   17–55 *The . . . 'scape* [F omits]   22 *Now* [Q2] [F omits] no [Q]   25 *bourn* [Capell] [F omits] broome [Q] 34 *cushions* [F omits] cushings [Q]   47 *she kicked* [Q2] [F omits] kicked [Q]   53 *made on* [Capell] [F omits] made an [Q]   67 *lym*

[Hanmer] Hym [F] him [Q] 68 *tike, or trundle* tight, or
Troundle 72 *Sessa!* [Malone] sese [F] [Q omits] 84 s.d. *Enter
Gloucester* [placed by Capell] [F prints after 1. 80] 97–100 *Op-
pressèd . . . behind* [F omits] 101–14 *When . . . lurk* [F omits]

3.7. *Scene 7* Scena Septima 21 s.d. *Exit Oswald* [Staunton] [F
and Q omit] 23 s.d. *Exeunt . . . Edmund* [Staunton] [F (Exit) and
Q (Exit Gon. and Bast.) print after 1. 22] 28 s.d. *Enter . . . three*
[Q, which prints after "traitor"] Enter Gloucester, and Servants [F,
which prints as here after "control"] 59 *rash* sticke 64 *dearn*
sterne 79 s.d. *Draw and fight* [F omits] 81 s.d. *She . . . him*
Killes him [F] Shee . . . behind [Q] 100–108 *I'll . . . him* [F omits]
100 *Second Servant* [Capell] [F omits] Servant [Q] 101 *Third
Servant* [Capell] [F omits] 2 Servant [Q] 104 *Second Servant*
[Capell] [F omits] 1 Ser. [Q] 105 *roguish* [Q2] [Q omits] 107
Third Servant [Capell] [F omits] 2 Ser. [Q] 108 s.d. *Exeunt severally* [F omits] Exit [Q]

4.1. *Act 4 Scene 1* Actus Quartus. Scena Prima 9 s.d. *led by an
Old Man* [Q, which prints after 1. 12] and an Old man [F, which
places after 1. 9, as here] 41 *Then, prithee, get thee gone* Get thee
away 60–65 *Five . . . master* [F omits] 62–63 *Flibbertigibbet*
[Pope] Stiberdigebit [Q] 63 *mopping and mowing* [Theobald]
Mobing, & Mohing [Q]

4.2. *Scene 2* Scena Secunda 1 s.d. *Enter Goneril and Edmund*
Enter Gonerill, Bastard, and Steward 2 s.d. [after "way"] *Enter
Oswald* [placed by Theobald] [Q prints after "master," 1.2] [F
omits] 25 s.d. *Exit Edmund* [placed by Rowe] Exit [F, which
prints after "death"] [Q omits] 28 s.d. *Exit* [F omits] Exit Stew.
[Q] 31–50 *I . . . deep* [F omits] 32 *its* ith [Q] 45 *benefited* [Q
corrected] beniflicted [Q uncorrected] 47 *these* [Jennens; Heath
conj.] the [Q uncorrected] this [Q corrected] 49 *Humanity* [Q cor-
rected] Humanly [Q uncorrected] 53–59 *that . . . so* [F omits]
56 *noiseless* [Q corrected] noystles [Q uncorrected] 57 *thy state
begins to threat* [Jennens] thy slayer begin threats [Q uncorrected]
thy state begins thereat [Q corrected] thy slaier begins threats [Q2]
58 *Whilst* [Q corrected] Whil's [Q uncorrected] 62–69 *Thou . . .
news* [F omits] 65 *dislocate* [Q3] dislecate [Q2.1,2] 68 *mew* [Q
corrected] now [Q uncorrected] 68 s.d. *Enter a Messenger* [F
prints after 1. 61] Enter a Gentleman [Q, which prints after 1. 69;
and Q2, which prints after 1. 68, as here] 75 *thereat enraged*
threat-enrag'd 79 *justicers* [Q corrected] Iustices [F, Q] 87 s.d.
Exit [F omits]

4.3. *Scene 3* Scena Tertia [for Scene IV] 1 s.d. *Enter . . . Gentleman* [F omits the entire scene] 12 *sir* [Theobald] say 17 *strove*
[Pope] streme 21 *seemed* [Pope: "seem'd"] seeme 30 *believed*

[Q2] *beleeft*   32 *moistened* [Capell] moystened her   56 *Exeunt*
[Pope] Exit

4.4. *Scene 4* [Pope] Scena Tertia [F] [Q omits]   1 s.d. *Cordelia,
Doctor, and Soldiers* Cordelia, Gentlemen, and Souldiours [F]
Cordelia, Doctor and others [Q]   3 *femiter* Fenitar   6 *century*
Centery   18 *distress* desires   28 *right* Rite

4.5. *Scene 5* [Pope] Scena Quarta [F] [Q omits]   39 *meet him* meet

4.6. *Scene 6* [Pope] Scena Quinta [Q omits]   17 *walk* walk'd
34 s.d.   *He kneels* [F omits]   41 s.d.   *He falls* [F omits]
71 *whelked* wealk'd   71 *enridgèd* enraged   83 *coining* crying   97 *had white* had the white   166 *Through* Thorough *small*
great   167 *Plate sin* [Theobald] Place sinnes [Q omits]   199
Ay . . . dust [F omits]   200 *Good sir* [Q2] [F and Q omit]   206 s.d.
Exit . . . follow Exit [F] Exit King running [Q]   208 *one*
a   244 *I'se* [Johnson: "Ise"] ice [F] ile [Q]   247 s.d. *They fight*
[F omits]   255 s.d.   *He dies* [F omits]   274 *and . . . venture*
[Q reads "Venter"] [F omits] [This line, from the First Quarto, is
almost universally omitted from editions of the play]   276 *indistinguished* indinguish'd   289 s.d.   *Drum afar off* [F prints after
l. 287] A drum a farre off [Q, which prints as here]

4.7. *Scene 7* Scena Septima   1 s.d.   *Enter . . . Gentleman*
Enter Cordelia, Kent, and Gentleman [F] Enter Cordelia, Kent,
and Doctor [Q]   24 *doubt not* doubt   24–25 *Very . . . there*
[F omits]   32 *warring* iarring   33–36 *To . . . helm* [F omits]
79–80 *and . . . lost* [F omits]   85 s.d.   *Exeunt . . . Gentleman*
Exeunt   86–98 *Holds . . . fought* [F omits]

5.1. *Act 5 Scene 1* Actus Quintus. Scena Prima   11–13 *That . . .
hers* [F omits]   16 *Fear me not* Feare not   18–19 *I . . . me*
[F omits]   23–28 *Where . . . nobly* [F omits]   33 *I . . . tent*
[F omits]   36 *pray you* pray   39 s.d. *To those going out* [F and Q
omit] *To Edgar* [F and Q omit] *Exeunt* [placed by Cambridge edi-
tion] [Q prints after "word," l. 39] [F omits]   46 *love* loues
50 s.d. *Exit* [placed by Dyce] [F and Q print after l. 49]

5.2. *Scene 2* Scena Secunda

5.3. *Scene 3* Scena Tertia   13 *hear poor rogues* heere (poore
Rogues) [reference in F is to Lear and Cordelia]   26 s.d. *Exeunt . . .
guarded* Exit [F] [Q omits]   39–40 *I . . . do't*   [F omits]   40 s.d.
Exit Captain [F prints after 1.38] [Q omits]   48 *and appointed
guard* [Q corrected, and Q2] [F and Q omit]   55–60 *At . . . place*
[F omits]   56 *We* [Q corrected, and Q2] mee [Q]   58 *sharpness*
[Q corrected, and Q2] sharpes [Q]   84 *attaint* arrest   85 *sister*
Sisters   98 *he is* hes   103 *Edmund . . . ho, a herald* [F
omits]   108 s.d.   *Enter a Herald* [placed by Hanmer] [F prints
after l. 102] [Q omits]   110 *Sound, trumpet* [F omits]   110 s.d.

A trumpet sounds [F prints after 1. 109] [Q omits] trumpet [F2]
Tumpet   116 *Sound* [F omits]   116 s.d.   *First trumpet* [F prints
after 1. 115] [Q omits]   118 s.d.   *Enter ... him* Enter Edgar
armed [F] Enter Edgar at the third sound, a trumpet before
him [Q]   137 *illustrious* illustirous   145 *some   say* (some
say)   152 s.d.   *fight* Fights [F, which prints after 1. 153,
"him"] [Q omits]   162 *Ask ... know* [F gives to Edmund]
162 s.d. *Exit* [placed here by Q: "Exit. Gonorill"] [F prints after 1.
161, "for't"]   206–23 *This ... slave* [F omits]   215 *him* [Theobald]
me [Q] [F omits]   223 s.d.   *Enter ... knife* Enter a Gentleman [F]
Enter one with a bloudie knife [Q]   234 s.d.   *Enter Kent* [placed
by Q2] [F prints after 1. 231, "Kent"] [Q prints after "allow" in 1.
235]   240 s.d.   *The ... in* Gonerill and Regans bodies brought out
[F, which prints after 1. 232]   253 s.d.   *Exit Messenger*
[Theobald] [F and Q omit]   259 *Howl, howl, howl, howl* Howle,
howle, howle *you are* your are   279 *them* him   291 *You are* [Q2]
Your   are   [F]   You'r   [Q]   296 s.d.   *Enter   a   Messenger*
[F, which prints after "him"] Enter Captaine [Q, placed as here]

The Date and Sources of
King Lear

King Lear was probably written between 1603 and 1606. The evidence is as follows. Under the date of November 26, 1607, the printers Nathaniel Butter and John Busby entered the play in the Stationers' Register, thereby asserting their right to print it. That right was exercised in the following year, with the appearance of the First Quarto of 1608. The title page of that quarto (Q1) announces a performance of the play as having taken place before the King on St. Stephen's Night (December 26) in the Christmas holidays. The entry in the Stationers' Register (1607), since it refers to the Court performance as occurring on "Christmas Last," fixes the date of that performance as December 26, 1606. This date is therefore the *terminus ad quem* for the composition of the play. The earliest date, that of 1603, is more difficult to establish. Probably it is fixed by the entry in the Stationers' Register, on March 16, 1603, of Samuel Harsnett's *Declaration of Egregious Popishe Impostures*. Harsnett's work, a treatise on diabolism and an attack on the Jesuits, was written in 1602–03. It is utilized by Shakespeare in his play, chiefly for the names of the demons who lurk about Poor Tom. Assume—and it is reasonable to do so—that Shakespeare did not have access to Harsnett's *Declaration* before the date of publication, and 1603 becomes the *terminus a quo* for the writing of *King Lear*.

Astrological reference furnishes another clue. Gloucester, citing as portentous "These late eclipses in the sun and moon" (1.2.112), is commonly thought to be speaking of a contemporary event. There were in fact eclipses in 1601 and, more pertinently, in September (the moon) and October (the sun) of 1605. It has been suggested, moreover, that a publication of 1606, telling of "The Earth's and Moone's late and horrible obscurations," lies directly behind Gloucester's superstitious mutterings. The pamphlet in question, translated from the High Dutch and edited by the almanac writer Edward Gresham, is entitled *Strange fearful & true news which happened at Carlstadt, in the Kingdome of Croatia.* Its preface is dated February 11, 1606.

Finally, there is the re-emergence, in the period just before the first recorded performance of Shakespeare's play, of the older dramatic version of his story, *The True Chronicle History of King Leir.* Though this play was probably written about 1590, and was on the boards in 1594, it was published and perhaps acted again in 1605: on May 8, 1605, it is entered in the Stationers' Register. Presumably Shakespeare used the edition appearing in that year, in writing his own play.

The publication, then, of the old chronicle history in 1605, the notable eclipses occurring in the fall of the same year, and the appearance of Gresham's pamphlet early in 1606 seem to point to the winter of 1605–06 as the period in which Shakespeare wrote *King Lear.*

The ultimate source of the play is an ancient folk tale existing in many versions. It first appears as literature in the twelfth-century *Historia Regum Britanniae* (ii, 11–15), by Geoffrey of Monmouth. Throughout the Middle Ages and on into the Renaissance, the Lear story retained its popularity, appearing in some fifty different accounts. Shakespeare was familiar with it from the retelling in what is perhaps his most important source book, the second edition (1587) of *The Chronicles of England, Scotlande, and Irelande* by Raphael Holinshed, first compiled in 1577. From Edmund Spenser, in *The Faerie Queene* (1590), Shakespeare derived the name of Cordelia in its present form, and also the detail of her death by hanging (II.x.27–32). Other suggestions were furnished by John Higgins, in *A Mirror for Magistrates* (1574), that immensely popular collection of stories of the falls of princes; and of course, by *The True Chronicle History of King Leir and his three daughters*. John Marston, in *The Malcontent* (1604), dramatizes a feigned suicide (4.3) that seems to parallel Gloucester's, at the Cliffs of Dover (4.6). The author of *The London Prodigal* (1605), a play once attributed to Shakespeare and performed by his company, anticipates the rustic dialogue affected by Edgar in his combat with Oswald (4.6). As previously noted, Harsnett and, possibly, Gresham were also of use to Shakespeare. So, in less tangible ways, was his great French contemporary, Montaigne, whose *Essais* were translated into English by John Florio in 1603. Numerous words and passages in Florio's translation (which Shakespeare may have read in manuscript) are echoed in *King Lear*. More impressive, however, is the impact on Shakespeare of Montaigne's skeptical thought, as expressed particularly in the *Apology for Raymond Sebonde*.

None of these sources of *Lear* includes the analogous story of Gloucester and his two sons. That story Shakespeare adapted from Sir Philip Sidney's account of the unhappy King of Paphlagonia, in his famous romantic narrative *Arcadia* (ii, 10), written early in the 1580s but not published until 1590. The tying of the subplot to the old and sufficiently horrid tale of King Lear and his daughters has, of course, the effect of engrossing the horror, until the audience is almost persuaded that ferocious cruelty is not so much an aberration as the norm. Certainly, if Lear is childed as Edgar is fathered it is no longer possible to see as merely sensational or idiosyncratic the evil that Shakespeare anatomizes in the play. Earlier writers, handling one or the other story, allow of that view. Shakespeare, in fusing the two stories, is at pains to controvert it. What is more, he darkens consistently, in manipulating his sources, whatever dark suggestion is latent in them. In the old *Leir*, in Holinshed, in Spenser, in the *Mirror for Magistrates*, the travails of the King are intermitted at last. Vice is punished and virtue rewarded: Cordelia triumphs over her wicked sisters; her father, restored to the throne, dies at the apogee, and in peace. It is true that, in some sources, Cordelia ends a suicide. But that is an irrelevant epilogue: the chief business of the tale is happily resolved.

It is left to Shakespeare to cancel that happy resolution. He is the first to educe tragedy from what is essentially a melodramatic romance. The madness of Lear is altogether his own contribution. So is the pathetic figure of the Fool. So is the murder of Cordelia, that cruelest stroke of all, which is made to fall just as the good are preparing to taste the wages of their virtue. Some sense of Shakespeare's lack of ruth, of his invention, and not least, of his tact may be gathered from a perusal of the source material on which he worked.

RAPHAEL HOLINSHED

Selections from The Chronicles of England, Scotland, and Ireland

Leir the son of Baldud was admitted ruler over the Britains, in the year of the world 3105, at what time Joas reigned in Juda. This Leir was a prince of right noble demeanor, governing his land and subjects in great wealth. He made the town of Caerleir now called Leicester, which standeth upon the river of Sore. It is written that he had by his wife three daughters without other issue, whose names were Gonorilla, Regan, and Cordeilla, which daughters he greatly loved, but specially Cordeilla the youngest far above the two elder. When this Leir therefore was come to great years, & began to wax unwieldy through age, he thought to understand the affections of his daughters towards him, and prefer her whom he best loved, to the succession over the kingdom. Whereupon he first asked Gonorilla the eldest, how well she loved him: who calling her gods to record, protested that she loved him more than her own life, which by right and reason should be most dear unto her. With which answer the father, being well pleased, turned to the second, and demanded of her how well she loved him: who answered (confirming her sayings with great oaths) that she loved him more than tongue could express, and far above all other creatures of the world.

Then called he his youngest daughter Cordeilla before him, and asked of her what account she made of him, unto whom she made this answer as followeth: "Knowing the great love and fatherly zeal that you have always borne towards me (for the which I may not answer you otherwise than I think, and as my conscience leadeth me) I protest unto you, that I have loved you ever, and will continually (while I live) love you as my natural father. And if you would more understand of the love that I bear you, ascertain yourself, that so much as you have, so much you are worth, and so much I love you, and no more." The father being nothing content with this answer, married his two eldest daughters, the one unto Henninus, the duke of Cornwall, and the other unto Maglanus, the duke of Albania, betwixt whom he willed and ordained that his land should be divided after his death, and the one half thereof immediately should be assigned to them in hand: but for the third daughter Cordeilla he reserved nothing.

Nevertheless it fortuned that one of the princes of Gallia (which now is called France), whose name was Aganippus, hearing of the beauty, womanhood, and good conditions of the said Cordeilla, desired to have her in marriage, and sent over to her father, requiring that he might have her to wife; to whom answer was made, that he might have his daughter, but as for any dower he could have none, for all was promised and assured to her other sisters already. Aganippus notwithstanding this answer of denial to receive anything by way of dower with Cordeilla, took her to wife, only moved thereto (I say) for respect of her person and amiable virtues. This Aganippus was one of the twelve kings that ruled Gallia in those days, as in British history it is recorded. But to proceed.

After that Leir was fallen into age, the two dukes that had married his two eldest daughters, thinking it long ere the government of the land did come to their hands, arose against him in armor, and reft from him the governance of the land, upon conditions to be continued for term of life: by the which he was put to his portion, that is, to live after a rate assigned to him for the maintenance of his estate, which in process of time was diminished as well by Maglanus as by Henninus. But the greatest grief that Leir took was to see the unkindness of his daughters, which seemed to think that all was too much which their father had, the same being never so little: in so much that going from the one to the other, he was brought to that misery, that scarcely they would allow him one servant to wait upon him.

In the end, such was the unkindness, or (as I may say) the unnaturalness which he found in his two daughters, notwithstanding their fair and pleasant words uttered in time past, that being constrained of necessity, he fled the land, & sailed into Gallia, there to seek some comfort of his youngest daughter Cordeilla, whom beforetime he hated. The lady Cordeilla hearing that he was arrived in poor estate, she first sent to him privily a certain sum of money to apparel himself withal, and to retain a certain number of servants that might attend upon him in honorable wise, as appertained to the estate which he had borne: and then so accompanied, she appointed him to come to the court, which he did, and was so joyfully, honorably, and lovingly received, both by his son-in-law Aganippus, and also by his daughter Cordeilla, that his heart was greatly comforted: for he was no less honored, than if he had been king of the whole country himself.

Now when he had informed his son-in-law and his daughter in what sort he had been used by his other daughters, Aganippus caused a mighty army to be put in a readiness, and likewise a great navy of ships to be rigged, to pass over into Britain with Leir his father-in-law, to see him again restored to his kingdom. It was accorded, that Cordeilla should also go with him to take possession of the land, the which he promised to leave unto her, as the rightful inheritor after his decease, notwithstanding any former grant made to her sisters or to their husbands in any manner of wise.

Hereupon, when this army and navy of ships were ready, Leir and his daughter Cordeilla with her husband took the sea, and arriving in Britain, fought with their enemies, and discomfited them in battle, in the which Maglanus and Henninus were slain; and then was Leir restored to his kingdom, which he ruled after this by the space of two years, and then died, forty years after he first began to reign.

SIR PHILIP SIDNEY

From Arcadia

The pitiful state, and story of the Paphlagonian unkind King, and his kind son, first related by the son, then by the blind father.

It was in the kingdom of Galacia, the season being (as in the depth of winter) very cold, and as then suddenly grown to so extreme and foul a storm, that never any winter (I think) brought forth a fouler child: so that the Princes were even compelled by the hail, that the pride of the wind blew into their faces, to seek some shrouding place within a certain hollow rock offering it unto them, they made it their shield against the tempest's fury. And so staying there, till the violence thereof was passed, they heard the speech of a couple, who not perceiving them (being hid within that rude canopy) held a strange and pitiful disputation which made them step out; yet in such sort, as they might see unseen. There they perceived an aged man, and a young, scarcely come to the age of a man, both poorly arrayed, extremely weatherbeaten; the old man blind, the young man leading him: and yet through all those miseries, in both these seemed to appear a kind of nobleness, not suitable to that affliction. But the first words they heard were these of the old man. Well Leonatus (said he) since I cannot persuade thee to lead me to that which should end my grief, &

thy trouble, let me now entreat thee to leave me: fear not, my misery cannot be greater than it is, & nothing doth become me but misery; fear not the danger of my blind steps. I cannot fall worse than I am. And do not, I pray thee, do not obstinately continue to infect thee with my wretchedness. But fly, fly from this region, only worthy of me. Dear father (answered he) do not take away from me the only remnant of my happiness: while I have power to do you service, I am not wholly miserable. Ah my son (said he, and with that he groaned, as if sorrow strove to break his heart), how evil fits it me to have such a son, and how much doth thy kindness upbraid my wickedness? These doleful speeches, and some others to like purpose (well showing they had not been borne to the fortune they were in), moved the Princes to go out unto them, and ask the younger what they were? Sirs (answered he, with a good grace, and made the more agreeable by a certain noble kind of piteousness) I see well you are strangers, that know not our misery so well here known, that no man dare know, but that we must be miserable. Indeed our state is such, as though nothing is so needful unto us as pity, yet nothing is more dangerous unto us, than to make ourselves so known as may stir pity. But your presence promiseth, that cruelty shall not overrun hate. And if it did, in truth our state is sunk below the degree of fear.

This old man (whom I lead) was lately rightful Prince of this country of Paphlagonia, by the hard-hearted ungratefulness of a son of his, deprived, not only of his kingdom (whereof no foreign forces were ever able to spoil him) but of his sight, the riches which Nature grants to the poorest creatures. Whereby, & by other his unnatural dealings, he hath been driven to such grief, as even now he would have had me to have led him to the top of this rock, thence to cast himself headlong to death: and so would have made me (who received my life of him) to be the worker of his destruction. But noble Gentlemen (said he) if either of you have a father, and feel what dutiful affection is engraffed in a son's heart, let me entreat you to convey this afflicted Prince to some place of rest & security. Amongst your worthy acts it shall be none of the least, that a King, of such might and fame, and so unjustly oppressed, is in any sort by you relieved.

But before they could make him answer, his father began to speak, Ah my son (said he) how evil an historian are you, that leave out the chief knot of all the discourse? my wickedness, my wickedness. And if thou doest it to spare my ears, (the only sense now left me proper for knowledge) assure thy self thou dost mistake me. And I take witness of that sun which you see (with that he cast up his blind eyes, as if he would hunt for light), and wish myself in worse case than I do wish myself, which is as evil as may be, if I speak untruly; that nothing is so welcome to my thoughts, as the publishing of my shame. Therefore know you Gentlemen (to whom from my heart I wish that it may not prove ominous foretoken of misfortune to have met with such a miser as I am) that whatsoever my son (O God, that truth binds me to reproach him with the name of my son) hath said, is true. But besides those truths this also is true, that having had in lawful marriage, of a mother fit to bear royal children, this son (such one as partly you see, and better shall know by my short declaration) and so enjoyed the expectations in the world of him, till he was grown to justify their expectations (so as I needed envy no father for the chief comfort of mortality, to leave another oneself after me) I was carried by a bastard son of mine (if at least I be bound to believe the words of that base woman my concubine, his mother) first to mislike, then to hate, lastly to destroy, to do my best to destroy, this son (I think you think) undeserving destruction. What ways he used to bring me to it, if I should tell you, I should tediously trouble you with as much poisonous hypocrisy, desperate fraud, smooth malice, hidden ambition, & smiling envy, as in any living person could be harbored. But I list it not, no remembrance, (no, of naughtiness) delights me, but mine own; & me thinks, the accusing his trains might in some manner excuse my fault, which certainly I loathe to do. But the conclusion is, that I gave order to some servants of mine, whom I thought as apt for such charities as myself, to lead him out into a forest, & there to kill him.

But those thieves (better natured to my son than myself)

spared his life, letting him go, to learn to live poorly: which he did, giving himself to be a private soldier, in a country hereby. But as he was ready to be greatly advanced for some noble pieces of service which he did, he heard news of me: who (drunk in my affection to that unlawful and un-natural son of mine) suffered myself so to be governed by him, that all favors and punishments passed by him, all of-fices, and places of importance, distributed to his favorites; so that ere I was aware, I had left myself nothing but the name of a King: which he shortly weary of too, with many indignities (if anything may be called an indignity, which was laid upon me) threw me out of my seat, and put out my eyes; and then (proud in his tyranny) let me go, neither imprisoning, nor killing me: but rather delighting to make me feel my misery; misery indeed, if ever there were any: full of wretchedness, fuller of disgrace, and fullest of guiltiness. And as he came to the crown by so unjust means, as unjustly he kept it, by force of stranger soldiers in citadels, the nests of tyranny, & murderers of liberty; disarming all his own countrymen, that no man durst show himself a well-willer of mine: to say the truth (I think) few of them being so (considering my cruel folly to my good son, and foolish kindness to my unkind bastard): but if there were any who fell to pity of so great a fall, and had yet any sparks of unstained duty left in them towards me, yet durst they not show it, scarcely with giving me alms at their doors; which yet was the only sustenance of my dis-tressed life, nobody daring to show so much charity, as to lend me a hand to guide my dark steps: Till this son of mine (God knows, worthy of a more virtuous, and more fortunate father) forgetting my abominable wrongs, not recking danger, & neglecting the present good way he was in doing himself good, came hither to do this kind office you see him perform towards me, to my unspeakable grief; not only because his kindness is a glass even to my blind eyes, of my naughtiness, but that above all griefs, it grieves me he should desperately adventure the loss of his soul-deserving life for mine, that yet owe more to fortune for my deserts, as if he would carry mud in a chest of crystal. For well I know, he that now reigneth, how much soever (and with good reason) he despiseth me, of all men despised; yet he will not let slip any advantage to make away him, whose just title (ennobled by courage and goodness) may one day shake the seat of a never secure tyranny. And for this cause I craved of him to lead me to the top of this rock, indeed I must confess, with meaning to free him from so serpentine a companion as I am. But he finding what I purposed only therein since he was born, showed himself disobedient unto me. And now Gentlemen, you have the true story, which I pray you publish to the world, that my mischievous proceedings may be the glory of his filial piety, the only reward now left for so great a merit. And if it may be, let me obtain that of you, which my son denies me: for never was there more pity in saving any, than in ending me; both because therein my agonies shall end, and so shall you preserve this excellent young man, who else willfully follows his own ruin.

The matter in itself lamentable, lamentably expressed by the old Prince (which needed not take to himself the gestures of pity, since his face could not put off the marks thereof) greatly moved the two Princes to compassion, which could not stay in such hearts as theirs without seeking remedy. But by and by the occasion was presented: for Plexirtus (so was the bastard called) came thither with forty horse, only of purpose to murder this brother; of whose coming he had soon advertisement, and thought no eyes of sufficient credit in such a matter, but his own; and therefore came himself to be actor, and spectator. And as soon as he came, not regarding the weak (as he thought) guard of but two men, commanded some of his followers to set their hands to his, in the killing of Leonatus. But the young Prince (though not otherwise armed but with a sword) how falsely soever he was dealt with by others, would not betray himself: but bravely drawing it out, made the death of the first that assaulted him, warn his fellows to come more warily after him. But then Pyrocles and Musidorus were quickly become parties (so just a defense deserving as much as old friendship) and so did behave them among that company (more injurious, than valiant) that many of them lost their lives for their wicked master.

Yet perhaps had the number of them at last prevailed, if the King of Pontus (lately by them made so) had not come unlooked for to their succor. Who (having had a dream which had fixed his imagination vehemently upon some great danger, presently to follow those two Princes whom he most dearly loved) was come in all haste, following as well as he could their track with a hundred horses in that country, which he thought (considering who then reigned) a fit place enough to make the stage of any tragedy.

But then the match had been so ill made for Plexirtus, that his ill-led life, & worse-gotten honor should have tumbled together to destruction; had there not come in Tydeus & Telenor, with forty or fifty in their suit, to the defense of Plexirtus. These two were brothers, of the noblest house of that country, brought up from their infancy with Plexirtus: men of such prowess, as not to know fear in themselves, and yet to teach it others that should deal with them: for they had often made their lives triumph over most terrible dangers; never dismayed and ever fortunate; and truly no more settled in their valor, than disposed to goodness and justice, if either they had lighted on a better friend, or could have learned to make friendship a child, and not the father of virtue. But bringing up (rather than choice) having first knit their minds unto him, (indeed crafty enough, either to hide his faults, or never to show them, but when they might pay home) they willingly held out the course, rather to satisfy him, than all the world; and rather to be good friends, than good men: so as though they did not like the evil he did, yet they liked him that did the evil; and though not councilors of the offense, yet protectors of the offender. Now they having heard of this sudden going out, with so small a company, in a country full of evil-wishing minds toward him (though they knew not the cause) followed him; till they found him in such case as they were to venture their lives, or else he to lose his: which they did with such force of mind and body, that truly I may justly say, Pyrocles & Musidorus had never till then found any, that could make them so well repeat their hardest lesson in the

feats of arms. And briefly so they did, that if they overcame
not; yet were they not overcome, but carried away that ungrateful master of theirs to a place of security; howsoever
the Princes labored to the contrary. But this matter being
thus far begun, it became not the constancy of the Princes
so to leave it; but in all haste making forces both in Pontus
and Phrygia, they had in few days, left him but only that
one strong place where he was. For fear having been the
only knot that had fastened his people unto him, that once
untied by a greater force, they all scattered from him; like
so many birds, whose cage had been broken.

In which season the blind King (having in the chief city
of his realm, set the crown upon his son Leonatus' head)
with many tears (both of joy and sorrow) setting forth to
the whole people, his own fault & his son's virtue, after he
had kissed him, and forced his son to accept honor of him
(as of his new-become subject) even in a moment died, as
it should seem: his heart broken with unkindness & affliction, stretched so far beyond his limits with this excess of
comfort, as it was able no longer to keep safe his royal
spirits. But the new King (having no less lovingly performed all duties to him dead, than alive) pursued on the
siege of his unnatural brother, as much for the revenge of
his father, as for the establishing of his own quiet. In which
siege truly I cannot but acknowledge the prowess of those
two brothers, than whom the Princes never found in all
their travel two men of greater ability to perform, nor of
abler skill for conduct.

But Plexirtus finding, that if nothing else, famine would
at last bring him to destruction, thought better by humble-
ness to creep, where by pride he could not march. For certainly so had nature formed him, & the exercise of craft
conformed him to all turnings of sleights, that though no
man had less goodness in his soul than he, no man could
better find the places whence arguments might grow of
goodness to another: though no man felt less pity, no man
could tell better how to stir pity: no man more impudent to
deny, where proofs were not manifest; no man more ready
to confess with a repenting manner of aggravating his own
evil, where denial would but make the fault fouler. Now he

took this way, that having gotten a passport for one (that pretended he would put Plexirtus alive into his hands) to speak with the King his brother, he himself (though much against the minds of the valiant brothers, who rather wished to die in brave defense) with a rope about his neck, barefooted, came to offer himself to the discretion of Leonatus. Where what submission he used, how cunningly in making greater the fault he made the faultiness the less, how artificially he could set out the torments of his own conscience, with the burdensome cumber he had found of his ambitious desires, how finely seeming to desire nothing but death, as ashamed to live, he begged life, in the refusing it, I am not cunning enough to be able to express: but so fell out of it, that though at first sight Leonatus saw him with no other eye, than as the murderer of his father; & anger already began to paint revenge in many colors, ere long he had not only gotten pity, but pardon, and if not an excuse of the fault past, yet an opinion of future amendment: while the poor villains (chief ministers of his wickedness, now betrayed by the author thereof) were delivered to many cruel sorts of death; he so handling it, that it rather seemed, he had rather come into the defense of an unremediable mischief already committed, than that they had done it at first by his consent.

From The True Chronicle History of King Leir

Scene XXIV

Enter the Gallian King and Queen, and Mumford, with a basket, disguised like country folk.

King. This tedious journey all on foot, sweet Love,
    Cannot be pleasing to your tender joints,
    Which ne'er were used to these toilsome walks.

Cordella. I never in my life took more delight
    In any journey, than I do in this:
    It did me good, when as we hapt to light
    Amongst the merry crew of country folk,
    To see what industry and pains they took,
    To win them commendations 'mongst their friends.
    Lord, how they labor to bestir themselves,
    And in their quirks to go beyond the moon,
    And so take on them with such antic fits,
    That one would think they were beside their wits!
    Come away, Roger, with your basket.

Mumford. Soft, Dame, here comes a couple of old
        youths,
    I must needs make myself fat with jesting at them.

Cordella. Nay, prithy do not, they do seem to be
    Men much o'ergone with grief and misery.
    Let's stand aside, and harken what they say.

    [*Enter Leir and Perillus very faintly.*]

Leir. Ah, my Perillus, now I see we both
    Shall end our days in this unfruitful soil.
    Oh, I do faint for want of sustenance:
    And thou, I know, in little better case.
    No gentle tree affords one taste of fruit,
    To comfort us, until we meet with men:
    No lucky path conducts our luckless steps
    Unto a place where any comfort dwells.
    Sweet rest betide unto our happy souls;
    For here I see our bodies must have end.

Perillus. Ah, my dear Lord, how doth my heart
    lament,
  To see you brought to this extremity!
  O, if you love me, as you do profess,
  Or ever thought well of me in my life,
        [*He strips up his arm.*]
  Feed on this flesh, whose veins are not so dry
  But there is virtue left to comfort you.
  O, feed on this, if this will do you good,
  I'll smile for joy, to see you suck my blood.

Leir. I am no Cannibal, that I should delight
  To slake my hungry jaws with human flesh:
  I am no devil, or ten times worse than so,
  To suck the blood of such a peerless friend.
  O, do not think that I respect my life
  So dearly, as I do thy loyal love.
  Ah, Britain, I shall never see thee more,
  That hast unkindly banishèd thy King;
  And yet thou dost not make me to complain,
  But they which were more near to me than thou.

Cordella. What do I hear? this lamentable voice,
  Me thinks, ere now I oftentimes have heard.

Leir. Ah, Gonorill, was half my kingdom's gift
  The cause that thou didst seek to have my life?
  Ah, cruel Ragan, did I give thee all,
  And all could not suffice without my blood?
  Ah, poor Cordella, did I give thee nought,
  Nor never shall be able for to give?
  O, let me warn all ages that ensueth,
  How they trust flattery, and reject the truth.
  Well, unkind girls, I here forgive you both,
  Yet the just heavens will hardly do the like;
  And only crave forgiveness at the end
  Of good Cordella, and of thee, my friend;
  Of God, whose maiesty I have offended,
  By my transgression many thousand ways:
  Of her, dear heart, whom I for no occasion
  Turned out of all, through flatterers' persuasion:
  Of thee, kind friend, who but for me, I know,

Hadst never come unto this place of woe.

Cordella. Alack, that ever I should live to see
My noble father in this misery.

King. Sweet Love, reveal not what thou art as yet,
Until we know the ground of all this ill.

Cordella. O, but some meat, some meat: do you not see,
How near they are to death for want of food?

Perillus. Lord, which didst help thy servants at their need.
Or now or never send us help with speed.
Oh comfort, comfort! yonder is a banquet,
And men and women, my Lord: be of good cheer;
For I see comfort coming very near.
O my Lord, a banquet, and men and women!

Leir. O, let kind pity mollify their hearts,
That they may help us in our great extremes.

Perillus. God save you, friends; & if this blessèd banquet
Affordeth any food or sustenance,
Even for his sake that saved us all from death,
Vouchsafe to save us from the grip of famine.

[*She bringeth him to the table.*]

Cordella. Here father, sit and eat, here sit and drink:
And would it were far better for your sakes.

    Perillus takes Leir by the hand to the table.

Perillus. I'll give you thanks anon: my friend doth faint,
And needeth present comfort.

[*Leir drinks.*]

Mumford. I warrant, he ne'er stays to say grace:
O, there's no sauce to a good stomach.

Perillus. The blessed God of heaven hath thought upon us.

Leir. The thanks be his, and these kind courteous folk,
By whose humanity we are preserved.

They eat hungrily, Leir drinks.

Cordella. And may that draught be unto him, as was
    That which old Eson drank, which did renew
    His withered age, and made him young again.
    And may that meat be unto him, as was
    That which Elias ate, in strength whereof
    He walkèd forty days, and never fainted.
    Shall I conceal me longer from my father?
    Or shall I manifest myself to him?

King. Forbear a while, until his strength return,
    Lest being overjoyed with seeing thee,
    His poor weak senses should forsake their office,
    And so our cause of joy be turned to sorrow.

Perillus. What cheer, my Lord? how do you feel
    yourself?

Leir. Me thinks, I never ate such savory meat:
    It is as pleasant as the blessed manna,
    That rained from heaven amongst the Israelites:
    It hath recalled my spirits home again,
    And made me fresh, as erst I was before.
    But how shall we congratulate their kindness?

Perillus. In faith, I know not how sufficiently;
    But the best mean that I can think on, is this:
    I'll offer them my doublet in requital;
    For we have nothing else to spare.

Leir. Nay, stay, Perillus, for they shall have mine.

Perillus. Pardon, my Lord, I swear they shall have
    mine.

    Perillus proffers his doublet: they will not take it.

Leir. Ah, who would think such kindness should
    remain
    Among such strange and unacquainted men:
    And that such hate should harbor in the breast
    Of those, which have occasion to be best?

Cordella. Ah, good old father, tell to me thy grief,
    I'll sorrow with thee, if not add relief.

Leir. Ah, good young daughter, I may call thee so;
    For thou art like a daughter I did owe.

Cordella. Do you not owe her still? what, is she dead?

Leir. No, God forbid: but all my interest's gone,
    By showing myself too much unnatural:
    So have I lost the title of a father,
    And may be called a stranger to her rather.

Cordella. Your title's good still; for 'tis always known,
    A man may do as him list with his own.
    But have you but one daughter then in all?

Leir. Yes, I have more by two, than would I had.

Cordella. O, say not so, but rather see the end:
    They that are bad, may have the grace to mend:
    But how have they offended you so much?

Leir. If from the first I should relate the cause,
    'Twould make a heart of adamant to weep;
    And thou, poor soule, kindhearted as thou art,
    Dost weep already, ere I do begin.

Cordella. For God's love tell it, and when you have
        done,
    I'll tell the reason why I weep so soon.

Leir. Then know this first, I am a Briton born,
    And had three daughters by one loving wife;
    And though I say it, of beauty they were sped;
    Especially the youngest of the three,
    For her perfections hardly matched could be:
    On these I doted with a jealous love,
    And thought to try which of them loved me best,
    By asking them, which would do most for me?
    The first and second flattered me with words,
    And vowed they loved me better than their lives:
    The youngest said, she loved me as a child
    Might do: her answer I esteemed most vile,
    And presently in an outrageous mood,
    I turned her from me to go sink or swim:
    And all I had, even to the very clothes,
    I gave in dowry with the other two:
    And she that best deserved the greatest share,
    I gave her nothing, but disgrace and care.
    Now mark the sequel: When I had done thus,

I sojourned in my eldest daughter's house,
Where for a time I was entreated well,
And lived in state sufficing my content:
But every day her kindness did grow cold,
Which I with patience put up well enough,
And seemed not to see the things I saw:
But at the last she grew so far incensed
With moody fury, and with causeless hate,
That in most vile and contumelious terms,
She bade me pack, and harbor somewhere else.
Then was I fain for refuge to repair
Unto my other daughter for relief,
Who gave me pleasing and most courteous words;
But in her actions showed herself so sore,
As never any daughter did before:
She prayed me in a morning out betime,
To go to a thicket two miles from the court,
Pointing that there she would come talk with me:
There she had set a shag-haired murdering wretch,
To massacre my honest friend and me.
Then judge yourself, although my tale be brief,
If ever man had greater cause of grief.

King. Nor never like impiety was done,
Since the creation of the world begun.

Leir. And now I am constrained to seek relief
Of her, to whom I have been so unkind;
Whose censure, if it do award me death,
I must confess she pays me but my due:
But if she show a loving daughter's part,
It comes of God and her, not my desert.

Cordella. No doubt she will, I dare be sworn she will.

Leir. How know you that, not knowing what she is?

Cordella. Myself a father have a great way hence,
Used me as ill as ever you did her;
Yet, that his reverend age I once might see,
I'd creep along, to meet him on my knee.

Leir. O, no men's children are unkind but mine.

Cordella. Condemn not all, because of other's crime:

But look, dear father, look, behold and see
Thy loving daughter speaketh unto thee.

[*She kneels.*]

Leir. O, stand thou up, it is my part to kneel,
And ask forgiveness for my former faults.

[*He kneels.*]

Cordella. O, if you wish I should enjoy my breath,
Dear father rise, or I receive my death.

[*He riseth.*]

Leir. Then I will rise, to satisfy your mind,
But kneel again, till pardon be resigned.

[*He kneels.*]

Cordella. I pardon you: the word beseems not me:
But I do say so, for to ease your knee.
You gave me life, you were the cause that I
Am what I am, who else had never been.

Leir. But you gave life to me and to my friend,
Whose days had else, had an untimely end.

Cordella. You brought me up, when as I was but
young,
And far unable for to help myself.

Leir. I cast thee forth, when as thou wast but young,
And far unable for to help thyself.

Cordella. God, world and nature say I do you wrong,
That can endure to see you kneel so long.

King. Let me break off this loving controversy,
Which doth rejoice my very soul to see.
Good father, rise, she is your loving daughter,

[*He riseth.*]

And honors you with as respective duty.
As if you were the monarch of the world.

Cordella. But I will never rise from off my knee,
Until I have your blessing, and your pardon
Of all my faults committed any way,
From my first birth unto this present day.

Leir. The blessing, which the God of Abraham gave

Unto the tribe of Juda, light on thee,
And multiply thy days, that thou mayst see
Thy children's children prosper after thee.
Thy faults, which are just none that I do know,
God pardon on high, and I forgive below.

[*She riseth.*]

Cordella. Now is my heart at quiet, and doth leap
Within my breast, for joy of this good hap:
And now (dear father) welcome to our court,
And welcome (kind Perillus) unto me,
Mirror of virtue and true honesty.

Leir. O, he hath been the kindest friend to me,
That ever man had in adversity.

Perillus. My tongue doth fail, to say what heart
doth think,
I am so ravished with exceeding joy.

King. All you have spoke: now let me speak my mind,
And in few words much matter here conclude:

[*He kneels.*]

If ere my heart do harbor any joy,
Or true content repose within my breast,
Till I have rooted out this viperous sect,
And repossessed my father of his crown,
Let me be counted for the perjuredest man,
That ever spoke word since the world began.

[*Rise.*]

Mumford. Let me pray too, that never prayed before;

[*Mumford kneels.*]

If ere I resalute the British earth,
(As [ere't be long] I do presume I shall)
And do return from thence without my wench,
Let me gelded from my recompense.

[*Rise.*]

King. Come, let's to arms for to redress this wrong:
Till I am there, me thinks, the time seems long.

[*Exeunt.*]

Commentaries

SAMUEL JOHNSON

From Preface to Shakespeare *and "King Lear"*

PREFACE TO SHAKESPEARE

Nothing can please many, and please long, but just representations of general nature. Particular manners can be known to few, and therefore few only can judge how nearly they are copied. The irregular combinations of fanciful invention may delight awhile, by that novelty of which the common satiety of life sends us all in quest; but the pleasures of sudden wonder are soon exhausted, and the mind can only repose on the stability of truth.

Shakespeare is above all writers, at least above all modern writers, the poet of nature; the poet that holds up to his readers a faithful mirror of manners and of life. His characters are not modified by the customs of particular places, unpracticed by the rest of the world; by the peculiarities of studies or professions, which can operate but upon small numbers; or by the accidents of transient fashions or temporary opinions: they are the genuine progeny of common humanity, such as the world will always supply, and observation will always find. His persons act and speak by the influence of those general passions and principles by which all minds are agitated, and the whole system of life is continued in motion. In the writings of other poets a character is too often an individual; in those of Shakespeare it is commonly a species.

It is from this wide extension of design that so much instruction is derived. It is this which fills the plays of Shakespeare with practical axioms and domestic wisdom. It was said of Euripides, that every verse was a precept; and

From *The Plays of William Shakespeare,* London, 1765.

it may be said of Shakespeare, that from his works may be collected a system of civil and economical prudence. Yet his real power is not shown in the splendor of particular passages, but by the progress of his fable, and, the tenor of his dialogue; and he that tries to recommend him by select quotations, will succeed like the pedant in *Hierocles*, who, when he offered his house to sale, carried a brick in his pocket as a specimen. . . .

Other dramatists can only gain attention by hyperbolical or aggravated characters, by fabulous and unexampled excellence or depravity, as the writers of barbarous romances invigorated the reader by a giant and a dwarf; and he that should form his expectations of human affairs from the play, or from the tale, would be equally deceived. Shakespeare has no heroes; his scenes are occupied only by men, who act and speak as the reader thinks that he should himself have spoken or acted on the same occasion: Even where the agency is supernatural the dialogue is level with life. Other writers disguise the most natural passions and most frequent incidents; so that he who contemplates them in the book will not know them in the world: Shakespeare approximates the remote, and familiarizes the wonderful; the event which he represents will not happen, but if it were possible, its effects would be probably such as he has assigned; and it may be said, that he has not only shown human nature as it acts in real exigencies, but as it would be found in trials, to which it cannot be exposed.

This therefore is the praise of Shakespeare, that his drama is the mirror of life; that he who has mazed his imagination, in following the phantoms which other writers raise up before him, may here be cured of his delirious ecstasies, by reading human sentiments in human language; by scenes from which a hermit may estimate the transactions of the world, and a confessor predict the progress of the passions. . . .

The censure which he has incurred by mixing comic and tragic scenes, as it extends to all his works, deserves more consideration. Let the fact be first stated, and then examined.

Shakespeare's plays are not in the rigorous and critical sense either tragedies or comedies, but compositions of a distinct kind; exhibiting the real state of sublunary nature, which partakes of good and evil, joy and sorrow, mingled with endless variety of proportion and innumerable modes of combination; and expressing the course of the world, in which the loss of one is the gain of another; in which, at the same time, the reveler is hasting to his wine, and the mourner burying his friend; in which the malignity of one is sometimes defeated by the frolic of another; and many mischiefs and many benefits are done and hindered without design.

Out of this chaos of mingled purposes and casualties the ancient poets, according to the laws which custom had prescribed, selected some the crimes of men, and some their absurdities; some the momentous vicissitudes of life, and some the lighter occurrences; some the terrors of distress, and some the gaieties of prosperity. Thus rose the two modes of imitation, known by the names of *tragedy* and *comedy*, compositions intended to promote different ends by contrary means, and considered as so little allied, that I do not recollect among the Greeks or Romans a single writer who attempted both.

Shakespeare has united the powers of exciting laughter and sorrow not only in one mind but in one composition. Almost all his plays are divided between serious and ludicrous characters, and, in the successive evolutions of the design, sometimes produce seriousness and sorrow, and sometimes levity and laughter.

That this is a practice contrary to the rules of criticism will be readily allowed; but there is always an appeal open from criticism to nature. The end of writing is to instruct; the end of poetry is to instruct by pleasing. That the mingled drama may convey all the instruction of tragedy or comedy cannot be denied, because it includes both in its alternations of exhibition, and approaches nearer than either to the appearance of life, by showing how great machinations and slender designs may promote or obviate one another, and the high and the low cooperate in the general system by unavoidable concatenation.

It is objected, that by this change of scenes the passions are interrupted in their progression, and that the principal event, being not advanced by a due gradation of preparatory incidents, wants at last the power to move, which constitutes the perfection of dramatic poetry. This reasoning is so specious, that it is received as true even by those who in daily experience feel it to be false. The interchanges of mingled scenes seldom fail to produce the intended vicissitudes of passion. Fiction cannot move so much, but that the attention may be easily transferred; and though it must be allowed that pleasing melancholy be sometimes interrupted by unwelcome levity, yet let it be considered likewise, that melancholy is often not pleasing, and that the disturbance of one man may be the relief of another; that different auditors have different habitudes; and that, upon the whole, all pleasure consists in variety. . . .

Shakespeare engaged in dramatic poetry with the world open before him; the rules of the ancients were yet known to few; the public judgment was unformed; he had no example of such fame as might force him upon imitation, nor critics of such authority as might restrain his extravagance: He therefore indulged his natural disposition, and his disposition, as Rymer has remarked, led him to comedy. In tragedy he often writes with great appearance of toil and study, what is written at last with little felicity; but in his comic scenes, he seems to produce without labor, what no labor can improve. In tragedy he is always struggling after some occasion to be comic, but in comedy he seems to repose, or to luxuriate, as in a mode of thinking congenial to his nature. In his tragic scenes there is always something wanting, but his comedy often surpasses expectation or desire. His comedy pleases by the thoughts and the language, and his tragedy for the greater part by incident and action. His tragedy seems to be skill, his comedy to be instinct.

The force of his comic scenes has suffered little diminution from the changes made by a century and a half, in manners or in words. As his personages act upon principles arising from genuine passion, very little modified by particular forms, their pleasures and vexations are communicable to all times and to all places; they are natural, and therefore durable; the adventitious peculiarities of personal habits are only superficial dyes, bright and pleasing for a little while, yet soon fading to a dim tinct, without any remains of former luster; but the discriminations of true passion are the colors of nature; they pervade the whole mass, and can only perish with the body that exhibits them. The accidental compositions of heterogeneous modes are dissolved by the chance which combined them; but the uniform simplicity of primitive qualities neither admits increase, nor suffers decay. The sand heaped by one flood is scattered by another, but the rock always continues in its place. The stream of time, which is continually washing the dissoluble fabrics of other poets, passes without injury by the adamant of Shakespeare.

If there be, what I believe there is, in every nation, a style which never becomes obsolete, a certain mode of phraseology so consonant and congenial to the analogy and principles of its respective language as to remain settled and unaltered; this style is probably to be sought in the common intercourse of life, among those who speak only to be understood, without ambition of elegance. The polite are always catching modish innovations, and the learned depart from established forms of speech, in hope of finding or making better; those who wish for distinction forsake the vulgar, when the vulgar is right; but there is a conversation above grossness and below refinement, where propriety resides, and where this poet seems to have gathered his comic dialogue. He is therefore more agreeable to the ears of the present age than any other author equally remote, and among his other excellencies deserves to be studied as one of the original masters of our language. . . .

Shakespeare with his excellencies has likewise faults, and faults sufficient to obscure and overwhelm any other merit. I shall show them in the proportion in which they appear to me, without envious malignity or superstitious veneration. No question can be more innocently discussed than a dead poet's pretensions to renown; and little regard is due to that bigotry which sets candor higher than truth.

His first defect is that to which may be imputed most of the evil in books or in men. He sacrifices virtue to convenience, and is so much more careful to please than to instruct, that he seems to write without any moral purpose. From his writings indeed a system of social duty may be selected, for he that thinks reasonably must think morally; but his precepts and axioms drop casually from him; he makes no just distribution of good or evil, nor is always careful to show in the virtuous a disapprobation of the wicked; he carries his persons indifferently through right and wrong, and at the close dismisses them without further care, and leaves their examples to operate by chance. This fault the barbarity of his age cannot extenuate; for it is always a writer's duty to make the world better, and justice is a virtue independent on time or place.

The plots are often so loosely formed, that a very slight consideration may improve them, and so carelessly pursued, that he seems not always fully to comprehend his own design. He omits opportunities of instructing or delighting which the train of his story seems to force upon him, and apparently rejects those exhibitions which would be more affecting, for the sake of those which are more easy.

It may be observed, that in many of his plays the latter part is evidently neglected. When he found himself near the end of his work, and in view of his reward, he shortened the labor, to snatch the profit. He therefore remits his efforts where he should most vigorously exert them, and his catastrophe is improbably produced or imperfectly represented.

He had no regard to distinction of time or place, but gives to one age or nation, without scruple, the customs, institutions, and opinions of another, at the expense not only of likelihood, but of possibility. . . .

In tragedy his performance seems constantly to be worse, as his labor is more. The effusions of passion which exigence forces out are for the most part striking and energetic; but whenever he solicits his invention, or strains his faculties, the offspring of his throes is tumor, meanness, tediousness, and obscurity.

In narration he affects a disproportionate pomp of diction and a wearisome train of circumlocution, and tells the incident imperfectly in many words, which might have been more plainly delivered in few. Narration in dramatic poetry is naturally tedious, as it is unanimated and inactive, and obstructs the progress of the action; it should therefore always be rapid, and enlivened by frequent interruption. Shakespeare found it an encumbrance, and instead of lightening it by brevity, endeavored to recommend it by dignity and splendor.

His declamations or set speeches are commonly cold and weak, for his power was the power of nature; when he endeavored, like other tragic writers, to catch opportunities of amplification, and instead of inquiring what the occasion demanded, to show how much his stores of knowledge could supply, he seldom escapes without the pity or resentment of his reader.

It is incident to him to be now and then entangled with an unwieldy sentiment, which he cannot well express, and will not reject; he struggles with it a while, and if it continues stubborn, comprises it in words such as occur, and leaves it to be disentangled and evolved by those who have more leisure to bestow upon it.

Not that always where the language is intricate the thought is subtle, or the image always great where the line is bulky; the equality of words to things is very often neglected, and trivial sentiments and vulgar ideas disappoint the attention, to which they are recommended by sonorous epithets and swelling figures.

But the admirers of this great poet have never less reason to indulge their hopes of supreme excellence, than when he seems fully resolved to sink them in dejection, and mollify them with tender emotions by the fall of greatness, the danger of innocence, or the crosses of love. He is not long soft and pathetic without some idle conceit, or contemptible equivocation. He no sooner begins to move, than he counteracts himself; and terror and pity, as they are rising in the mind, are checked and blasted by sudden frigidity.

A quibble is to Shakespeare, what luminous vapors are to the traveler; he follows it at all adventures, it is sure to lead him out of his way, and sure to engulf him in the mire. It has some malignant power over his mind, and its fascinations are irresistible. Whatever be the dignity or profundity of his disquisition, whether he be enlarging knowledge or exalting affection, whether he be amusing attention with incidents, or enchaining it in suspense, let but a quibble spring up before him, and he leaves his work unfinished. A quibble is the golden apple for which he will always turn aside from his career, or stoop from his elevation. A quibble, poor and barren as it is, gave him such delight, that he was content to purchase it, by the sacrifice of reason, propriety and truth. A quibble was to him the fatal Cleopatra for which he lost the world, and was content to lose it.

It will be thought strange, that, in enumerating the defects of this writer, I have not yet mentioned his neglect of the unities; his violation of those laws which have been instituted and established by the joint authority of poets and critics.

For his other deviations from the art of writing I resign him to critical justice, without making any other demand in his favor, than that which must be indulged to all human excellence; that his virtues be rated with his failings: But, from the censure which this irregularity may bring upon him, I shall, with due reverence to that learning which I must oppose, adventure to try how I can defend him.

His histories, being neither tragedies nor comedies, are not subject to any of their laws; nothing more is necessary to all the praise which they expect, than that the changes of action be so prepared as to be understood, that the incidents be various and affecting, and the characters consistent, natural and distinct. No other unity is intended, and therefore none is to be sought.

In his other works he has well enough preserved the unity of action. He has not, indeed, an intrigue regularly perplexed and regularly unraveled; he does not endeavor to hide his design only to discover it, for this is seldom the order of real events, and Shakespeare is the poet of nature: But his plan has commonly what Aristotle requires, a beginning, a middle, and an end; one event is concatenated with another, and the conclusion follows by easy consequence. There are perhaps some incidents that might be spared, as in other poets there is much talk that only fills up time upon the stage; but the general system makes gradual advances, and the end of the play is the end of expectation.

To the unities of time and place he has shown no regard, and perhaps a nearer view of the principles on which they stand will diminish their value, and withdraw from them the veneration which, from the time of Corneille, they have very generally received by discovering that they have given more trouble to the poet, than pleasure to the auditor.

The necessity of observing the unities of time and place

arises from the supposed necessity of making the drama credible. The critics hold it impossible, that an action of months or years can be possibly believed to pass in three hours; or that the spectator can suppose himself to sit in the theater, while ambassadors go and return between distant kings, while armies are levied and towns besieged, while an exile wanders and returns, or till he whom they saw courting his mistress, shall lament the untimely fall of his son. The mind revolts from evident falsehood, and fiction loses its force when it departs from the resemblance of reality.

From the narrow limitation of time necessarily arises the contraction of place. The spectator, who knows that he saw the first act at Alexandria, cannot suppose that he sees the next at Rome, at a distance to which not the dragons of Medea could, in so short a time, have transported him; he knows with certainty that he has not changed his place; and he knows that place cannot change itself; that what was a house cannot become a plain; that what was Thebes can never be Persepolis.

Such is the triumphant language with which a critic exults over the misery of an irregular poet, and exults commonly without resistance or reply. It is time therefore to tell him by the authority of Shakespeare, that he assumes, as an unquestionable principle, a position, which, while his breath is forming it into words, his understanding pronounces to be false. . . .

There is no reason why a mind thus wandering in ecstasy should count the clock, or why an hour should not be a century in that calenture of the brains that can make the stage a field.

The truth is, that the spectators are always in their senses, and know, from the first act to the last, that the stage is only a stage, and that the players are only players. They came to hear a certain number of lines recited with just gesture and elegant modulation. The lines relate to some action, and an action must be in some place; but the different actions that complete a story may be in places very remote from each other. . . .

Time is, of all modes of existence, most obsequious to the imagination; a lapse of years is as easily conceived as a passage of hours. In contemplation we easily contract the time of real actions, and therefore willingly permit it to be contracted when we only see their imitation.

It will be asked, how the drama moves, if it is not credited. It is credited with all the credit due to a drama. It is credited, whenever it moves, as a just picture of a real original; as representing to the auditor what he would himself feel, if he were to do or suffer what is there feigned to be suffered or to be done. The reflection that strikes the heart is not, that the evils before us are real evils, but that they are evils to which we ourselves may be exposed. If there be any fallacy, it is not that we fancy the players, but that we fancy ourselves unhappy for a moment; but we rather lament the possibility than suppose the presence of misery, as a mother weeps over her babe, when she remembers that death may take it from her. The delight of tragedy proceeds from our consciousness of fiction; if we thought murders and treasons real, they would please no more. . . .

[Shakespeare's] plots, whether historical or fabulous, are always crowded with incidents, by which the attention of a rude people was more easily caught than by sentiment or argumentation; and such is the power of the marvelous even over those who despise it, that every man finds his mind more strongly seized by the tragedies of Shakespeare than of any other writer; others please us by particular speeches, but he always makes us anxious for the event, and has perhaps excelled all but Homer in securing the first purpose of a writer, by exciting restless and unquenchable curiosity and compelling him that reads his work to read it through.

The shows and bustle with which his plays abound have the same original. As knowledge advances, pleasure passes from the eye to the ear, but returns, as it declines, from the ear to the eye. Those to whom our author's labors were exhibited had more skill in pomps or processions than in poetical language, and perhaps wanted some visible and discriminated events, as comments on the dialogue. He knew how he should most please; and whether his practice is more agreeable to nature, or whether his example has prejudiced the nation, we still find that on our stage something must be done as well as said, and inactive declamation is very coldly heard, however musical or elegant, passionate or sublime. . . .

"KING LEAR"

The Tragedy of *Lear* is deservedly celebrated among the dramas of Shakespeare. There is perhaps no play which keeps the attention so strongly fixed; which so much agitates our passions and interests our curiosity. The artful involutions of distinct interests, the striking opposition of contrary characters, the sudden changes of fortune, and the quick succession of events, fill the mind with a perpetual tumult of indignation, pity, and hope. There is no scene which does not contribute to the aggravation of the distress or conduct of the action, and scarce a line which does not conduce to the progress of tne scene. So powerful is the current of the poet's imagination, that the mind, which once ventures within it, is hurried irresistibly along.

On the seeming improbability of Lear's conduct, it may be observed that he is represented according to histories at that time vulgarly received as true. And perhaps if we turn our thoughts upon the barbarity and ignorance of the age to which this story is referred, it will appear not so unlikely as while we estimate Lear's manners by our own. Such preference of one daughter to another, or resignation of dominion on such conditions, would be yet credible, if told of a petty prince of Guinea or Madagascar. Shakespeare, indeed, by the mention of his Earls and Dukes, has given us the idea of times more civilized, and of life regulated by softer manners; and the truth is, that though he so nicely discriminates, and so minutely describes the characters of men, he commonly neglects and confounds the characters of age, by mingling customs ancient and modern, English and foreign.

My learned friend Mr. Warton, who has in the *Adventurer* very minutely criticized this play, remarks, that the instances of cruelty are too savage and shocking, and that the intervention of Edmund destroys the simplicity of the story. These objections may, I think, be answered, by repeating, that the cruelty of the daughters is an historical fact, to which the poet has added little, having only drawn it into a series by dialogue and action. But I am not able to apologize with equal plausibility for the extrusion of Gloucester's eyes, which seems an act too horrid to be endured in dramatic exhibition, and such as must always compel the mind to relieve its distress by incredulity. Yet let it be remembered that our author well knew what would please the audience for which he wrote.

The injury done by Edmund to the simplicity of the action is abundantly recompensed by the addition of variety, by the art with which he is made to cooperate with the chief design, and the opportunity which he gives the poet of combining perfidy with perfidy, and connecting the wicked son with the wicked daughters, to impress this important moral, that villainy is never at a stop, that crimes lead to crimes, and at last terminate in ruin.

But though this moral be incidentally enforced, Shakespeare has suffered the virtue of Cordelia to perish in a just cause, contrary to the natural ideas of justice, to the hope of the reader, and what is yet more strange, to the faith of chronicles. Yet this conduct is justified by the Spectator, who blames Tate for giving Cordelia success and happiness in his alteration, and declares, that in his opinion, *the tragedy has lost half its beauty.* Dennis has remarked, whether justly or not, that, to secure the favorable reception of *Cato, the town was poisoned with much false and abominable criticism,* and that endeavors had been used to discredit and decry poetical justice. A play in which the wicked prosper, and the virtuous miscarry, may doubtless be good, because it is a just representation of the common events of human life: but since all reasonable beings naturally love justice, I cannot easily be persuaded, that the observation of justice makes a play worse; or, that if other excellencies are equal, the audience will not always rise better pleased from the final triumph of persecuted virtue.

In the present case the public has decided. Cordelia, from the time of Tate, has always retired with victory and felicity. And, if my sensations could add anything to the general suffrage, I might relate, that I was many years ago shocked by Cordelia's death, that I know not whether I ever endured to read again the last scenes of the play till I undertook to revise them as an editor.

A. C. BRADLEY

From Shakespearean Tragedy

. . . [The] chief value [of the double action in *King Lear*] is not merely dramatic. It lies in the fact—in Shakespeare without a parallel—that the subplot simply repeats the theme of the main story. Here, as there, we see an old man "with a white beard." He, like Lear, is affectionate, unsuspicious, foolish, and self-willed. He, too, wrongs deeply a child who loves him not less for the wrong. He, too, meets with monstrous ingratitude from the child whom he favors, and is tortured and driven to death. This repetition does not simply double the pain with which the tragedy is witnessed: it startles and terrifies by suggesting that the folly of Lear and the ingratitude of his daughters are no accidents or merely individual aberrations, but that in that dark cold world some fateful malignant influence is abroad, turning the hearts of the fathers against their children and of the children against their fathers, smiting the earth with a curse, so that the brother gives the brother to death and the father the son, blinding the eyes, maddening the brain, freezing the springs of pity, numbing all powers except the nerves of anguish and the dull lust of life.

Hence too, as well as from other sources, comes that feeling which haunts us in *King Lear*, as though we were

From *Shakespearean Tragedy* by A. C. Bradley. (London: Macmillan & Co., Ltd., 1904). Reprinted by permission of Macmillan & Co., Ltd. (London), St Martin's Press, Inc. (New York), and the Macmillan Company of Canada, Ltd.

witnessing something universal—a conflict not so much of particular persons as of the powers of good and evil in the world. And the treatment of many of the characters confirms this feeling. Considered simply as psychological studies few of them, surely, are of the highest interest. Fine and subtle touches could not be absent from a work of Shakespeare's maturity; but, with the possible exception of Lear himself, no one of the characters strikes us as psychologically a *wonderful* creation, like Hamlet or Iago or even Macbeth; one or two seem even to be somewhat faint and thin. And, what is more significant, it is not quite natural to us to regard them from this point of view at all. Rather we observe a most unusual circumstance. If Lear, Gloster and Albany are set apart, the rest fall into two distinct groups,. which are strongly, even violently, contrasted: Cordelia, Kent, Edgar, the Fool on one side, Goneril, Regan, Edmund, Cornwall, Oswald on the other. These characters are in various degrees individualized, most of them completely so; but still in each group there is a quality common to all the members, or one spirit breathing through them all. Here we have unselfish and devoted love, there hard self-seeking. On both sides, further, the common quality takes an extreme form; the love is incapable of being chilled by injury, the selfishness of being softened by pity; and, it may be added, this tendency to extremes is found again in the characters of Lear and Gloster, and is the main source of the accusations of improbability directed against their conduct at certain points. Hence the members of each group tend to appear, at least in part, as varieties of one species; the radical differences of the two species are emphasized in broad hard strokes; and the two are set in conflict, almost as if Shakespeare, like Empedocles, were regarding Love and Hate as the two ultimate forces of the universe.

The presence in *King Lear* of so large a number of characters in whom love or self-seeking is so extreme, has another effect. They do not merely inspire in us emotions of unusual strength, but they also stir the intellect to wonder and speculation. How can there be such men and women? we ask ourselves. How comes it that humanity can take such absolutely opposite forms? And, in particular, to what omission of elements which should be present in human nature; or, if there is no omission, to what distortion of these elements is it due that such beings as some of these come to exist? This is a question which Iago (and perhaps no previous creation of Shakespeare's) forces us to ask, but in *King Lear* it is provoked again and again. And more, it seems to us that the author himself is asking this question: "Then let them anatomize Regan, see what breeds about her heart. Is there any cause in nature that makes these hard hearts?"—the strain of thought which appears here seems to be present in some degree throughout the play. We seem to trace the tendency which, a few years later, produced Ariel and Caliban, the tendency of imagination to analyze and abstract, to decompose human nature into its constituent factors, and then to construct beings in whom one or more of these factors is absent or atrophied or only incipient. This, of course, is a tendency which produces symbols, allegories, personifications of qualities and abstract ideas; and we are accustomed to think it quite foreign to Shakespeare's genius, which was in the highest degree concrete. No doubt in the main we are right here; but it is hazardous to set limits to that genius. The Sonnets, if nothing else, may show us how easy it was to Shakespeare's mind to move in a world of "Platonic" ideas; and, while it would be going too far to suggest that he was employing conscious symbolism or allegory in *King Lear*, it does appear to disclose a mode of imagination not so very far removed from the mode with which, we must remember, Shakespeare was perfectly familiar in Morality plays and in the *Fairy Queen*.

This same tendency shows itself in *King Lear* in other forms. To it is due the idea of monstrosity—of beings, actions, states of mind, which appear not only abnormal but absolutely contrary to nature; an idea, which, of course, is common enough in Shakespeare, but appears with unusual frequency in *King Lear*, for instance in the lines:

Ingratitude, thou marble-hearted fiend,
More hideous when thou show'st thee in a child
Than the sea-monster!   (1.4.267–68)

or in the exclamation,

Filial ingratitude!
Is it not as this mouth should tear this hand
For lifting food to't?   (3.4.14–16)

It appears in another shape in that most vivid passage where Albany, as he looks at the face which had bewitched him, now distorted with dreadful passions, suddenly sees it in a new light and exclaims in horror:

Thou changed and self-cover'd thing, for shame,
Bemonster not thy feature. Were't my fitness
To let these hands obey my blood,
They are apt enough to dislocate and tear
Thy flesh and bones: howe'er thou art a fiend,
A woman's shape doth shield thee.   (4.3.62–67)

It appears once more in that exclamation of Kent's, as he listens to the description of Cordelia's grief:

It is the stars,
The stars above us, govern our conditions;
Else one self mate and mate could not beget
Such different issues.   (33–36)

(This is not the only sign that Shakespeare had been musing over heredity, and wondering how it comes about that the composition of two strains of blood or two parent souls can produce such astonishingly different products.)

This mode of thought is responsible, lastly, for a very striking characteristic of *King Lear*—one in which it has no parallel except *Timon*—the incessant references to the lower animals and man's likeness to them. These references are scattered broadcast through the whole play as though Shakespeare's mind were so busy with the subject that he could hardly write a page without some allusion to it. The dog, the horse, the cow, the sheep, the hog, the lion, the bear, the wolf, the fox, the monkey, the polecat, the civet cat, the pelican, the owl, the crow, the chough, the wren, the fly, the butterfly, the rat, the mouse, the frog, the tadpole, the wall newt, the water newt, the worm—I am sure I cannot have completed the list, and some of them are mentioned again and again. Often, of course, and especially in the talk of Edgar as the Bedlam, they have no symbolical meaning; but not seldom, even in his talk, they are expressly referred to for their typical qualities—"hog in sloth, fox in stealth, wolf in greediness, dog in madness, lion in prey," "The fitchew nor the soiled horse goes to't with a more riotous appetite." Sometimes a person in the drama is compared, openly or implicitly, with one of them. Goneril is a kite: her ingratitude has a serpent's tooth: she has struck her father most serpentlike upon the very heart: her visage is wolfish: she has tied sharp-toothed unkindness like a vulture on her father's breast: for her husband she is a gilded serpent: to Gloster her cruelty seems to have the fangs of a boar. She and Regan are dog-hearted: they are tigers, not daughters: each is an adder to the other: the flesh of each is covered with the fell of a beast. Oswald is a mongrel, and the son and heir of a mongrel: ducking to everyone in power, he is a wagtail: white with fear, he is a goose. Gloster, for Regan, is an ingrateful fox: Albany, for his wife, has a cowish spirit and is milk-liver'd: when Edgar as the Bedlam first appeared to Lear he made him think a man a worm. As we read, the souls of all the beasts in turn seem to us to have entered the bodies of these mortals; horrible in their venom, savagery, lust, deceitfulness, sloth, cruelty, filthiness; miserable in their feebleness, nakedness, defenselessness, blindness; and man, "consider him well," is even what they are. Shakespeare, to whom the idea of the transmigration of souls was familiar and had once been material for jest,[1] seems to have been brooding on humanity, in the light of it. It is remarkable, and somewhat sad, that he seems to find none of man's better qualities in the world of the brutes (though he might well have found the prototype of the selfless love of Kent and Cordelia in the dog whom he so habitually maligns); but he seems to have been asking himself whether that which he loathes in man may not be due to some strange wrenching of this frame of things, through which the lower animal souls have found a lodgment in human forms, and there found—to the horror and confusion of the thinking mind—brains to forge, tongues to speak, and hands to act, enormities which no mere brute can conceive or execute. He shows us in *King Lear* these terrible forces bursting into monstrous life and flinging themselves upon those human beings who are weak and defenseless, partly from old age, but partly because they *are* human and lack the dreadful undivided energy of the beast. And the only comfort he might seem to hold out to us is the prospect that at least this bestial race, strong only where it is vile, cannot endure: though stars and gods are powerless, or careless, or empty dreams, yet there must be an end of this horrible world:

[1]*E.g.* in *As You Like It*, 3.2.187, "I was never so berhymed since Pythagoras' time, that I was an Irish rat, which I can hardly remember"; *Twelfth Night*, 4.2.55, "*Clown.* What is the opinion of Pythagoras concerning wild fowl? *Mal.* That the soul of our grandam might haply inhabit a bird.   *Clown.* What thinkest thou of his opinion? *Mal.* I think nobly of the soul, and no way approve his opinion," etc. But earlier comes a passage which reminds us of *King Lear*, *Merchant of Venice*, 4.1.128:

> O be thou damn'd, inexecrable dog!
> And for thy life let justice be accused.
> Thou almost makest me waver in my faith
> To hold opinion with Pythagoras,
> That souls of animals infuse themselves
> Into the trunks of men: thy currish spirit
> Govern'd a wolf, who, hang'd for human slaughter,
> Even from the gallows did his fell soul fleet,
> And, whilst thou lay'st in thy unhallow'd dam,
> Infused itself in thee; for thy desires
> Are wolvish, bloody, starv'd and ravenous.

It will come;
Humanity must perforce prey on itself
Like monsters of the deep.   (4.2.48–50)

The influence of all this on imagination as we read
King Lear is very great; and it combines with other influences to convey to us, not in the form of distinct ideas but
in the manner proper to poetry, the wider or universal significance of the spectacle presented to the inward eye.
But the effect of theatrical exhibition is precisely the re-
verse. There the poetic atmosphere is dissipated; the
meaning of the very words which create it passes half-
realized; in obedience to the tyranny of the eye we conceive the characters as mere particular men and women;
and all that mass of vague suggestion, if it enters the mind
at all, appears in the shape of an allegory which we immediately reject. A similar conflict between imagination
and sense will be found if we consider the dramatic center of the whole tragedy, the Storm-scenes. The temptation of Othello and the scene of Duncan's murder may
lose upon the stage, but they do not lose their essence,
and they gain as well as lose. The Storm-scenes in *King
Lear* gain nothing and their very essence is destroyed. It
is comparatively a small thing that the theatrical storm,
not to drown the dialogue, must be silent whenever a human being wishes to speak, and is wretchedly inferior to
many a storm we have witnessed. Nor is it simply that, as
Lamb observed, the corporal presence of Lear, "an old
man tottering about the stage with a walking stick," dis-
turbs and depresses that sense of the greatness of his
mind which fills the imagination. There is a further reason, which is not expressed, but still emerges, in these
words of Lamb's: "the explosions of his passion are terrible as a volcano: they are storms turning up and disclos-
ing to the bottom that sea, his mind, with all its vast
riches." Yes, "they are *storms*." For imagination, that is
to say, the explosions of Lear's passion, and the bursts of
rain and thunder, are not, what for the senses they must
be, two things, but manifestations of one thing. It is the
powers of the tormented soul that we hear and see in the

"groans of roaring wind and rain" and the "sheets of fire";
and they that, at intervals almost more overwhelming, sink
back into darkness and silence. Nor yet is even this all; but,
as those incessant references to wolf and tiger made us see
humanity "reeling back into the beast" and ravening against
itself, so in the storm we seem to see Nature herself convulsed by the same horrible passions; the "common mother,"

> Whose womb unmeasurable and infinite breast
> Teems and feeds all;
>
> (Timon of Athens, 4.3.179–80)

turning on her children, to complete the ruin they have
wrought upon themselves. Surely something not less, but
much more, than these helpless words convey, is what comes
to us in these astounding scenes; and if, translated thus into
the language of prose, it becomes confused and inconsistent,
the reason is simply that it itself is poetry, and such poetry as
cannot be transferred to the space behind the footlights, but
has its being only in imagination. Here then is Shakespeare at
his very greatest, but not the mere dramatist Shakespeare.

And now we may say this also of the catastrophe, which
we found questionable from the strictly dramatic point of
view. Its purpose is not merely dramatic. This sudden blow
out of the darkness, which seems so far from inevitable,
and which strikes down our reviving hopes for the victims
of so much cruelty, seems now only what we might have
expected in a world so wild and monstrous. It is as if
Shakespeare said to us: "Did you think weakness and innocence have any chance here? Were you beginning to dream
that? I will show you it is not so."

I come to a last point. As we contemplate this world, the
question presses on us, What can be the ultimate power
that moves it, that excites this gigantic war and waste, or,
perhaps, that suffers them and overrules them? And in
King Lear this question is not left to *us* to ask, it is raised
by the characters themselves. References to religious or ir-
religious beliefs and feelings are more frequent than is
usual in Shakespeare's tragedies, as frequent perhaps as in
his final plays. He introduces characteristic differences in

the language of the different persons about fortune or the
stars or the gods, and shows how the question, What rules
the world? is forced upon their minds. They answer it in
their turn: Kent, for instance:

> It is the stars,
> The stars above us, govern our condition:
>
> (4.3.33–34)

Edmund:

> Thou, nature, art my goddess; to thy law
> My services are bound: (1.2.1–2)

and again,

> This is the excellent foppery of the world, that, when we
> are sick in fortune—often the surfeits of our own behavior—
> we make guilty of our disasters the sun, the moon and the
> stars; as if we were villains by necessity, fools by heavenly
> compulsion, . . . and all that we are evil in by a divine thrust-
> ing on: (128–36)

Gloster:

> As flies to wanton boys, are we to the gods,
> They kill us for their sport;   (4.1.36–37)

Edgar:

> Think that the clearest gods, who make them honours
> Of men's impossibilities, have preserved thee.
>
> (4.6.73–74)

Here we have four distinct theories of the nature of the
ruling power. And besides this, in such of the characters
as have any belief in gods who love good and hate evil,
the spectacle of triumphant injustice or cruelty provokes
questionings like those of Job, or else the thought, often
repeated, of divine retribution. To Lear at one moment
the storm seems the messenger of heaven:

> Let the great gods,
> That keep this dreadful pother o'er our heads,

> Find out their enemies now. Tremble, thou wretch,
> That hast within thee undivulged crimes. . . .
>
> (3.2.49–52)

At another moment those habitual miseries of the poor, of which he has taken too little account, seem to him to accuse the gods of injustice:

> Take physic, pomp;
> Expose thyself to feel what wretches feel,
> That thou mayst shake the superflux to them
> And show the heavens more just;
>
> (3.4.33–35)

and Gloster has almost the same thought (4.1.67 ff.). Gloster again, thinking of the cruelty of Lear's daughters, breaks out,

> but I shall see
> The winged vengeance overtake such children.
>
> (3.7.66–67)

The servants who have witnessed the blinding of Gloster by Cornwall and Regan, cannot believe that cruelty so atrocious will pass unpunished. One cries,

> I'll never care what wickedness I do,
> If this man come to good;
>
> (100–1)

and another,

> if she live long,
> And in the end meet the old course of death,
> Women will all turn monsters.
>
> (101–3)

Albany greets the news of Cornwall's death with the exclamation,

> This shows you are above,
> You justicers, that these our nether crimes
> So speedily can venge;   (4.2.78–80)

and the news of the deaths of the sisters with the words,

> This judgment of the heavens, that makes us tremble,
> Touches us not with pity.   (5.3.233–34)

Edgar, speaking to Edmund of their father, declares

> The gods are just, and of our pleasant vices
> Make instruments to plague us,   (173–74)

and Edmund himself assents. Almost throughout the latter
half of the drama we note in most of the better characters
a preoccupation with the question of the ultimate power,
and a passionate need to explain by reference to it what
otherwise would drive them to despair. And the influence
of this preoccupation and need joins with other influences
in affecting the imagination, and in causing it to receive
from *King Lear* an impression which is at least as near of
kin to the *Divine Comedy* as to *Othello*.

For Dante that which is recorded in the *Divine Comedy*
was the justice and love of God. What did *King Lear*
record for Shakespeare? Something, it would seem, very
different. This is certainly the most terrible picture that
Shakespeare painted of the world. In no other of his
tragedies does humanity appear more pitiably infirm or
more hopelessly bad. What is Iago's malignity against an
envied stranger compared with the cruelty of the son of
Gloster and the daughters of Lear? What are the sufferings
of a strong man like Othello to those of helpless age? Much
too that we have already observed—the repetition of the
main theme in that of the underplot, the comparisons of
man with the most wretched and the most horrible of the
beasts, the impression of Nature's hostility to him, the
irony of the unexpected catastrophe—these, with much
else, seem even to indicate an intention to show things at
their worst, and to return the sternest of replies to that
question of the ultimate power and those appeals for retribution. Is it an accident, for example, that Lear's first
appeal to something beyond the earth,

> O heavens,
> If you do love old men, if your sweet sway
> Allow obedience, if yourselves are old,
> Make it your cause: (2.4.188–91)

is immediately answered by the iron voices of his daughters, raising by turns the conditions on which they will give him a humiliating harborage; or that his second appeal, heart-rending in its piteousness,

> You see me here, you gods, a poor old man,
> As full of grief as age; wretched in both: (271–72)

is immediately answered from the heavens by the sound of the breaking storm? Albany and Edgar may moralize on the divine justice as they will, but how, in the face of all that we see, shall we believe that they speak Shakespeare's mind? Is not his mind rather expressed in the bitter contrast between their faith and the events we witness, or in the scornful rebuke of those who take upon them the mystery of things as if they were God's spies? Is it not Shakespeare's judgment on his kind that we hear in Lear's appeal,

> And thou, all-shaking thunder,
> Smite flat the thick rotundity o' the world!
> Crack nature's moulds, all germens spill at once,
> That make ingrateful man!   (3.2.6–9)

and Shakespeare's judgment on the worth of existence that we hear in Lear's agonized cry, "No, no, no life!"?

Beyond doubt, I think, some such feelings as these possess us, and, if we follow Shakespeare, ought to possess us, from time to time as we read *King Lear*. And some readers will go further and maintain that this is also the ultimate and total impression left by the tragedy. *King Lear* has been held to be profoundly "pessimistic" in the full meaning of that word—the record of a time when contempt and loathing for his kind had overmastered the poet's soul, and in despair he pronounced man's life to be simply hateful and hideous. And if we exclude the biographical part of this view, the rest may claim some support even from the greatest of Shakespearean critics since the days of Coleridge, Hazlitt and Lamb. Mr. Swinburne, after observing that *King Lear* is "by far the most Aeschylean" of Shakespeare's works, proceeds thus:

"But in one main point it differs radically from the work and the spirit of Aeschylus. Its fatalism is of a darker and harder nature. To Prometheus the fetters of the lord and enemy of mankind were bitter; upon Orestes the hand of heaven was laid too heavily to bear; yet in the not utterly infinite or everlasting distance we see beyond them the promise of the morning on which mystery and justice shall be made one; when righteousness and omnipotence at last shall kiss each other. But on the horizon of Shakespeare's tragic fatalism we see no such twilight of atonement, such pledge of reconciliation as this. Requital, redemption, amends, equity, explanation, pity and mercy, are words without a meaning here.

> As flies to wanton boys are we to the gods;
> They kill us for their sport.   (4.1.36–37)

Here is no need of the Eumenides, children of Night everlasting; for here is very Night herself.

"The words just cited are not casual or episodical; they strike the keynote of the whole poem, lay the keystone of the whole arch of thought. There is no contest of conflicting forces, no judgment so much as by casting of lots: far less is there any light of heavenly harmony or of heavenly wisdom, of Apollo or Athene from above. We have heard much and often from theologians of the light of revelation: and some such thing indeed we find in Aeschylus; but the darkness of revelation is here."[2]

It is hard to refuse assent to these eloquent words, for they express in the language of a poet what we feel at times in reading *King Lear* but cannot express. But do they rep-

[2]*A Study of Shakespeare* (1880), pp. 171, 172.

resent the total and final impression produced by the play? If they do, this impression, so far as the substance of the drama is concerned (and nothing else is in question here), must, it would seem, be one composed almost wholly of painful feelings—utter depression, or indignant rebellion, or appalled despair. And that would surely be strange. For *King Lear* is admittedly one of the world's greatest poems, and yet there is surely no other of these poems which produces on the whole this effect, and we regard it as a very serious flaw in any considerable work of art that this should be its ultimate effect. So that Mr. Swinburne's description, if taken as final, and any description of *King Lear* as "pessimistic" in the proper sense of that word, would imply a criticism which is not intended, and which would make it difficult to leave the work in the position almost universally assigned to it.

But in fact these descriptions, like most of the remarks made on *King Lear* in the present lecture, emphasize only certain aspects of the play and certain elements in the total impression; and in that impression the effect of these aspects, though far from being lost, is modified by that of others. I do not mean that the final effect resembles that of the *Divine Comedy* or the *Oresteia*: how should it, when the first of these can be called by its author a "Comedy," and when the second, ending (as doubtless the *Prometheus* trilogy also ended) with a solution, is not in the Shakespearean sense a tragedy at all? Nor do I mean that *King Lear* contains a revelation of righteous omnipotence or heavenly harmony, or even a promise of the reconciliation of mystery and justice. But then, as we saw, neither do Shakespeare's other tragedies contain these things. Any theological interpretation of the world on the author's part is excluded from them; and their effect would be disordered or destroyed equally by the ideas of righteous or of unrighteous omnipotence. Nor, in reading them, do we think of "justice" or "equity" in the sense of a strict requital or such an adjustment of merit and prosperity as our moral sense is said to demand; and there never was vainer labor than that of critics who try to make out that the persons in these dramas meet with "justice" or their "deserts." But, on the other hand, man is not represented in these tragedies as the mere plaything of a blind or capricious power, suffering woes which have no relation to his character and actions; nor is the world represented as given over to darkness. And in these respects *King Lear*, though the most terrible of these works, does not differ in essence from the rest. Its keynote is surely to be heard neither in the words wrung from Gloster in his anguish, nor in Edgar's words "the gods are just." Its final and total result is one in which pity and terror, carried perhaps to the extreme limits of art, are so blended with a sense of law and beauty that we feel at last, not depression and much less despair, but a consciousness of greatness in pain, and of solemnity in the mystery we cannot fathom. . . .

But there is another aspect of Lear's story, the influence of which modifies, in a way quite different and more peculiar to this tragedy, the impressions called pessimistic and even this impression of law. There is nothing more noble and beautiful in literature than Shakespeare's exposition of the effect of suffering in reviving the greatness and eliciting the sweetness of Lear's nature. The occasional recurrence, during his madness, of autocratic impatience or of desire for revenge serves only to heighten this effect, and the moments when his insanity becomes merely infinitely piteous do not weaken it. The old King who in pleading with his daughters feels so intensely his own humiliation and their horrible ingratitude, and who yet, at fourscore and upward, constrains himself to practice a self-control and patience so many years disused; who out of old affection for his Fool, and in repentance for his injustice to the Fool's beloved mistress, tolerates incessant and cutting reminders of his own folly and wrong; in whom the rage of the storm awakes a power and a poetic grandeur surpassing even that of Othello's anguish; who comes in his affliction to think of others first, and to seek, in tender solicitude for his poor boy, the shelter he scorns for his own bare head; who learns to feel and to pray for the miserable and houseless poor, to discern the falseness of flattery and the brutality of authority, and to pierce below the differences of rank and raiment to the common humanity

beneath; whose sight is so purged by scalding tears that it
sees at last how power and place and all things in the world
are vanity except love; who tastes in his last hours the extremes both of love's rapture and of its agony, but could
never, if he lived on or lived again, care a jot for aught beside—there is no figure, surely, in the world of poetry at
once so grand, so pathetic, and so beautiful as his. Well,
but Lear owes the whole of this to those sufferings which
made us doubt whether life were not simply evil, and men
like the flies which wanton boys torture for their sport.
Should we not be at least as near the truth if we called this
poem *The Redemption of King Lear*, and declared that the
business of "the gods" with him was neither to torment
him, nor to teach him a "noble anger," but to lead him to at-
tain through apparently hopeless failure the very end and
aim of life? One can believe that Shakespeare had been
tempted at times to feel misanthropy and despair, but it is
quite impossible that he can have been mastered by such
feelings at the time when he produced this conception. . . .

. . . Lear's insanity, which destroys the coherence, also
reduces the poetry of his imagination. What it stimulates is
that power of moral perception and reflection which had already been quickened by his sufferings. This, however partial and however disconnectedly used, first appears, quite
soon after the insanity has declared itself, in the idea that
the naked beggar represents truth and reality, in contrast
with those conventions, flatteries, and corruptions of the
great world, by which Lear has so long been deceived and
will never be deceived again. . . .

. . . *King Lear* . . . is the tragedy in which evil is shown
in the greatest abundance; and the evil characters are pecu-
liarly repellent from their hard savagery, and because so
little good is mingled with their evil. The effect is therefore
more startling than elsewhere; it is even appalling. But in
substance it is the same as elsewhere. . . .

On the one hand we see a world which generates terrible
evil in profusion. Further, the beings in whom this evil appears at its strongest are able, to a certain extent, to thrive.
They are not unhappy, and they have power to spread misery and destruction around them. All this is undeniable fact.

On the other hand this evil is *merely* destructive: it founds nothing, and seems capable of existing only on foundations laid by its opposite. It is also self-destructive. . . . These . . . are undeniable facts; and, in face of them, it seems odd to describe *King Lear* as "a play in which the wicked prosper" (Johnson).

Thus the world in which evil appears seems to be at heart unfriendly to it. And this impression is confirmed by the fact that the convulsion of this world is due to evil, mainly in the worst forms here considered, partly in the milder forms which we call the errors or defects of the better characters. Good, in the widest sense, seems thus to be the principle of life and health in the world; evil, at least in these worst forms, to be a poison. The world reacts against it violently, and, in the struggle to expel it, is driven to devastate itself.

If we ask why the world should generate that which convulses and wastes it, the tragedy gives no answer, and we are trying to go beyond tragedy in seeking one. But the world, in this tragic picture, *is* convulsed by evil, and rejects it.

. . . I might almost say that the "moral" of *King Lear* is presented in the irony of this collocation:

> *Albany.* The gods defend her!
> *Enter Lear with Cordelia dead in his arms.*   (5.3.258)

The "gods," it seems, do *not* show their approval by "defending" their own from adversity or death, or by giving them power and prosperity. These, on the contrary, are worthless, or worse; it is not on them, but on the renunciation of them, that the gods throw incense. They breed lust, pride, hardness of heart, the insolence of office, cruelty, scorn, hypocrisy, contention, war, murder, self-destruction. The whole story beats this indictment of prosperity into the brain. Lear's great speeches in his madness proclaim it like the curses of Timon on life and man. But here, as in *Timon*, the poor and humble are, almost without exception, sound and sweet at heart, faithful and pitiful. And here adversity, to the blessed in spirit, is blessed. It wins fragrance from the crushed flower. It melts in aged hearts sympathies which prosperity had frozen. It purges the soul's sight by blinding that of the eyes.[3] Throughout that stupendous Third Act the good are seen growing better through suffering, and the bad worse through success. The warm castle is a room in hell, the storm-swept heath a sanctuary. The judgment of this world is a lie; its goods, which we covet, corrupt us; its ills, which break our bodies, set our souls free;

> Our means secure us, and our mere defects
> Prove our commodities.   (4.1.20–21)

Let us renounce the world, hate it, and lose it gladly. The only real thing in it is the soul, with its courage, patience, devotion. And nothing outward can touch that.

This, if we like to use the word, is Shakespeare's "pessimism" in *King Lear*. . . .

[3] "I stumbled when I saw," says Gloster.

From Prefaces to Shakespeare

THE MAIN LINES OF CONSTRUCTION

King Lear, alone among the great tragedies, adds to its plot a subplot fully developed. And it suffers somewhat under the burden. After a few preliminary lines—Shakespeare had come to prefer this to the grand opening, and in this instance they are made introductory to plot and subplot too—we have a full and almost formal statement of the play's main theme and a show of the characters that are to develop it, followed by a scene which sets out the subplot as fully. The two scenes together form a sort of double dramatic prologue: and they might, by modern custom, count as a first act, for after them falls the only clearly indicated time-division in the play. The Folio, however, adds the quarrel with Goneril before an act-pause is allowed: then—whatever its authority, but according to its usual plan—sets out four more acts, the second allotted to the parallel quarrel with Regan, the third to the climax of the main theme; the fourth we may call a picture of the wreck of both Lear and Gloucester, and in it subplot and main plot are blended, and the fifth act is given to the final and rather complex catastrophe. This division, then, has thus much dramatic validity, and a producer may legitimately choose to abide by it. On the other hand, one may contend, the play's action flows unchecked throughout (but for the one check which does not coincide with the act-division of the Folio). Still it is not to be supposed that a Jacobean audience did, or a modern audience would, sit through a per-

Reprinted from *Prefaces to Shakespeare*, I, by Harley Granville-Barker. Reprinted by permission of Princeton University Press. Copyright 1946 by Princeton University Press.

formance without pause. Yet again, it does not follow that
the Folio's act-divisions were observed as intervals in which
the audience dispersed and by which the continuity of dramatic effect was altogether broken. A producer must, I
think, exercise his own judgment. There may be something
to be said for more "breathing-spaces," but I should myself
incline to one definite interval only, to fall after Act 3. . . .

The scene in which Lear divides his kingdom is a magnificent statement of a magnificent theme. It has a proper
formality, and there is a certain megalithic grandeur about
it, Lear dominating it, that we associate with Greek
tragedy. Its probabilities are neither here nor there. A
dramatist may postulate any situation he has the means to
interpret, if he will abide by the logic of it after.[1] The producer should observe and even see stressed the scene's
characteristics; Lear's two or three passages of such an eloquence as we rather expect at a play's climax than its opening, the strength of such single lines as

> The bow is bent and drawn, make from the shaft
> (1.1.145)

with its hammering monosyllables; and the hard-bitten

> Nothing: I have sworn; I am firm   (247)

together with the loosening of the tension in changes to
rhymed couplets, and the final drop into prose by that busi-
nesslike couple, Goneril and Regan. Then follows, with a
lift into lively verse for a start, as a contrast and as the right
medium for Edmund's sanguine conceit, the development

---

[1] Later, on p. 313 of his volume, Barker says: "We must not . . . [more-
over], appraise either . . . [Gloucester's initial] simplicity or Edgar's . . .
with detachment—for by that light, no human being, it would seem, between infancy and dotage, could be so gullible. Shakespeare asks us to
allow him the fact of the deception, even as we have allowed him Lear's
partition of the kingdom. It is his starting point, the dramatist's let's pretend, which is as essential to the beginning of a play as a "let it be
granted" to a proposition of Euclid. And, within bounds, the degree of
pretence makes surprisingly little difference. It is what the assumption
will commit him to that counts."

of the Gloucester theme. Shakespeare does this at his ease, allows himself diversion and time. He has now both the plot of the ungrateful daughters and the subplot of the treacherous son under way.

But the phenomenon for which Shakespeareans learn to look has not yet occurred, that inexplicable "springing to life"—a springing, it almost seems, into a life of its own— of character or theme. Very soon it does occur; Lear's entrance, disburdened from the care of state, is its natural signal. On his throne, rightly enough, he showed formal and self-contained. Now he springs away; and now the whole play in its relation to him takes on a liveliness and variety; nor will the energy be checked or weakened, or, if checked, only that the next stroke may be intenser, till the climax is past, till his riven and exhausted nature is granted the oblivion of sleep. This is the master movement of the play, which enshrines the very soul of the play—and in the acting, as I have suggested, there should be no break allowed. To read and give full imaginative value to those fifteen hundred lines at a stretch is certainly exhausting; if they were written at one stretch of inspiration the marvel is that Shakespeare, with his Lear, did not collapse under the strain, yet the exactions of his performance he tempers with all his skill. Lear is surrounded by characters, which each in a different way take a share of the burden from him. Kent, the Fool, and Edgar as Poor Tom are a complement of dramatic strength; and the interweaving of the scenes concerning Oswald, Edmund, and Gloucester saves the actor's energy for the scenes of the rejection and the storm.

As the Lear theme expanded under his hand Shakespeare had begun, and perforce, to economize his treatment of the Gloucester-Edgar-Edmund story. Edgar himself is indeed dismissed from the second scene upon no more allowance of speech than

                    I'm sure on't, not a word.   (2.1.29)

—with which the best of actors may find it hard to make his presence felt; and at our one view of him before he had been

left negative enough. Edmund is then brought rapidly into relation with the main plot, and the blending of main plot and
subplot begins. Edgar also is drawn into Lear's orbit; and, for
the time, to the complete sacrifice of his own interests in
the play. "Poor Tom" is in effect an embodiment of Lear's
frenzy, the disguise no part of Edgar's own development.

As we have seen, while Act 3 is at the height of its argument, Shakespeare is careful to keep alive the lower-
pitched theme of Edmund's treachery, his new turn to the
betrayal of his father. He affords it two scenes, of twenty-
five lines each, wedged between the three dominant scenes
of the storm and Lear's refuge from it. They are sufficient
and no more for their own purpose; in their sordidness they
stand as valuable contrast to the spiritual exaltation of the
others. The supreme moment for Lear himself, the turning
point, therefore, of the play's main theme, is reached in the
second of the three storm-scenes, when the proud old king
kneels humbly and alone in his wretchedness to pray. This
is the argument's absolute height; and from now on we
may feel (as far as Lear is concerned) the tension relax,
through the first grim passage of his madness, slackening
still through the fantastic scene of the arraignment of the
joint-stools before that queer bench of justices, to the moment of his falling asleep and his conveyance away—his
conveyance, we find it to be, out of the main stream of the
play's action. Shakespeare then deals the dreadful blow to
Gloucester. The very violence and horror of this finds its
dramatic justification in the need to match in another
sort—since he could not hope to match it in spiritual inten-
sity—the catastrophe to Lear. And now we may imagine
him, if we please, stopping to consider where he was.
Anticlimax, after this, is all but inevitable. Let the producer
take careful note how Shakespeare sets out to avoid the
worst dangers of it.

Had the play been written upon the single subject of Lear
and his daughters, we should now be in sight of its end. But
the wealth of material Shakespeare has posited asks for use,
and his own imagination, we may suppose, is still teeming.
But by the very nature of the material (save Cordelia) left
for development the rest of the play must be pitched in a

lower key. Shakespeare marshals the action by which the
wheel of Gloucester's weakness and Edmund's treachery is
brought full circle with extraordinary skill and even more
extraordinary economy. Yet for all this, except in a fine
flash or two, the thing stays by comparison pedestrian. He is
only on the wing again when Lear and Cordelia are his concern; in the scenes of their reconciliation and of the detached tragedy of Lear's death with the dead Cordelia in his
arms, as in the still more detached and—as far as the mere
march of the action is concerned—wholly unjustifiable
scene of Lear mad and fantastically crowned with wild
flowers. We must add, though, to the inspired passages the
immediately preceding fantasy of Gloucester's imaginary
suicide, an apt offset to the realistic horror of his blinding,
and occasion for some inimitable verse. The chief fact to
face, then, is that for the rest of the play, the best will be incidental and not a necessary part of the story. The producer
therefore must give his own best attention to Albany,
Goneril, and Regan and their close-packed contests, and to
the nice means by which Edgar is shaped into a hero; and in
general must see that this purposeful disciplined necessary
stuff is given fullness and, as far as may be, spontaneity of
life in its interpretation. If he will take care of this the marvelous moments will tend to take care of him.

Shakespeare strengthens the action at once with the
fresh interest of the Edmund-Goneril-Regan intrigue, daring as it is to launch into this with the short time left him
for its development and resolving. He is, indeed, driven to
heroic compressions, to implications, effects by "business," action "off," almost to "love-making by reference
only." Goneril's first approach to Edmund (or his to her;
but we may credit the lady, I think, with the throwing of
the handkerchief) is only clearly marked out for the actors
by Regan's reference to it five scenes later, when she tells
us that at Goneril's

> late being here
> She gave strange oeilliads and most speaking looks
> To noble Edmund.   (4.5.24–26)

(Regan credits her with what, if we prefer our Shakespeare modernized, we might literally translate into "giving the glad eye.") But this silent business of the earlier scene is important and must be duly marked if the arrival of the two together and Edmund's turning back to avoid meeting Albany, the "mild husband," is to have its full effect. For the first and last of their spoken love-making, excellently characteristic as it is, consists of Goneril's

> Our wishes on the way
> May prove effects. . . .
>   This trusty servant
> Shall pass between us: ere long you are like to hear,
> If you dare venture in your own behalf,
> A mistress's command. Wear this; spare speech;
> Decline your head: this kiss, if it durst speak,
> Would stretch thy spirits up into the air.
> Conceive, and fare thee well.   (4.2.14–24)

and Edmund's ("Spare speech," indeed!)

> Yours in the ranks of death!   (25)

—all spoken in Oswald's presence too. It is, of course, not only excellent but sufficient. The regal impudency of the woman, the falsely chivalrous flourish of the man's response—pages of dialogue might not tell us more of their relations; and, of these relations, is there much more that is dramatically worth knowing? The point for the producer is that no jot of such a constricted dramatic opportunity must be missed.

For the whole working-out of this lower issue of the play the same warning stands true; an exact and unblurred value must be given to each significant thing. The interaction of circumstance and character is close-knit and complex, but it is clear. Keep it clear and it can be made effective to any audience that will listen, and is not distracted from listening. Let us underline this last phrase and now make the warning twofold. In working out a theme so full of incident and of contending characters Shakespeare allows for no distraction of attention at all, certainly not for the breaking of continuity which the constant shifting of realistically localized scenery must involve. The action, moreover, of these later scenes is exceptionally dependent upon to-ings and fro-ings. Given continuity of performance and no more insistence upon whereabouts than the action itself will indicate, the impression produced by the constant busy movement into our sight and out again of purposeful, passionate or distracted figures, is in itself of great dramatic value, and most congruous to the plot and counterplot of the play's ending. The order for Lear's and Cordelia's murder, the quarrel over Edmund's precedence, Albany's sudden self-assertion, Regan's sickness, Edgar's appearance, the fight, his discovery of himself, Goneril's discomfiture, the telling of Kent's secret, Regan's and Goneril's death, the alarm to save Lear and Cordelia—Shakespeare, by the Folio text, gets all this into less than two hundred lines, with a fair amount of rhetoric and incidental narrative besides. He needs no more, though bareness does nearly turn to banality sometimes. But unless we can be held in an unrelaxed grip we may not submit to the spell.

He has kept a technical master stroke for his ending:

Enter Lear with Cordelia in his arms.

There should be a long, still pause, while Lear passes slowly in with his burden, while they all stand respectful as of old to his majesty. We may have wondered a little that Shakespeare should be content to let Cordelia pass from the play as casually as she seems to in the earlier scene. But this is the last of her, not that. Dumb and dead, she that was never apt of speech—what fitter finish for her could there be? What fitter ending to the history of the two of them, which began for us with Lear on his throne, conscious of all eyes on him, while she shamed and angered him by her silence? The same company are here, or all but the same, and they await his pleasure. Even Regan and Goneril are here to pay him a ghastly homage. But he knows none of them—save for a blurred moment Kent whom he banished—none but Cordelia. And again he reproaches her silence; for

> Her voice was ever soft,
> Gentle and low, an excellent thing in woman.   (5.3.274–75)

Then his heart breaks. . . .

THE CHARACTERS AND THEIR INTERPLAY

LEAR

But it is upon Lear's own progress that all now centers, upon his passing from that royal defiance of the storm to the welcomed shelter of the hovel. He passes by the road of patience:

> No, I will be the pattern of all patience;
> I will say nothing,   (3.2.37–38)

of—be it noted—a thankfulness that he is at last simply

> a man
> More sinn'd against than sinning . . .   (59–60)

to the humility of

> My wits begin to turn.
> Come on, my boy. How dost, my boy? Art cold?
> I am cold myself. Where is this straw, my fellow?
> The art of our necessities is strange
> That can make vile things precious. Come, your
> hovel . . .   (67–71)

and, a little later yet, mind and body still further strained towards breaking point, to the gentle dignity, when Kent would make way for him—to the more than kingly dignity of

> Prithee, go in thyself: seek thine own ease.
> This tempest will not give me leave to ponder
> On things would hurt me more. But I'll go in:
> In, boy; go first.   (3.4.22–25)

Now comes the crowning touch of all:

> I'll pray, and then I'll sleep.   (27)

In the night's bleak exposure he kneels down, like a child at bedtime, to pray. .

> Poor naked wretches, wheresoe'er you are,
> That bide the pelting of this pitiless storm,
> How shall your houseless heads and unfed sides,
> Your loop'd and window'd raggedness, defend you
> From seasons such as these? O, I have ta'en
> Too little care of this! Take physic, pomp;
> Expose thyself to feel what wretches feel,
> That thou mayst shake the superflux to them,
> And show the heavens more just.   (28–36)

To this heaven of the spirit has he come, the Lear of un-bridled power and pride. And how many dramatists, could they have achieved so much, would have been content to leave him here! Those who like their drama rounded and trim might approve of such a finish, which would leave us a play more compassable in performance no doubt. But the wind of a harsher doctrine is blowing through Shake-speare. Criticism, as we have seen, is apt to fix upon the episode of the storm as the height of his attempt and the point of his dramatic defeat; but it is this storm of the mind here beginning upon which he expends skill and imagination most recklessly till inspiration has had its will of him; and the drama of desperate vision ensuing it is hard indeed for actors to reduce to the positive medium of their art—without reducing it to ridicule. The three coming scenes of Lear's madness show us Shakespeare's art at its boldest. They pass beyond the needs of the plot, they belong to a larger synthesis. Yet the means they employ are simple enough; of a kind of absolute simplicity, indeed.

The boldest and simplest is the provision of Poor Tom, that living instance of all rejection. Here, under our eyes, is Lear's new vision of himself.

> What! have his daughters brought him to this pass? Could'st thou save nothing? Did'st thou give them all?   (63–64)

Side by side stand the noble old man, and the naked, scarce human wretch.

> Is man no more than this? Consider him
> well. Thou ow'st the worm no silk, the beast no
> hide, the sheep no wool, the cat no perfume. Ha!
> here's three on's are sophisticated. Thou art the
> thing itself; unaccommodated man is no more
> but such a poor, bare, forked animal as thou art.
> Off, off, you lendings! Come, unbutton here.
>
> (105–111)

Here is a volume of argument epitomized as only drama can epitomize it, flashed on us by word and action combined. And into this, one might add, has Shakespeare metamorphosed the didactics of those old Moralities which were the infancy of his art.

> What, hath your grace no better company?   (145)

gasps poor Gloucester, bewailing at once the King's wrongs and his own, as he offers shelter from the storm. But Lear, calmness itself now, will only pace up and down, arm in arm with this refuse of humanity:—nor will he seek shelter without him. So they reach the outhouse, all of his own castle that Gloucester dare offer. What a group! Kent, sturdy and thrifty of words; Gloucester, tremulous; the bedraggled and exhausted Fool; and Lear, magnificently courteous and deliberate, keeping close company with his gibbering fellow-man.

They are in shelter. Lear is silent; till the Fool—himself never overfitted, we may suppose, in body or mind for the rough and tumble of the world—rallies, as if to celebrate their safety, to a semblance of his old task. Edgar, for his own safety's sake, must play Poor Tom to the life now. Kent has his eyes on his master, watching him—at what new fantastic trick? The old king is setting two joint-stools side by side; they are Regan and Goneril, and the Fool and the beggar are to pass judgment upon them.

The lunatic mummery of the trial comes near to something we might call pure drama—as one speaks of pure mathematics or pure music—since it cannot be rendered into other terms than its own. Its effect depends upon the combination of the sound and meaning of the words and the sight of it being brought to bear as a whole directly upon our sensibility. The sound of the dialogue matters almost more than its meaning. Poor Tom and the Fool chant antiphonally; Kent's deep and kindly tones tell against the higher, agonized, weakening voice of Lear. But the chief significance is in the show. Where Lear, such a short while since, sat in his majesty, there sit the Fool and the outcast, with Kent whom he banished beside them; and he, witless, musters his failing strength to beg justice upon a joint-stool. Was better justice done, the picture ironically asks, when he presided in majesty and sanity and power?

But what, as far as Lear is concerned, is to follow? You cannot continue the development of a character in terms of lunacy—in darkness, illuminated by whatever brilliant flashes of lightning. Nor can a madman well dominate a play's action. From this moment Lear no longer is a motive force; and the needs of the story—the absolute needs of the character—would be fulfilled if, from this exhausted sleep upon the poor bed in the outhouse, he only woke to find Cordelia at his side. But Shakespeare contrives another scene of madness for him, and one which lifts the play's argument to a yet rarer height. It is delayed; and the sense of redundancy is avoided partly by keeping Lear from the stage altogether for a while, a short scene interposed sufficiently reminding us of him.

His reappearance is preluded—with what consonance! —by the fantastically imaginative episode of Gloucester's fall from the cliff. There also is Edgar, the aura of Poor Tom about him still. Suddenly Lear breaks in upon them. The larger dramatic value of the ensuing scene can hardly be overrated. For in it, in this encounter between mad Lear and blind Gloucester, the sensual man robbed of his eyes, and the despot, the light of his mind put out, Shakespeare's sublimation of the two old stories is consummated. No moral is preached to us. It is presented as it was when king and beggar fraternized in the storm and beggar and Fool were set on the bench of justice, and we are primarily to feel the significance. Yet this does not lack interpretation; less explicit than when Lear, still sane, could read the lesson of the storm, clearer than was the commentary on the mock trial. It is Edgar here that sets us an example of sympathetic listening. His asides enforce it, and the last one:

> O! matter and impertinency mixed,
> Reason in madness!   (4.6.176–77)

will reproach us if we have not understood. The train of fancies fired by the first sight of Gloucester, with its tragically comic

> Ha! Goneril with a white beard!   (97)

(Goneril, disguised, pursuing him still!) asks little gloss.

> They flattered me like a dog. . . . To say 'Ay' and 'No' to everything I said! . . . When the rain came to wet me once and the wind to make me chatter; when the thunder would not peace at my bidding; there I found 'em, there I smelt 'em out. Go to, they are not men o' their words: they told me I was everything; 'tis a lie, I am not agueproof.
> (97–107)

Gloucester's dutiful

> Is't not the king?   (109)

begins to transform him in those mad eyes. And madness sees a Gloucester there that sanity had known and ignored.

> I pardon that man's life. What was thy cause?
> Adultery?
> Thou shalt not die: die for adultery! No:
> The wren goes to't, and the small gilded fly
> Does lecher in my sight.
> Let copulation thrive; for Gloucester's bastard son
> Was kinder to his father than my daughters
> Got 'tween the lawful sheets.   (111–18)

Gloucester knows better; but how protest so to the mere erratic voice? Besides which there is only the kindly stranger-peasant near. A slight unconscious turn of the sightless eyes toward him, a simple gesture—unseen—in response from Edgar, patiently biding his time, will illuminate the irony and the pathos.

Does the mad mind pass logically from this to some uncanny prevision of the ripening of new evil in Regan and Goneril? Had it in its sanity secretly surmised what lay beneath the moral surface of their lives, so ready to emerge?

> Behold yon simp'ring dame,
> Whose face between her forks presages snow,
> That minces virtue and does shake the head
> To hear of pleasure's name.
> The fitchew, nor the soilèd horse, goes to't
> With a more riotous appetite.   (120–25)

But a man—so lunatic logic runs—must free himself from the tyrannies of the flesh if he is to see the world clearly:

> Give me an ounce of civet; good apothecary, sweeten my
> imagination.   (132–33)

And then a blind man may see the truth of it, so he tells the ruined Gloucester:

> Look with thine ears: see how yond justice rails upon yond
> simple thief. Hark, in thine ear: change places, and, handy-
> dandy, which is the justice, which is the thief? Thou hast seen
> a farmer's dog bark at a beggar? . . . And the creature run
> from the cur? There thou might'st behold the great image of
> authority: a dog's obeyed in office.   (153–57, 159–61)

It is the picture of the mock trial given words. But with a difference! There is no cry now for vengeance on the wicked. For what are we that we should smite them?

> Thou rascal beadle, hold thy bloody hand!
> Why dost thou lash that whore? Strip thine own back;

That hotly lusts to use her in that kind
For which thou whip'st her. The usurer hangs the
   cozener.
Through tattered clothes small vices do appear;
Robes and furred gowns hide all. Plate sin with gold,
And the strong lance of justice hurtless breaks;
Arm it in rags, a pigmy's straw doth pierce it.   (162–69)

<u>Shakespeare has led Lear</u> to compassion for sin as well
<u>as suffering, has led him mad to where he could not hope</u>
<u>to lead him sane</u>—to where sound common sense will
hardly let us follow him:

> None does offend, none, I say, none.   (170)

To a deep compassion for mankind itself.

> I know thee well enough; thy name is Gloucester:
> Thou must be patient; we came crying hither:
> Thou know'st, the first time that we smell the air
> We wawl and cry. I will preach to thee: mark. . . .
> When we are born, we cry that we are come
> To this great stage of fools.   (179–82, 184–85)

This afterpart of Lear's madness may be redundant,
then, to the strict action of the play, but to its larger issues
it is most germane. It is perhaps no part of the play that
Shakespeare set out to write. The play that he found himself writing would be how much the poorer without it!

The simple perfection of the scene that restores Lear to
Cordelia one can leave unsullied by comment. What need
of any? Let the producer only note that there is reason in
the Folio's stage direction:

> *Enter Lear in a chair carried by servants.*

For when he comes to himself it is to find that he is royally
attired and as if seated on his throne again. It is from this
throne that he totters to kneel at Cordelia's feet. Note, too,
the pain of his response to Kent's

> In your own kingdom, sir.
> Do not abuse me.   (4.7.76–77)

Finally, Lear must pass from the scene with all the ceremony due to royalty; not mothered—please!—by Cordelia.

Cordelia found again and again lost, what is left for Lear but to die? But for her loss, however, his own death might seem to us an arbitrary stroke; since the old Lear, we may say, is already dead. Shakespeare, moreover, has transported him beyond all worldly issues. This is, perhaps, why the action of the battle which will seemingly defeat his fortunes is minimized. What does defeat matter to him—or even victory? It is certainly the key to the meaning of the scene which follows. Cordelia, who would "outfrown false fortune's frown," is ready to face her sisters and to shame them—were there a chance of it!—with the sight of her father's wrongs. But Lear himself has no interest in anything of the sort.

> No, no, no, no! Come, let's away to prison:
> We two alone will sing like birds i' the cage:
> When thou dost ask me blessing, I'll kneel down,
> And ask of thee forgiveness: so we'll live,
> And pray, and sing, and tell old tales, and laugh
> At gilded butterflies, and hear poor rogues
> Talk of court news.   (5.3.8–14)

He has passed beyond care for revenge or success, beyond even the questioning of rights and wrongs. Better indeed to be oppressed, if so you can be safe from contention. Prison will bring him freedom.

> Upon such sacrifices, my Cordelia,
> The gods themselves throw incense. Have I caught
>   thee?
> He that parts us shall bring a brand from heaven,
> And fire us hence like foxes. Wipe thine eyes;
> The good years shall devour them, flesh and fell,
> Ere they shall make us weep. We'll see 'em starved
>   first.   (20–25)

Lear's death, upon one ground or another, is artistically inevitable. Try to imagine his survival; no further argument will be needed. The death of Cordelia has been condemned as a wanton outrage upon our feelings and so as an aesthetic blot upon the play. But the dramatic mind that was working to the tune of

> As flies to wanton boys, are we to th' gods,
> They kill us for their sport,   (4.1.36–37)

was not likely to be swayed by sentiment. The tragic truth about life, to the Shakespeare that wrote *King Lear*, included its capricious cruelty. And what meeter sacrifice to this than Cordelia? Besides, as we have seen, he must provide this new Lear with a tragic determinant, since "the great rage . . . is kill'd in him," which precipitated catastrophe for the old Lear. And what but Cordelia's loss would suffice?

We have already set Lear's last scene in comparison with his first; it will be worth while to note a little more particularly the likeness and the difference. The same commanding figure; he bears the body of Cordelia as lightly as ever he carried robe, crown and scepter before. All he had undergone has not so bated his colossal strength but that he could kill her murderer with his bare hands.

> I kill'd the slave that was a-hanging thee.
> 'Tis true, my lords, he did,   (5.3.276–77)

says the officer in answer to their amazed looks. Albany, Edgar, Kent and the rest stand silent and intent around 'iim; Regan and Goneril are there, silent too. He stands, with the limp body close clasped, glaring blankly at them for a moment. When speech is torn from him, in place of the old kingly rhetoric we have only the horrible, half human

> Howl, howl, howl, howl!   (259)

Who these are, for all their dignity and martial splendor, for all the respect they show him, he neither knows nor cares. They are men of stone and murderous traitors; though, after a little, through the mist of his suffering, comes a word for Kent. All his world, of power and passion and will, and the wider world of thought over which his mind in its ecstasy had ranged, is narrowed now to Cordelia; and she is dead in his arms.

Here is the clue to the scene; this terrible concentration upon the dead, and upon the unconquerable fact of death. This thing was Cordelia; she was alive, she is dead. Here is human tragedy brought to its simplest terms, fit ending to a tragic play that has seemed to out-leap human experience. From power of intellect and will, from the imaginative sweep of madness, Shakespeare brings Lear to this; to no moralizing nor high thoughts, but just to

> She's gone for ever.
> I know when one is dead and when one lives;
> She's dead as earth. Lend me a looking-glass;
> If that her breath will mist or stain the stone,
> Why, then she lives.   (261–65)

Lacking a glass, he catches at a floating feather. That stirs on her lips; a last mockery. Kent kneels by him to share his grief. Then to the bystanders comes the news of Edmund's death; the business of life goes forward, as it will, and draws attention from him for a moment. But what does he heed? When they turn back to him he has her broken body in his arms again.

MAYNARD MACK

From King Lear in Our Time

I turn now to a closer scrutiny of the play. In the remarks that follow I shall address myself primarily to three topics, which I believe to be both interesting in themselves and well suited to bring before us other qualities of this tragedy which stir the twentieth-century imagination. The first topic is the externality of Shakespeare's treatment of action in *King Lear*; the second is the profoundly social orientation of the world in which he has placed this action; and the third is what I take to be the play's dominant tragic theme, summed up best in Lear's words to Gloucester in Dover fields: "We came crying hither."

As we watch it in the theatre, the action of *King Lear* comes to us first of all as an experience of violence and pain. No other Shakespearean tragedy, not even *Titus*, contains more levels of raw ferocity, physical as well as moral. In the action, the exquisite cruelties of Goneril and Regan to their father are capped by Gloucester's blinding onstage, and this in turn by the wanton indignity of Cordelia's murder. In the language, as Miss Caroline Spurgeon has pointed out, allusions to violence multiply and accumulate into a pervasive image as of "a human body in anguished movement—tugged, wrenched, beaten, pierced, stung, scourged, dislocated, flayed, gashed, scalded, tortured, and finally broken on the rack."[1]

Miss Spurgeon's comment tends to formulate the play

From *King Lear in Our Time,* by Maynard Mack, © 1965 The Regents of the University of California. Used by permission of the University of California Press, Berkeley, California.
[1]*Shakespeare's Iterative Imagery* (1935), p. 342.

in terms of passiveness and suffering. But the whole truth
is not seen unless it is formulated also in terms of agency
and aggression. If the *Lear* world is exceptionally anguished, it is chiefly because it is exceptionally contentious. Tempers in *King Lear* heat so fast that some
critics are content to see in it simply a tragedy of wrath.
Unquestionably, it does contain a remarkable number of
remarkably passionate collisions. Lear facing Cordelia,
and Kent facing Lear, in the opening scene; Lear con-
fronting Goneril at her house with his terrifying curse;
Kent tangling with Oswald outside Gloucester's castle;
Cornwall run through by his own servant, who warns Regan that if she had a beard he'd "shake it on this quarrel";
Edgar and Edmund simulating a scuffle in the first act, and
later, in the last act, hurling charge and countercharge
in the scene of their duel; the old king himself defying the
storm: these are only the more vivid instances of a pattern
of pugnacity which pervades this tragedy from beginning
to end, shrilling the voices that come to us from the stage
and coloring their language even in the tenderest scenes.
The pattern gives rise to at least one locution which in
frequency of occurrence is peculiar to *King Lear*—
to "outface the winds and persecutions of the sky," to
"outscorn the to-and-fro contending wind and rain," to
"outjest his heart-struck injuries," to "outfrown false Fortune's frown." And it appears as a motif even in that pitiful scene at Dover, where the old king, at first alone,
throws down his glove before an imaginary opponent—
"There's my gauntlet, I'll prove it on a giant"—and, afterward, when the blind Gloucester enters, defies him, too:
"No, do thy worst, blind Cupid, I'll not love." So powerful is this vein of belligerence in the linguistic texture of
the play that pity itself is made, in Cordelia's words,
something that her father's white hair must "challenge."
Even "had you not been their father," she says in an apostrophe to the sleeping king, referring to the suffering he
has been caused by his other daughters, "these white
flakes did challenge pity of them."

It goes without saying that in a world of such contentiousness most of the *dramatis personae* will be outra-

geously self-assured. The contrast with the situation in *Hamlet*, in this respect, is striking and instructive. There, as I have argued in another place, the prevailing mood tends to be interrogative.[2] Doubt is real in *Hamlet*, and omnipresent. Minds, even villainous minds, are inquiet and uncertain. Action does not come readily to anyone except Laertes and Fortinbras, who are themselves easily deflected by the stratagems of the king, and there is accordingly much emphasis on the fragility of the human will. All this is changed in *King Lear*. Its mood, I would suggest (if it may be caught in a single word at all), is imperative. The play asks questions, to be sure, as *Hamlet* does, and far more painful questions because they are so like a child's, so simple and unmediated by the compromises to which much experience usually impels us: "Is man no more than this?" "Is there any cause in nature that makes these hard hearts?" "Why should a dog, a horse, a rat have life And thou no breath at all?" Such questionings in *King Lear* stick deep, like Macbeth's fears in Banquo.

Yet it is not, I think, the play's questions that establish its distinctive coloring onstage. (Some of its questions we shall return to later.) It is rather its commands, its invocations and appeals that have the quality of commands, its flat-footed defiances and refusals: "Come not between the dragon and his wrath." "You nimble lightnings, dart your blinding flames into her scornful eyes!" "Blow, winds, and crack your cheeks! rage! blow!" "Thou shalt not die; die for adultery, no!" "A plague upon you, murderers, traitors, all! I might have sav'd her . . ." In the psychological climate that forms round a protagonist like this, there is little room for doubt, as we may see from both Lear's and Goneril's scorn of Albany. No villain's mind is inquiet. Action comes as naturally as breathing and twice as quick. And, what is particularly unlike the situation in the earlier tragedies, the hero's destiny is self-made. Lear does not inherit his predicament like Hamlet; he is not duped by an antagonist like Othello. He walks into disaster head on.

This difference is of the first importance. *King Lear*, to

follow R. W. Chambers in applying Keats's memorable
phrase, is a vale of soul-making,[3] where to all appearances
the will is agonizingly free. As if to force the point on our
attention, almost every character in the play, including
such humble figures as Cornwall's servant and the old
tenant who befriends Gloucester, is impelled soon or late
to take some sort of stand—to show, in Oswald's words,
"what party I do follow." One cannot but be struck by
how much positioning and repositioning of this kind the
play contains. Lear at first takes up his position with
Goneril and Regan, France and Kent take theirs with
Cordelia, Albany takes his with Goneril, and Gloucester
(back at his own house), with Cornwall and Regan. But
then all reposition. Kent elects to come back as his master's humblest servant. The Fool elects to stay with the
great wheel, even though it runs downhill. Lear elects
to become a comrade of the wolf and owl rather than return to his elder daughters. Gloucester likewise has second thoughts and comes to Lear's rescue, gaining his
sight though he loses his eyes. Albany, too, has second
thoughts, and lives, he says, only to revenge those eyes. In
the actions of the old king himself, the taking of yet a
third position is possibly implied. For after the battle,
when Cordelia asks, "Shall we not see these daughters
and these sisters?" Lear replies (with the vehemence characteristic of him even in defeat), "No, no, no, no!" and
goes on to build, in his famous following lines, that world
entirely free of pugnacity and contentiousness in which he
and Cordelia will dwell: "We two alone will sing like
birds i' th' cage."

Movements of the will, then, have a featured place in
King Lear. But what is more characteristic of the play than
their number is the fact that no one of them is ever exhibited to us in its inward origins or evolution. Instead of
scenes recording the genesis or gestation of an action—
scenes of introspection or persuasion or temptation like
those which occupy the heart of the drama in *Hamlet*,
Othello, and *Macbeth*—*King Lear* offers us the moment at

---

[3] *King Lear* (W. P. Ker Memorial Lecture), p. 48.

which will converts into its outward expressions of action and consequence; and this fact, I suspect, helps account for the special kind of painfulness that the play always communicates to its audiences. In *King Lear* we are not permitted to experience violence as an externalization of a psychological drama which has priority in both time and significance, and which therefore partly palliates the violence when it comes. This is how we do experience, I think, Hamlet's vindictiveness to his mother, Macbeth's massacres, Othello's murder: the act in the outer world is relieved of at least part of its savagery by our understanding of the inner act behind it. The violences in *King Lear* are thrust upon us quite otherwise—with the shock that comes from evil which has nowhere been inwardly accounted for, and which, from what looks like a studiedly uninward point of view on the playwright's part, must remain unaccountable, to characters and audience alike: "Is there any cause in nature that makes these hard hearts?"

The relatively slight attention given in *King Lear* to the psychological processes that ordinarily precede and determine human action suggests that here we are meant to look for meaning in a different quarter from that in which we find it in the earlier tragedies. In *Hamlet*, Shakespeare had explored action in its aspect of dilemma. Whether or not we accept the traditional notion that Hamlet is a man who cannot make up his mind, his problem is clearly conditioned by the unsatisfactory nature of the alternatives he faces. Any action involves him in a kind of guilt, the more so because he feels an already existing corruption in himself and in his surroundings which contaminates all action at the source. "Virtue cannot so inoculate our old stock but we shall relish of it." Hence the focus of the play is on those processes of consciousness that can explain and justify suspension of the will. In *Othello*, by contrast, Shakespeare seems to be exploring action in its aspect of error. Othello faces two ways of understanding love: Iago's and Desdemona's—which is almost to say, in the play's terms, two systems of valuing and two ways of being—but we are left in no doubt that one of the ways is wrong. Even if we take Iago and Desdemona, as some critics do, to be dramatic emblems of conflicting aspects in Othello's own nature, the play remains a tragedy of error, not a tragedy of dilemma. "The pity of it, Iago" is that Othello makes the wrong choice when the right one is open to him and keeps clamoring to be known for what it is even to the very moment of the murder. The playwright's focus in this play is therefore on the corruptions of mind by which a man may be led into error, and he surrounds Iago and Desdemona with such overtones of damnation and salvation as ultimately must attend any genuine option between evil and good.

King Lear, as I see it, confronts the perplexity and mystery of human action at a later point. Choice remains in the forefront of the argument, but its psychic antecedents have been so effectively shrunk down in this primitivized world that action seems to spring directly out of the bedrock of personality. We feel sure no imaginable psychological process could make Kent other than loyal, Goneril other then cruel, Edgar other than "a brother noble." Such characters, as we saw earlier, are qualities as well as persons: their acts have consequences but little history. The meaning of action here, therefore, appears to lie rather in effects than in antecedents, and particularly in its capacity, as with Lear's in the opening scene, to generate energies that will hurl themselves in unforeseen and unforeseeable reverberations of disorder from end to end of the world.

The elements of that opening scene are worth pausing over, because they seem to have been selected to bring before us precisely such an impression of unpredictable effects lying coiled and waiting in an apparently innocuous posture of affairs. The atmosphere of the first episode in the scene, as many a commentator has remarked, is casual, urbane, even relaxed. In the amenities exchanged by Kent and Gloucester, Shakespeare allows no hint to penetrate of Gloucester's later agitation about "these late eclipses," or about the folly of a king's abdicating his responsibilities and dividing up his power. We are momentarily lulled into a security that is not immediately broken even when the court assembles and Lear informs us that he will shake off

all business and "unburthen'd crawl toward death." I suspect we are invited to sense, as Lear speaks, that this is a
kingdom too deeply swaddled in forms of all kinds—too
comfortable and secure in its "robes and furr'd gowns"; in
its rituals of authority and deference (of which we have just
heard and witnessed samples as Gloucester is dispatched
offstage, the map demanded, and a "fast intent" and "constant will" thrust on our notice by the king's imperious personality); and in its childish charades, like the one about to
be enacted when the daughters speak. Possibly we are invited to sense, too, that this is in some sort an emblematic
kingdom—almost a paradigm of hierarchy and rule, as indeed the scene before us seems to be suggesting, with its
wide display of ranks in both family and state. Yet perhaps
too schematized, too regular—a place where complex re-
alities have been too much reduced to formulas, as they are
on a map: as they are on that visible map, for instance, on
which Lear three times lays his finger in this scene ("as if
he were marking the land itself," says Granville-Barker),
while he describes with an obvious pride its tidy catalogue
of "shadowy forests" and "champains," "plenteous rivers
and wide-skirted meads." Can it be that here, as on that
map, is a realm where everything is presumed to have been
charted, where all boundaries are believed known, including those of nature and human nature; but where no account has been taken of the heath which lies in all countries
and in all men and women just beyond the boundaries they
think they know?

However this may be, into this emblematic, almost dream-
like situation erupts the mysterious thrust of psychic energy
that we call a choice, an act; and the waiting coil of consequences leaps into threatening life, bringing with it, as
every act considered absolutely must, the inscrutable where
we had supposed all was clear, the unexpected though we
thought we had envisaged all contingencies and could never
be surprised. Perhaps it is to help us see this that the consequences in the play are made so spectacular. The first consequence is Lear's totally unlooked-for redistribution of his
kingdom into two parts instead of three, and his rejection of
Cordelia. The second is his totally unlooked-for banishment

of his most trusted friend and counselor. The third is the
equally unlooked-for rescue of his now beggared child to
be the Queen of France; and what the unlooked-for fourth
and fifth will be, we already guess from the agreement between Goneril and Regan, as the scene ends, that something
must be done, "and i' th' heat." Thereafter the play seems to
illustrate, with an almost diagrammatic relentlessness and
thoroughness, the unforeseen potentials that lie waiting to be
hatched from a single choice and act: nakedness issues out of
opulence, madness out of sanity and reason out of madness,
blindness out of seeing and insight out of blindness, salvation out of ruin. The pattern of the unexpected is so completely worked out, in fact, that, as we noticed in the
preceding chapter, it appears to embrace even such minor
devices of the plot as the fact that Edmund, his fortune made
by two letters, is undone by a third.

Meantime, as we look back over the first scene, we may
wonder whether the gist of the whole matter has not been
placed before us, in the play's own emblematic terms, by
Gloucester, Kent, and Edmund in that brief conversation
with which the tragedy begins. This conversation touches
on two actions, we now observe, each loaded with menac-
ing possibilities, but treated with a casualness at this point
that resembles Lear's in opening his trial of love. The first
action alluded to is the old king's action in dividing his
kingdom, the dire effects of which we are almost instantly
to see. The other action is Gloucester's action in begetting
a bastard son, and the dire effects of this will also speedily
be known. What is particularly striking, however, is that in
the latter instance the principal effect is already on the
stage before us, though its nature is undisclosed, in the person of the bastard son himself. Edmund, like other "consequences," looks tolerable enough till revealed in full: "I
cannot wish the fault undone, the issue of it being so
proper," says Kent, meaning by proper "handsome"; yet
there is a further dimension of meaning in the word that we
will only later understand, when Edgar relates the darkness
of Edmund to the darkness wherein he was got and the
darkness he has brought to his father's eyes. Like other
consequences, too, Edmund looks to be predictable and

manageable—in advance. "He hath been out nine years," says Gloucester, who has never had any trouble holding consequences at arm's length before, "and away he shall again." Had Shakespeare reflected on the problem consciously—and it would be rash, I think, to be entirely sure he did not—he could hardly have chosen a more vivid way of giving dramatic substance to the unpredictable relationships of act and consequence than by this confrontation of a father with his unknown natural son—or to the idea of consequences come home to roost, than by this quiet youthful figure, studying "deserving" as he prophetically calls it, while he waits upon his elders.

In *King Lear* then, I believe it is fair to say, the inscrutability of the energies that the human will has power to release is one of Shakespeare's paramount interests. By the inevitable laws of drama, this power receives a degree of emphasis in all his plays, especially the tragedies. The difference in *King Lear* is that it is assigned the whole canvas. The crucial option, which elsewhere comes toward the middle of the plot, is here presented at the very outset. Once taken, everything that happens after is made to seem, in some sense, to have been set in motion by it, not excluding Gloucester's recapitulation of it in the subplot. Significantly, too, the act that creates the crisis, the act on which Shakespeare focuses our dramatic attention, is not (like Lear's abdication) one which could have been expected to germinate into such a harvest of disaster. The old king's longing for public testimony of affection seems in itself a harmless folly: it is not an outrage, not a crime, only a foolish whim. No more could Cordelia's death have been expected to follow from her truthfulness or Gloucester's salvation to be encompassed by a son whom he disowns and seeks to kill.

All this, one is driven to conclude, is part of Shakespeare's point. In the action he creates for Lear, the act of choice is cut loose not simply from the ties that normally bind it to prior psychic causes, but from the ties that usually limit its workings to commensurate effects. In this respect the bent of the play is mythic: it abandons verisimilitude to find out truth, like the story of Oedipus;

or like the *Rime of the Ancient Mariner*, with which, in fact, it has interesting affinities. Both works are intensely emblematic. Both treat of crime and punishment and reconciliation in poetic, not realistic, terms. In both the fall is sudden and unaccountable, the penalty enormous and patently exemplary. The willful act of the mariner in shooting down the albatross has a nightmarish inscrutability like Lear's angry rejection of the daughter he loves best; springs from a similar upsurge of egoistic willfulness; hurls itself against what was until that moment a natural "bond," and shatters the universe. Nor do the analogies end with this. When the mariner shoots the albatross, the dark forces inside him that prompted his deed project themselves and become the landscape, so to speak, in which he suffers his own nature: it is his own alienation, his own waste land of terror and sterility that he meets. Something similar takes place in Shakespeare's play. Lear, too, as we saw earlier, suffers his own nature, encounters his own heath, his own storm, his own nakedness and defenselessness, and by this experience, like the mariner, is made another man.

LINDA BAMBER

The Woman Reader in *King Lear*

When adults show children how to read a map, they say, "Here is *your* street (or state or nation)," and the habit of finding ourselves on the map persists when we are grown up. When travelers return with pictures of Cairo or Barcelona, they say, "That's the hotel we stayed in, there," as if it explained the picture. If a work of fiction is a map of its own world, the first question we ask of it is, "Where am *I* in here?" or "Who is like me?" This question is unsophisticated but important, because it shapes our most basic responses. Only when we have answered it do we know whom to love and hate and what to hope for.

For women the problem of locating ourselves in literature is complicated by the fact that so much of the literature of the past is written by men. Who is "like me" when the character offered as a version of the self is a man? When I began to read the great literature of the past I never thought to ask this question. My (excellent) teachers were almost all men, and I read stories and poems and plays by men without noticing the difference. In the end you could say I imprinted to a different species. I thought I was a man, just as Tarzan thought he was an ape. Of course, I also knew I wasn't. But my responses to literature were confused by an identity problem generated for me by literature itself.

In *King Lear*, the character who is "like me" is of course King Lear. Lear is passionate, articulate, capable of growth, capable of catastrophic error, important to himself and to everyone else in the play. He claims he is "more sinned against than sinning," and that's how I feel, too. But King Lear is a man while I am a woman. When I identify with him, an important part of my identity, my femininity, is homeless. If the *King Lear* world is organized around a man, what is the status of women in it? Are women important in this world, or are they (fictionally) second-class citizens? If I can find satisfactory answers to these questions I am free to identify with Lear as much as I can; otherwise, identifying with Lear means denigrating a part of myself.

The best solution would be finding an alternative, female home in the play. Is there a woman character who represents us as well as Lear himself? If so, we could breathe a sigh of relief and simply graph the play as an ellipse (which has two focal points) instead of a circle. But authors—women as well as men—tend to represent "us" much more fully in characters of their own sex than in characters of the opposite sex, and Shakespeare is no exception. In *King Lear* the women are either more or less than human. Goneril and Regan are too bad to live, much less to represent us, and Cordelia is perfect. The evil sisters present no temptations to the woman reader, but it is worth dealing in some detail with the problems of identifying with perfection.

Cordelia is never selfish or aggressive; when she hurts her father it is only because she is separate from him, not because of a failure of love:

> Good my lord,
> You have begot me, bred me, loved me. I
> Return those duties back as are right fit,
> Obey you, love you and most honor you.
> Why have my sisters husbands, if they say
> They love you all? Haply, when I shall wed,
> That lord whose hand must take my plight shall carry
> Half my love with him, half my care and duty.
> Sure I shall never marry like my sisters,
> To love my father all.   (1.1.97–106)

This is the only moment in the play in which Cordelia asserts herself, and even here she is not so much asserting herself as mediating between the claims of her father and

the claims of her future husband. Her characteristic gestures are of selfless love. No matter how well I think of myself, I would never go so far as to say that she is "like me."

Cordelia's perfection is maintained in this play by her
silence. First she refuses to speak the self-serving language
of flattery; next she listens in silence when her father dis-
inherits her. "The barbarous Scythian," he tells her,

> Or he that makes his generation messes
> To gorge his appetite, shall to my bosom
> Be as well neighbored, pitied, and relieved,
> As thou my sometime daughter.   (118–22)

The next voice to speak is not Cordelia's but Kent's. It is
Kent who protests the injustice and craziness of Lear's behavior, Kent who is angry and blunt in Cordelia's defense:

>   Be Kent unmannerly
> When Lear is mad. What wouldst thou do, old man?
> Think'st thou that duty shall have dread to speak
> When power to flattery bows? To plainness honor's bound
> When majesty falls to folly.   (147–51)

Why is it Kent who speaks aggressively to Lear rather
than Cordelia? Possibly because in the world of *King
Lear* an angry woman risks losing our sympathy, even
when anger is so clearly required that another character
must be enlisted to supply it. Nor is it only anger that
Cordelia notably fails to express. Later in the play, when
she receives the news of Lear's misery, she feels a great
deal but says very little. The whole description of her behavior turns Cordelia into a kind of icon of grief, precious
as a jewel but inarticulate. She controls her emotions,
reigns "queen / Over her passion," cries a few silent tears,
which part from her eyes "as pearls from diamonds."
"Made she no verbal question?" Kent asks the Gentleman,
who replies,

> Faith, once or twice she heaved the name of "father"
> Pantingly forth, as if it pressed her heart;

Cried, "Sisters! Sisters! Shame of ladies! Sisters!
Kent! Father! Sisters What, i' th' storm? i' th' night?
Let pity not be believed" There she shook
The holy water from her heavenly eyes,
And clamor moistened: then away she started
To deal with grief alone.   (4.3.26–33)

Cordelia's inarticulateness, the fewness and brokenness
of her words at times of great emotion, is her glory. Lear's
glory, by contrast, is to express his feelings fully, variously, and without restraint. The price of Cordelia's perfection seems to be her renunciation of language, and in
the medium of poetic drama, this is a heavy price to pay.
Cordelia may be as valuable, even as lovable as Lear, but
there is simply not enough of her to balance the enormous
pull of our sympathy to him. She doesn't represent me
because often she isn't even there.

There is no single woman character, then, who represents me in the play. But if we group the three sisters together and call them something like "the feminine" or "the
Other" (as opposed to Lear, who represents "the Self"), we
can find a kind of rough sexual justice in *King Lear*.
Women are important here not as I am important to myself
but as the outside world is important to me. They are like
the rock on which the hero is broken and remade; they are
the thing outside the Self that cannot be controlled and cannot be renounced. "The Other" is equal to the tragic hero as
the second term in a dialectic is equal to the first. Women
play the role of "the Other" not only in *King Lear* but in all
Shakespeare's plays. In all four genres—comedy, history,
tragedy, and romance—the nature of the feminine reflects
the nature of the world outside the Self. Before returning to
King Lear it is worth pausing to consider how this works.

In the comedies, the world outside us is manifestly reli-
able and orderly, a source of pleasure rather than a threat—
and so is the nature of the feminine. In *As They Liked It*,
Alfred Harbage has made a statistical survey of Shakespeare's characters, dividing them by groups into good and
bad. The highest percentage of good characters in any
group is the percentage of good women in the comedies:

96 percent good, 4 percent bad. The possibility of betrayal in this world is very slight. The women will not betray the men, the comic world will not betray its central characters, the playwright will not betray our expectations of a happy ending. The world of Shakespearean comedy is fundamentally safe and its women are fundamentally good. We are free in this world to play, to court danger in sport. Sometimes it seems as though the games have gotten out of hand: Oberon's cruel love games in *A Midsummer Night's Dream*, Shylock's murderous bond in *The Merchant of Venice*, and Orsino's threat to Cesario's life in *Twelfth Night*—all these give us some bad moments. But an invisible hand unravels everything and we enjoy the thrill of danger without its deadly consequences. Similarly, the women problem is raised only to be dismissed. We are titillated with reminders that women might be unfaithful; the cuckoldry jokes of *Much Ado About Nothing* and Portia's ring trick in *The Merchant of Venice* remind us of what could happen. But it never does. The women are as transparently faithful as the plot is transparently comic. We are always on our way to the happy ending, to marriage, to the love of good women.

In the romances, the world is a much more serious place—not, as in the tragedies, because it may betray us—but because it may be lost altogether. The protagonist of a Shakespearean romance loses his whole world; Pericles, Leontes, and Prospero live for a time in the absence of everything they care for. But although the world may be lost, it may also be found; and of course the most obvious property of the feminine in this genre is also its tendency to come and go. It is notable that in *The Winter's Tale* the two male characters who disappear from Sicilia, Mamillus and Antigonous, disappear for good. It is the women characters, Perdita and Hermione, who return. In Shakespearean romance, the feminine is infinitely valuable, capable of being utterly lost but capable also of miraculous self-renewal. Again, the nature of the feminine is congruent with the nature of the world outside the Self.

The feminine in the history plays is more difficult to characterize briefly than it is in the comedies and ro-

mances; perhaps it is best described as unproblematic. The
feminine Other may be unambiguously hated, as Joan is in
1 Henry VI; cheerfully courted, as Katherine is in *Henry
V*; or cleverly used to further a career, as Queen Elizabeth
is in *Richard III*. But whatever role she plays, she never
offers any metaphysical complications, never raises issues
of identity for the masculine Self. Emotions toward
women are unconfused; the feminine Other does not call
the masculine Self into question. Similarly, the world outside the Self in the histories is simple compared to the
world of the tragedies. Because it is almost wholly a political world, it, too, offers few metaphysical or psychological problems. The world divides up smartly into friends
and enemies; everyone is playing the same game, however
nastily. In tragedy, by contrast, the world becomes
murkier, the masculine-historical enterprise loses its cen-
trality, friends and enemies become hard to distinguish
from each other, and the feminine becomes a problem.

In Shakespearean tragedy, the world outside the Self
seems to thicken. It becomes hard to make out. It is not
necessarily evil, although it *may* be evil; in any case, it
causes so much suffering that it will at certain moments at
least *appear* evil. It is a world that is separate from us who
inhabit it; it will not yield to our desires and fantasies no
matter how desperately we need it to do so. This means
that in tragedy, recognition—*anagnorisis*, the banishing of
ignorance—is a major goal. We question the tragic universe to discover its laws, since they are what we must live
by. The worlds of comedy and romance, by contrast, are
shaped by our hearts' desires; and in history, we are busily
remaking the world to suit ourselves.

The feminine in the tragedies can be similarly defined in
terms of evil, obduracy, and the problem of *anagnorisis*.
First of all, women in the tragedies constitute the *single*
group in which Harbage finds more bad than good: 58 percent bad and only 42 percent good. Like the world outside
the Self, the feminine causes suffering, appears evil, and
may actually *be* evil. And like the world outside the Self,
women in the tragedies are notably separate from us, governed by their own laws whether their natures are good or

evil. The hero can only recognize them for what they are or fail to do so. The effort to control them is useless; neither the feminine Other nor the world outside the Self is within our power in Shakespeare's tragedy.

The idea of a congruence between women and the world can be taken even further. In *King Lear*, as in *Othello*, the world outside the hero is starkly divided between good and evil, and so are the principal women characters—Goneril, Regan, Cordelia, and Desdemona. In *Hamlet* and *Antony and Cleopatra*, by contrast, the outside world is a mixture of good and bad; it is hard to tell manly strength from mindless ambition, and restraint may be confused with weakness. The women in these two plays are similarly a confusing mixture of good and evil, and finally may be neither. We never know the extent of Gertrude's guilt, or whether Cleopatra, if offered better terms, would have sold out to Caesar. But we know all along that Desdemona and Cordelia are perfectly good and Goneril and Regan vile beasts. In *Lear* and *Othello*, kindness and constancy are to be found in their purest forms, as are their opposites, cruelty and malice.

It is time to return to my original question. Am I content with the role played in *King Lear* by the wandering portion of my identity, the part I cannot invest in King Lear? On the whole, I think I should be. For one thing, I am flattered to think that I may be capable of such thrilling modulations between good and evil as exist in the world of *King Lear*. It makes me interesting to myself. Identifying with the intensely problematic world outside the hero gives me another way of participating in the major questions of the play, questions about the violent extremes we find within ourselves and in our experience. More importantly, I am content to identify with the world outside the hero because the dialectic between King Lear and the outside world is what creates the satisfactions of tragedy. It is when Lear cannot get what he wants from the outside world that *he* becomes interesting. We do not really want the tragic world to yield to the hero's desires; we want to see what happens to him when his suffering cracks him open, and he goes out on the heath to become something new. There, thanks to the resistance offered by the tragic world, we are in the presence of exciting possibilities. The hero may triumph over his losses; naked, he may be more splendid than he appeared when he was clothed. Or, like Coriolanus, the hero of one of the Roman plays, he may collapse. Both the risk and the possibility of Shakespearean tragedy depend on the Otherness of the tragic universe to the masculine Self. In identifying with the world outside the hero, I am identifying with something as powerful in creating the drama as the hero himself.

What is the nature of the resistance offered by the feminine Other in *King Lear*? On the one hand, it is a matter of malice: Goneril and Regan are selfish beasts who wish their father ill. On the other hand, it is a matter of pure separateness. Cordelia, as we have seen, is guilty of nothing but being a separate person from her father, of having her own social role to play. In many ways the resistance Cordelia offers is more interesting. Cordelia simply resists Lear's claim to be the sun around which everything revolves. The mere presence of another inviolable person is enough to shatter Lear's identity. The tragic hero wants to be the only star in the sky.

The feminine Other creates drama by resisting the hero, but also by being endlessly desirable to him. The desire of the hero for women and the world keeps him both alive and vulnerable; it keeps open the possibility of both suffering and fulfillment. A comparison between Lear and Gloucester will illustrate the point. Gloucester, who has sons instead of daughters, loses his capacity for desire and with it both his vulnerability to his experience and his chance of happiness. He tries to kill himself, is rescued by Edgar, feels suicidal again when he witnesses Lear's madness, urges Oswald to kill him, and finally is parked by Edgar in "the shadow of this tree" (5.2.1). "A man may rot even here" (8), he tells Edgar when Edgar returns. Since Edgar and Gloucester are in the middle of a battle there is no time for an elaborate response. "Men must endure / Their going hence, even as their coming hither," Edgar tells his father briefly. "Ripeness is all. Come on." Gloucester gets up and plods on. "And that's

true, too," he says. (9–11) Nothing makes much differ-
ence to him anymore. Lear, by contrast, dies upon a wish.
"Do you see this?" he asks urgently, bent over the dead
Cordelia's head. "Look on her," he cries, tortured by hope.
"Look, her lips, / Look there, look there." (5.3.312–13)
Lear's feelings stay alive to the end of the play.

As many people have noticed, there is a sexual compo-
nent to Lear's desire for his daughters. When Lear is hurt
by Goneril and Regan, he denounces them as if he were
their lover, not their father:

> The fitchew, nor the soilèd horse, goes to 't
> With a more riotous appetite.
> Down from the waist they are Centaurs,
> Though women all above:
> But to the girdle do the gods inherit,
> Beneath is all the fiend's.
> There's hell, there's darkness, there is the sulphurous pit,
> Burning, scalding, stench, consumption; fie, fie, fie!
>
> (4.6.124–131)

Why does Lear blast women for their sexual appetites
rather than for their cruelty? Goneril and Regan are in fact
unfaithful wives, but Lear doesn't know that, and anyway
they haven't betrayed *him* sexually. But in Shakespeare's
mind any wound that really matters is felt as a sexual
wound. Sexual vulnerability, like sexual desire, is archetypal for Shakespeare. Lear's connection to his daughters
is like a sexual connection in that it keeps sending him
back for more. Finally Gloucester has had enough of life itself, but Lear can always think of something else to want
from his daughters. First he wants flattery, then revenge,
then recognition, kindness, forgiveness, companionship—
whatever he can get. Beaten and cornered by his enemies,
he comes up with yet another fantasy of being sustained by
his daughter's love:

> Come, let's away to prison:
> We two alone will sing like birds i'th'cage:
> When thou dost ask me blessing, I'll kneel down

And ask of thee forgiveness: so we'll live,
And pray, and sing, and tell old tales, and laugh
At gilded butterflies, and hear poor rogues
Talk of court news; and we'll talk with them too,
Who loses and who wins, who's in, who's out,
And take upon's the mystery of things,
As if we were God's spies. (5.3.8–17)

Lear is sometimes taken to task for this speech. It shows, according to a certain school of literary criticism, that Lear still hasn't learned his lesson, still thinks his desires are all-important, still can't face reality. But is it a tragic hero's job to learn his lesson, or is it his job to stay alive and kicking to the end of the play? Gloucester learns his lesson, but who cares what happens to him? Only Edgar. *We* lose interest in Gloucester when *he* loses interest in the world.

Women in *King Lear* are congruent with the tie that binds us to life itself. As the feminine Other, women are inviolably separate from the masculine Self, and they are as active and aggressive in creating the plot as the hero himself. Taken together, the three sisters range from one end to the other on the scale of human moral behavior; and if the feminine is, as so often in fiction by men, schizophrenically split up into good and evil, it must be admitted that so is everything else in the play. Edgar and Edmund are almost as deeply divided as Cordelia and her sisters. It is a play *about* extremes—of wealth and poverty, wisdom and folly, heights and depths. As individual characters the women in this play are very partial portraits; but as components of the feminine Other they do add up. Only when I refuse the role of Other altogether, only when nothing will satisfy but a female version of the Self, do I refuse to shelter the female portion of my identity with Shakespeare's women. At that point, if I'm smart, I take a break from Shakespeare and pick up *Middlemarch*.

JOHN RUSSELL BROWN

Staging Violence in *King Lear*

Incoherent and physical reaction to violence is almost the rule in *King Lear*. The suffering of Gloucester is prolonged, unremitting, and often silent. His interrogation and blinding are carried out by Regan and Cornwall with a precise verbal marking of physical brutality which is reminiscent of the much earlier *Titus Andronicus*: "Upon these eyes of thine, I'll set my foot" and "Out vile jelly! / Where is thy lustre now?" (3.7.69, 84–85). They provoke Gloucester's defiance and condemnation, but when he is finally thrust out of doors the blinded man is silent. Finding Edgar to guide him to Dover, he does not recognize his son's voice and so stumbles forward uncertainly, even when supported and shown the way; he is at anyone's mercy, and when he meets Lear, whom he recognizes by his voice, he cannot communicate with him. Eventually, after crying out "Alack, alack the day!" (4.6.183), he briefly begs to be killed by Oswald. When this crisis is over he does speak at greater length, envying the king for being mad:

> . . . how stiff is my vile sense,
> That I stand up, and have ingenious feeling
> Of my huge sorrows! Better I were distract:

From John Russell Brown, British Academy Annual Shakespeare Lecture, "Violence and Sensationalism in the Plays of Shakespeare and Other Dramatists," 21 April 1994, published in *Proceedings of the British Academy* 87 (1995): 101–18, used by permission of the author and of the British Academy.

So should my thoughts be severed from my griefs,
And woes by wrong imaginations lose
The knowledge of themselves.   (284–89)

When drums foretell battle he submits without words to being led away, and we can only guess at his feelings and
"imaginations." When first brought before Regan and Cornwall, Gloucester had seen himself as "tied to the stake" like
a bear which has to "stand the course" of being baited by
fierce dogs trained for the job (3.7.55): now, in the last battle, he is like one of the blind bears who were kept as more
special attractions, to be tied to a stake and then whipped—
only Gloucester remains motionless of his own free will by
the tree or shrub to which he has been led. Edgar tells him to
"pray that the right may thrive" (5.2.2) and then leaves. Now
all that happens is "*Alarm and retreat within*," and even that
will be in sound only if the noise of battle is heard from off
stage as the Folio text directs. As the action of the entire play
hangs in the balance, all that the audience is shown is a
worn-out old man, who can see nothing and do nothing, and
does not even understand who has brought him to where he
is. Does Gloucester react at all as the sound of battle rises
and dies away? We do not know, because Shakespeare has
withheld all further words and stage-directions. All we are
shown is the long-suffering body and sightless eyes.

This reliance on physical action was extraordinary and
risky, as three considerations show. First, we know that the
whipping of a blind bear in Paris Garden, not far from the
Globe Theatre, was:

performed by five or six men standing circularly with whips,
which they exercise upon him without any mercy, as he cannot escape because of his chain; he defends himself with all
his force and skill, throwing down all that come within his
reach and are not active enough to get out of it, and tearing
the whips out of their hands, and breaking them.[1]

[1] See Hentzner's *Itinerary* (1598); quoted, translated from the Latin, in
Joseph Strutt, *The Sports and Pastimes of the People of England* (London, 1801), ed. J. C. Cox (1903), p. 206.

No one approaches to whip Gloucester and this blind victim provides no entertainment. So what does this audience think, or do?

Secondly, consider productions of *King Lear* in present-day theatres where the hunched figure of Gloucester sits in a carefully chosen place, carefully cross-lit. Lights dim progressively, and a vast backcloth may redden to represent the off-stage battle; or perhaps carefully drilled soldiers with implements of war cross and recross in front of Gloucester; and all this time, appropriate music and semi-realistic sound will work on our minds with changing rhythm, pitch, and volume. The audience will sit in the dark, their eyes and ears controlled completely by the play's director working with a team of highly trained technicians. Then consider in contrast a performance at the Globe Theatre where the light on stage could not be changed or the sounds of battle orchestrated for maximum effect and meaning, and where all was what it happened to be as the play was revived for that one day only. The audience members, in the same light as the stage, were free to withdraw attention, move around (many were standing), and talk among themselves. The actor playing Gloucester had nothing to help him attract attention and not a word to say, as he sat alone with his eyes shut; he could have had only the vaguest idea of how long it would be before Edgar returned. The elaborate speeches of *Titus Andronicus*, holding the sufferer still and controlling the audience's thoughts, and the pyrotechnics of Pyrrhus's speech in *Hamlet*, are both missing. So too are the searching words of Romeo or Juliet, which simultaneously presented and veiled the horror of teenage suicide. Gloucester gains or loses attention because he is there, victim of violence and of his son's inability to speak to him of his presence and his love. The audience would have paid attention to Gloucester or not as they chose, and would have understood for themselves, or not. One might come to feel very alone, sitting in an audience which did not see what you saw, or did not care; then suffering would seem to exist in a disregarding world. If one sat in audience equally moved by what was silent on stage, then you might wonder if some words had been forgotten or if no words were the only possible response. Shakespeare has presented the consequences of violence so that the audience has to shoulder responsibility for its own reactions.

Thirdly, we should remember how mutilated old men are shown on television or film. Briefly they fill the screen in arresting and horrific images, and then disappear before attention can flag, leaving no trace behind; and that effect is created, not as part of the continuous performance of a play, but as something cunningly arranged, for that moment, by makeup artist, costume designer and fitter, the people in charge of set, lights, and sound, and, most significantly, by cameramen and editor. The result is no more than a few seconds of overwhelming horror or pathos, instead of being one part of a sustained performance by an actor who in some real ways has been living in the role. In the theatre, an actor represents the lived experience of violence, rather than achieving, with other people's help or hindrance, a moment or two of sensational effect.

SYLVAN BARNET

King Lear on Stage and Screen

In 1808 Charles Lamb wrote an essay that has become infamous, "On the Tragedies of Shakespeare, Considered with Reference to Their Fitness for Stage Representation." The most controversial portion runs as follows:

> To see Lear acted—to see an old man tottering about the stage with a walking-stick, turned out of doors by his daughters in a rainy night, has nothing in it but what is painful and disgusting. We want to take him into shelter and relieve him. That is all the feeling which the acting of Lear ever produced in me. But the Lear of Shakespeare cannot be acted. The contemptible machinery by which they mimic the storm which he goes out in, is not more inadequate to represent the horrors of the real elements, than any actor can be to represent Lear.... The greatness of Lear is not in corporal dimension, but in intellectual: the explosions of his passion are terrible as a volcano; they are storms turning up and disclosing to the bottom that sea, his mind, with all its vast riches. It is his mind which is laid bare.... On the stage we see nothing but corporal infirmities and weakness, the impotence of rage.

Many play readers and theatergoers have tested Lamb's response against their own; those who believe that even the best production of a play (if the play is great literature) is reductive have sided with Lamb; others, who believe that a play—even the greatest play—is essentially a script that achieves its fullest life only in performance, have dismissed him. The view of this second group is summed up in Ezra Pound's assertion: "The medium of drama is not words, but persons moving about on a stage using words." But those

249

who hold this view, and censure Lamb, should remember that Lamb never saw enacted a version of Shakespeare's *King Lear* that we would call acceptable. This statement requires some explanation, but first we should glance at the little that is known of productions in Shakespeare's day.

Although *King Lear* almost surely originally was performed at the Globe Theatre, the earliest recorded performance is at the court of King James I in Whitehall Palace, London, on December 26, 1606. A few references to the play during the first seventy-five years of its existence assure us that it was occasionally acted, but tell us nothing about how it was performed or how it was received. Performances of *Lear* ceased when civil war broke out in England in 1642 (the theaters were soon closed by Act of Parliament), but after Charles II was restored to the throne in 1660 the theaters were reopened, and we know that *Lear* was among the plays acted in the 1660s. If it evoked comment, however, the comment is lost; Samuel Pepys, the English diarist and the source for some of our sharpest glimpses of the theater in that period, does not mention *Lear.* In any case, in 1681 Nahum Tate presented his adaptation of the play in London, an adaptation that was to hold the stage for more than a century and a half.

In his dedication, Tate says that he found in Shakespeare's *Lear*

> a heap of jewels unstrung and unpolished, yet so dazzling in their disorder that I soon perceived I had seized a treasure. 'Twas my good fortune to light on one expedient to rectify what was wanting in the regularity and probability of the tale, which was to run through the whole a love betwixt Edgar and Cordelia. . . .

And so, as Shakespeare had freely rewritten the old anonymous play of *King Leir*, Tate now rewrote Shakespeare's play. He made changes throughout, for example modifications in Lear's curses, but the verbal changes seem small when compared with structural changes:

1) Tate manufactured a love interest for Edgar and Cordelia (Edgar, by the way, in this version saves Cordelia from

an attempted rape by Edmund) and therefore eliminated the King of France;
2) he deleted the Fool;
3) he added a happy ending, keeping Lear, Cordelia, and Gloucester alive, and marrying Cordelia and Edgar.

This version persisted on the stage throughout the eighteenth century and well into the nineteenth. Thus, even when David Garrick played *Lear* in 1756 with "restorations from Shakespeare," i.e. with the restoration of some of Shakespeare's lines, he nevertheless followed Tate in dropping the Fool, and in retaining not only Tate's love affair between Cordelia and Edgar but also Tate's happy ending. (For a detailed yet readable study of Garrick's version of *Lear,* see Kalman A. Burnim, *David Garrick, Director.*) From 1768 to 1773 George Colman's more faithful version was performed at Covent Garden, but this version, too, though adhering fairly closely to Shakespeare's first four acts, omitted the Fool and apparently made some sort of alteration in the ending. In 1823 Edmund Kean used much of Shakespeare's fifth act—but only for two performances, after which he returned to Tate's happy ending. In 1826 Kean and Robert W. Elliston restored the tragic ending—but they nevertheless kept the love story and omitted the Fool. Not until 1838, in William Macready's production, were all three of Tate's basic changes eliminated. That is, Macready eliminated the love story, restored the Fool (though he assigned the role to a woman) and restored the tragic ending. But it should be mentioned that even though Macready restored most of Shakespeare's lines, his version was still in some ways indebted to Tate; for example, he kept Gloucester alive at the end, and he retained Tate's telescoping of the scene in the hovel (3.4) with a corrupted version of the scene in the farmhouse (3.6).

With this background, then, perhaps we can better appreciate Lamb's position, expressed, one recalls, in 1808. Here is Lamb surveying the revisions—that is, the play in the form in which it was acted in his day:

The play is beyond all art, as the tamperings with it show: it is too hard and stony; it must have love-scenes, and a happy ending. It is not enough that Cordelia is a daughter;

she must shine as a lover too. Tate has put his hook in the nostrils of this Leviathan, for Garrick and his followers, the show-men of the scene, to draw the mighty beast about more easily. A happy ending—as if the living martyrdoms that Lear had gone through—the flaying of his feelings alive, did not make a fair dismissal from the stage of life the only decorous thing for him.

Although Macready's production, and the productions of his successors in the nineteenth century, continued to show traces of Tate (for instance, in keeping Gloucester alive at the end), if we speak broadly we can say that Macready restored the play to more or less its original form—"more or less" because even today almost all productions are somewhat abridged, and as the Textual Note suggests (page 146ff.), there is a good deal of uncertainty about what the original form of the play was. (For instance, the First Folio omits about three hundred lines that are found in the second Quarto.) Productions of *Lear* in the middle and later nineteenth century were given to emphasizing lavish spectacle that was said to be historically accurate. The aim (again, speaking roughly) was theatrical illusionism: the viewer looked, through the proscenium, at a highly detailed scene that was alleged to be an authentic reproduction of the past. Thus, Charles Kean's production in 1858 was said to be set in eighth-century Anglo-Saxon England. Architecture (a great raftered hall for the palace), decor (skins and heads of animals on the walls, gigantic crimson banners with pictures of animals on them) and costumes (for instance, Lear in a floor-length robe of gold, blue and purple, and France in a blue and red robe decorated with gold fleur-de-lys) were based on historical research—though today it is recognized that the sources Kean drew on range from the sixth through the eleventh centuries. Because it could take ten or fifteen minutes to erect on the stage a highly illusionistic set, scenes employing the same set were grouped together; intervening scenes with a different locale were either transposed or completely omitted, thus seriously distorting the rhythm of the play.

During the second half of the nineteenth century and the first quarter of the twentieth, *King Lear* was rarely played, perhaps because Lamb's essay was held to be authoritative, perhaps because the tragedy seemed too bleak, too savage—too resistant to any sort of moral interpretation. Henry Irving gave it a try in 1892, but his production was unsuccessful and he never revived it. Since 1920, however, *Lear* has often been staged, for instance by such major actors as Frank Benson, Ben Greet, John Gielgud, William Devlin, Donald Wolfit, Louis Calhern, Charles Laughton, Michael Redgrave, Orson Welles, Morris Carnovsky, Paul Scofield, and Laurence Olivier. For these actors, as well as for some in the nineteenth century, we often have rather full reports of performances. Thus, we know that Irving, confronted with deciding whether the Lear who banishes Cordelia is tyrannical or is mentally failing, decided on the second option. In an immensely informative book, *The Masks of "King Lear,"* Marvin Rosenberg lets us know how actors have interpreted the play, almost line by line. Here, for instance, is a tiny specimen (page 319). Rosenberg is talking about Lear's final gestures:

> The possible modes of Lear's dying, from ecstasy through dread, must be expressed solely in visual imagery; words fail now. A wide variety of possibilities has been suggested by actors as well as critics: so Gielgud, dying grandly in joy at his perception of apotheosis in Cordelia; Forrest, frankly hallucinating her reviving, staring vacantly into space; Carnovsky, shocked to death at the horror of Cordelia's stillness.

Obviously it is impossible in this short essay even to touch on all of the chief Lears, which range from conceptions of Lear as heroic to Lear as enfeebled and fretful (Gielgud and Wolfit, by the way, each did four Lears); rather, the rest of this space will be used, first, briefly to raise the question about how the play should be costumed and set, and second, at greater length, to discuss what probably are the two most praised recent efforts—the performances by Paul Scofield and Laurence Olivier.

In Shakespeare's day the setting was the bare stage, or, rather, the stage was adorned chiefly by the costumed players, banners, etc., and whatever portable furniture (chairs, a table, a throne) might be necessary for a scene. Although a play set in Rome would require some tokens of classical garb, most plays were performed by actors wearing contemporary clothing, i.e. Elizabethan or Jacobean clothing, not the clothing of the time of the action. The use of contemporary clothing persisted in the late seventeenth century and in the eighteenth. Garrick's 1756 production of *Lear* was said to be somewhat unusual because the characters were "judiciously habited" in "old English dresses," but the illustrations of the period suggest that only the smallest gesture was made in the direction of departing from modern dress. Some three-quarters of a century after Garrick, as we have seen, in the middle of the nineteenth century, the emphasis was on historical accuracy; and the illusionism this accuracy or realism aimed at could now be reinforced by spectacular effects (dawn, a storm, or whatever) made possible with gaslight and later with electric light. Henry Irving, in the preface to his acting edition for his version of 1892, reveals something of this concern for historical truth:

> As the period of King Lear, I have chosen ... a time shortly after the departure of the Romans, when the Britons would naturally inhabit the houses left vacant.

The souvenir program shows courtiers wearing suggestions of Roman armor, sometimes combined with horned helmets that one associates with Germanic peoples. The women wear elaborate gowns, and Lear wears a highly ornamented robe, all allegedly derived from medieval pictures.

Most productions of *King Lear* continue to evoke some vaguely medieval setting, usually by means of furs and leather, but one difficulty with this approach is that Lear's society may seem so primitive to begin with that as the play progresses there is little sense of a stripping away of conventional codes of behavior, with a descent into the depths. Partly to avoid a sense of primitiveness or remoteness that a medieval setting may be thought to convey, an occasional production uses modern dress or something close to it. For instance, Trevor Nunn's production for the Royal Shakespeare Company, in 1976, with Donald Sinden as Lear, was set in Victorian or Edwardian times: the King (smoking a cigar, to indicate that the division of the kingdom was a rather informal, private affair) wore a military uniform, with medals; Kent wore a frock coat, and others wore tweeds and riding boots. What is remarkable, and even paradoxical, is that this production was noted for its realism; real water poured from above onto the stage in the heath scenes. The idea behind the use of modern dress (in *King Lear* or in any other early play) commonly is that the play will become more real to the audience (presumably this means that the audience can more fully experience the play, can get more out of it) if the action is set in a real (easily identifiable) period. In practice, however, spectators often are distracted by the novelty of the costumes and occasionally by the incongruity between the action (say, a duel) and the later setting (say, 1900). If a detailed medieval setting (offered in the name of realism or authenticity) obscures what Maynard Mack calls "the archetypal character" of the play, so too—perhaps more so—does a modern setting.

At the other extreme, the *Lear* produced by George Devine in 1955, with John Gielgud as Lear, and with settings and costumes by the Japanese-American sculptor Isamu Noguchi, sought to avoid any indication of a specific time or place. The producer and the designer wrote that their

> object in this production has been to find a setting and costumes which would be free of historical or decorative associations, so that the timeless, universal and mythical quality of the story may be clear.

The set consisted of blocks of contrasting colors and shapes, which on occasion seemed to move on their own power. There were also symbolic forms: thus, an arch represented Lear's world, and a black shape stood for doom. The costumes were more troublesome. Noguchi had not previously designed costumes, and because of a misunderstanding he was forced to design these in a hurry. He settled on a style that has usually been described as "surrealistic," though some of the costumes show (as one can see by looking at Plate 5 in *Stage Directions*, one of John Gielgud's autobiographies) a considerable debt to the robes of Japanese Noh drama. Gielgud once remarked that the costumes looked like shower curtains. They were not only strange looking, but they also proved difficult to wear, and the performance was widely regarded as a disaster. If the costumes and the set freed the play from any specific historical time and place, the strange shapes nevertheless evoked the world of science fiction, fixing the play in an unreal world, an atmosphereless world utterly remote from the spectators. This is not what tragedy is about.

A similar charge—that the production was remote from tragedy—might be made against the version performed in 1962 at Stratford-upon-Avon, starring Paul Scofield and directed by Peter Brook. Later the company went to London, and then toured the United States. (The production became the basis for a film, but the film was not identical with the stage performance.) Brook's version, and Scofield's acting, were widely hailed by audiences and by reviewers in the popular press, though they evoked grumblings among academic critics. Because Brook was influenced by the discussion of the play in Jan Kott's book, *Shakespeare Our Contemporary*, we may begin with a glance at Kott's book. Kott's chapter on *King Lear*, called "King Lear or Endgame," begins by juxtaposing a quotation from *Lear* with a quotation from *Waiting for Godot*. Briefly, Kott sees *Lear* as an anticipation of the work of Ionesco, Duerrenmatt, and Beckett. Lear is kin, in various ways, to Beckett's Vladimir, Estragon, Hamm, and Clov; Shakespeare's play is assimilated to the Theater of the Absurd and the Theater of Cruelty. Kott does say that "of the twelve principal characters [in *King Lear*], half are just, the other half unjust," but perhaps because in his forty-page chapter he never explicitly mentions Cordelia or Kent, and never mentions Edgar's devotion to Gloucester, he says nothing about love or voluntary sacrifice in *King Lear*.

The set that Brook designed for his production was almost bare. The audience saw a grayish-white cyclorama, two movable white flats angled to the sides, three wooden benches, and a table with a few utensils. Over the table was a rusted bronze sheet, later used as a thunder sheet. The characters were dressed in leather. Charles Marowitz, Brook's assistant director, comments on the set in "Lear

Log," *Encore* 10 (1963), reprinted in *Tulane Drama Review* 8 (1963). "Apart from the rust, the leather and the old wood, there is nothing but space—giant white flats opening on to a blank cyclorama." Was attention being paid to the supposedly bare stage that many scholars have argued for? No. Rather, we were getting the angst-ridden stage of the Theater of the Absurd. At the opening of the play, Scofield's voice was rasping, imperious—there was nothing in it to gain any sympathy for him, nothing to suggest that Lear had ever known what it is to express affection. To speak more generally: Brook took as his text Gloucester's words:

> As flies to wanton boys, are we to th' gods,
> They kill us for their sport.   (4.1.36–37)

To this end, he tailored the play, apparently with no less confidence than Nahum Tate showed when he tailored the play to a different pattern. Thus, after the terrible scene in which Gloucester is blinded (3.7), Shakespeare shows us two servants who denounce the monstrosity of the action, commiserate with Gloucester, and do what little they can to alleviate his terrible pain: "I'll fetch some flax and whites of eggs / T'apply to his bleeding face. Now heaven help him." (107–8) These lines were cut, as were the lines in which Edmund, repenting his wickedness, goes so far as to say:

> Some good I mean to do,
> Despite of mine own nature. Quickly send,
> Be brief in it, to th' castle; for my writ
> Is on the life of Lear and on Cordelia:
> Nay, send in time.   (5.3.245–49)

Some actors interpret Lear's last words, "Look there, look there," as words of joy (however deluded a joyous Lear must be), but, not surprisingly, Scofield spoke the lines flatly, looked blankly into the auditorium, and died with his eyes remaining open. (The end of the film version differed.) The critic Kenneth Tynan, who hailed the production, offered an apt summary of the interpretation:

Lay him to rest, the royal Lear with whom generations of star actors have made us reverently familiar, the majestic

ancient, wronged and maddened by his vicious daughters;
the felled giant, beside whose bulk the other characters
crouch like pygmies. Lay also to rest the archaic notion that
Lear is automatically entitled to our sympathy because he
is a king who suffers.

Lay also to rest, Tynan might have added, the old idea that
an audience is supposed to be moved to woe and wonder at
the sight of the suffering humanity that it sees on the stage.
This production aimed not at moving the viewers, but at
alienating them.

In his film version (1969), Brook retained his overall interpretation, but the film in some ways is more satisfying than
was the stage version. Some of the landscape scenes (shot on
location chiefly in North Jutland, Denmark) possess great
beauty, though here too every effort was made to depict an
inhospitable world, an effort reinforced by using a film stock
that was grainy and that sometimes showed washed-out images. At the end of the film, Lear's head, in slow motion, falls
back, out of the frame, and we are confronted with bright
white light—that is, with nothing. And yet at least one scene
in this film was overpoweringly beautiful, the scene on the
beach with Lear and the blind Gloucester. Perhaps in this
scene alone one felt moved; during the rest of the film one
merely felt (as with the play) interested, and perhaps dis-
tressed that Shakespeare's play was so diminished. (A Rus-
sian film version of *King Lear*, made in 1970 by Grigori
Kozintsev, is also fairly free with Shakespeare's play, but its
emphasis is different from Brook's, for it concludes with
shots of peasants setting about the task of rebuilding the civ-
ilization that the aristocrats have ravaged. Kozintsev has said
that *King Lear* belongs not only to the Theater of Cruelty but
to the Theater of Mercy.)

The version of *Lear* produced by the British Broadcasting
Corporation and *Time-Life* Films in 1982 takes account of
both Cruelty and Mercy, and is in this respect nearly an ideal
presentation of the play. Jonathan Miller's intelligent direction keeps the director off stage, giving precedence to the
playwright. Michael Hordern makes a comprehensive hero,
running the gamut in his own emotions and attitudes and in

those excited in the audience. Dictatorial at first and every inch a king, he is at last humbled to Fortune's blows and becomes "pregnant to good pity." Very little of the play is altered or omitted. The actors, not engaging in verbal pyrotechnics—if anything, they understate—still less in bizarre readings of character, speak the lines, one feels, as Shakespeare meant them to be spoken. There is one exception to this, the mad speeches of Poor Tom, which ought to suggest madness but make the mistake of imitating the real thing, degenerate to "wild and whirling words." But the play recovers strongly from this lapsing into merely imitative form. Woe and wonder mark its conclusion, on the one hand almost too dreadful for report; on the other exhilarating in the rendering of human beings living their lives at full stretch.

Finally, something should be said about the televised production, made in 1982, with Laurence Olivier as Lear, Dorothy Tutin as Goneril, and Diana Rigg as Regan. In 1946, when Olivier at the age of thirty-nine had played Lear for the Old Vic, his performance evoked chiefly polite reviews, most of the high praise being reserved for Alec Guinness's performance as the Fool. Now, at the age of seventy-five, Olivier again took on Lear. He made some cuts—several on the authority of the First Folio—but the film nevertheless runs to two hours and forty minutes, and is far more faithful to Shakespeare's play than was Brook's production or film. But it is not a theater spectator's view of a theatrical performance recorded on film; rather, it is a version created for television cameras. Thus, when at the start of the play Lear's courtiers prostrate themselves, we get an overhead shot, a bird's-eye view. The set evokes Stonehenge, as did the sets of Henry Irving, Donald Wolfit, and Charles Laughton, but some viewers have found Olivier's studio Stonehenge—well, to come out with it—tacky. The director, Michael Elliott, has explained that he and Olivier decided not to make the film on location because the camera can dwell too lovingly on surfaces, on the real and perhaps irrelevant. The camera, that is, has a way of reminding viewers of limitless space, and of the rich abundance of life, and can be thought to be fundamentally inimical to the concentration and finiteness associated with tragedy. But in this television version the sets are essentially realistic (illusionistic), and so instead of the set helping us to concentrate on the tragic figures it distracts us by its imitation of the details of the real world.

What of Olivier's depiction of Lear? Perhaps one can say fairly that this television performance is touching rather than harrowing. Olivier had undergone a decade of severe illness (gout, cancer of the prostate, thrombosis of the leg, and a deteriorating muscular disease), and apparently lacked the strength that the role requires. There is much in the performance that is admirable, but on the whole this Lear lacks tragic stature. To use Aristotle's terms, Olivier evokes pity but not terror. In the beginning, in his dealings with his daughters at the love contest, he plays Lear as slightly eccentric, faintly senile, and even here one feels that Olivier the actor is drawing on his bag of tricks. Intimate scenes, notably the meeting with Gloucester and the reconciliation with Cordelia, are touching, but in the scenes calling for majestic anger it is evident that Olivier (whose voice has become shrill) no longer has the physical resources necessary for the role. One admires the skill, wishes that Olivier had attempted Lear a decade earlier, recognizes that this *Lear* (like many other productions) reveals qualities in the play that the reader otherwise might miss, but one also finds oneself wondering if, perhaps, when all is said and done, Charles Lamb may not have been right when he said that Shakespeare's Lear is diminished in performance.

Bibliographic Note: For wide-ranging discussions, see in Suggested References, the material listed under Shakespeare on Stage and Screen (page 265). Specialized discussions include: Marvin Rosenberg, *The Masks of "King Lear"* (1972); Gamini Salgado's book in the Text and Performance series, *King Lear* (1984); Alexander Leggatt's book in the Shakespeare in Performance series, *King Lear* (1991); James P. Lusardi and June Schlueter, *Reading Shakespeare in Performance* (1991); John Russell Brown's edition (1996) of *King Lear* ("a theatrical edition, . . . designed to help readers see and hear the plays in action"). On three films of *King Lear* (versions by Peter Brook, Grigori Kozintsev, and Akira Kurosawa), see R. B. Parker in *Shakespeare Quarterly* 42 (1991): 75–90.

Suggested References

The number of possible references is vast and grows alarmingly. (The *Shakespeare Quarterly* devotes one issue each year to a list of the previous year's work, and *Shakespeare Survey*—an annual publication—includes a substantial review of biographical, critical, and textual studies, as well as a survey of performances.) The vast bibliography is best approached through James Harner, *The World Shakespeare Bibliography on CD-Rom: 1900–Present*. The first release, in 1996, included more than 12,000 annotated items from 1990–93, plus references to several thousand book reviews, productions, films, and audio recordings. The plan is to update the publication annually, moving forward one year and backward three years. Thus, the second issue (1997), with 24,700 entries, and another 35,000 or so references to reviews, newspaper pieces, and so on, covered 1987–94.

Though no works are indispensable, those listed below have been found especially helpful. The arrangement is as follows:

1. Shakespeare's Times
2. Shakespeare's Life
3. Shakespeare's Theater
4. Shakespeare on Stage and Screen
5. Miscellaneous Reference Works
6. Shakespeare's Plays: General Studies
7. The Comedies
8. The Romances
9. The Tragedies
10. The Histories
11. *King Lear*

The titles in the first five sections are accompanied by brief explanatory annotations.

1. Shakespeare's Times

Andrews, John F., ed. *William Shakespeare: His World, His Work, His Influence,* 3 vols. (1985). Sixty articles, dealing not only with such subjects as "The State," "The Church," "Law," "Science, Magic, and Folklore," but also with the plays and poems themselves and Shakespeare's influence (e.g., translations, films, reputation)

Byrne, Muriel St. Clare. *Elizabethan Life in Town and Country* (8th ed., 1970). Chapters on manners, beliefs, education, etc., with illustrations.

Dollimore, John, and Alan Sinfield, eds. *Political Shakespeare: New Essays in Cultural Materialism* (1985). Essays on such topics as the subordination of women and colonialism, presented in connection with some of Shakespeare's plays.

Greenblatt, Stephen. *Representing the English Renaissance* (1988). New Historicist essays, especially on connections between political and aesthetic matters, statecraft and stagecraft.

Joseph, B. L. *Shakespeare's Eden: the Commonwealth of England 1558–1629* (1971). An account of the social, political, economic, and cultural life of England.

Kernan, Alvin. *Shakespeare, the King's Playwright: Theater in the Stuart Court 1603–1613* (1995). The social setting and the politics of the court of James I, in relation to *Hamlet, Measure for Measure, Macbeth, King Lear, Antony and Cleopatra, Coriolanus,* and *The Tempest.*

Montrose, Louis. *The Purpose of Playing: Shakespeare and the Cultural Politics of the Elizabethan Theatre* (1996). A poststructuralist view, discussing the professional theater "within the ideological and material frameworks of Elizabethan culture and society," with an extended analysis of *A Midsummer Night's Dream.*

Mullaney, Steven. *The Place of the Stage: License, Play, and Power in Renaissance England* (1988). New Historicist analysis, arguing that popular drama became a cultural institution "only by . . . taking up a place on the margins of society."

Schoenbaum, S. *Shakespeare: The Globe and the World*

(1979). A readable, abundantly illustrated introductory book on the world of the Elizabethans.

Shakespeare's England, 2 vols. (1916). A large collection of scholarly essays on a wide variety of topics, e.g., astrology, costume, gardening, horsemanship, with special attention to Shakespeare's references to these topics.

2. Shakespeare's Life

Andrews, John F., ed. *William Shakespeare: His World, His Work, His Influence,* 3 vols. (1985). See the description above.

Bentley, Gerald E. *Shakespeare: A Biographical Handbook* (1961). The facts about Shakespeare, with virtually no conjecture intermingled.

Chambers, E. K. *William Shakespeare: A Study of Facts and Problems,* 2 vols. (1930). The fullest collection of data.

Fraser, Russell. *Young Shakespeare* (1988). A highly readable account that simultaneously considers Shakespeare's life and Shakespeare's art.

———. *Shakespeare: The Later Years* (1992).

Schoenbaum, S. *Shakespeare's Lives* (1970). A review of the evidence and an examination of many biographies, including those of Baconians and other heretics.

———. *William Shakespeare: A Compact Documentary Life* (1977). An abbreviated version, in a smaller format, of the next title. The compact version reproduces some fifty documents in reduced form. A readable presentation of all that the documents tell us about Shakespeare.

———. *William Shakespeare: A Documentary Life* (1975). A large-format book setting forth the biography with facsimiles of more than two hundred documents, and with transcriptions and commentaries.

3. Shakespeare's Theater

Astington, John H., ed. *The Development of Shakespeare's Theater* (1992). Eight specialized essays on theatrical companies, playing spaces, and performance.

Beckerman, Bernard. *Shakespeare at the Globe, 1599–1609* (1962). On the playhouse and on Elizabethan dramaturgy, acting, and staging.

Bentley, Gerald E. *The Profession of Dramatist in Shakespeare's Time* (1971). An account of the dramatist's status in the Elizabethan period.

———. *The Profession of Player in Shakespeare's Time, 1590–1642* (1984). An account of the status of members of London companies (sharers, hired men, apprentices, managers) and a discussion of conditions when they toured.

Berry, Herbert. *Shakespeare's Playhouses* (1987). Usefully emphasizes how little we know about the construction of Elizabethan theaters.

Brown, John Russell. *Shakespeare's Plays in Performance* (1966). A speculative and practical analysis relevant to all of the plays, but with emphasis on *The Merchant of Venice, Richard II, Hamlet, Romeo and Juliet*, and *Twelfth Night*.

———. *William Shakespeare: Writing for Performance* (1996). A discussion aimed at helping readers to develop theatrically conscious habits of reading.

Chambers, E. K. *The Elizabethan Stage*, 4 vols. (1945). A major reference work on theaters, theatrical companies, and staging at court.

Cook, Ann Jennalie. *The Privileged Playgoers of Shakespeare's London, 1576–1642* (1981). Sees Shakespeare's audience as wealthier, more middle-class, and more intellectual than Harbage (below) does.

Dessen, Alan C. *Elizabethan Drama and the Viewer's Eye* (1977). On how certain scenes may have looked to spectators in an Elizabethan theater.

Gurr, Andrew. *Playgoing in Shakespeare's London* (1987). Something of a middle ground between Cook (above) and Harbage (below).

———. *The Shakespearean Stage, 1579–1642* (2nd ed., 1980). On the acting companies, the actors, the playhouses, the stages, and the audiences.

Harbage, Alfred. *Shakespeare's Audience* (1941). A study of the size and nature of the theatrical public, emphasizing the representativeness of its working class and middle-class audience.

Hodges, C. Walter. *The Globe Restored* (1968). A conjectural restoration, with lucid drawings.

Hosley, Richard. "The Playhouses," in *The Revels History of Drama in English*, vol. 3, general editors Clifford Leech and T. W. Craik (1975). An essay of a hundred pages on the physical aspects of the playhouses.

Howard, Jane E. "Crossdressing, the Theatre, and Gender Struggle in Early Modern England," *Shakespeare Quarterly* 39 (1988): 418–40. Judicious comments on the effects of boys playing female roles.

Orrell, John. *The Human Stage: English Theatre Design, 1567–1640* (1988). Argues that the public, private, and court playhouses are less indebted to popular structures (e.g., innyards and bear-baiting pits) than to banqueting halls and to Renaissance conceptions of Roman amphitheaters.

Slater, Ann Pasternak. *Shakespeare the Director* (1982). An analysis of theatrical effects (e.g., kissing, kneeling) in stage directions and dialogue.

Styan, J. L. *Shakespeare's Stagecraft* (1967). An introduction to Shakespeare's visual and aural stagecraft, with chapters on such topics as acting conventions, stage groupings, and speech.

Thompson, Peter. *Shakespeare's Professional Career* (1992). An examination of patronage and related theatrical conditions.

———. *Shakespeare's Theatre* (1983). A discussion of how plays were staged in Shakespeare's time.

4. Shakespeare on Stage and Screen

Bate, Jonathan, and Russell Jackson, eds. *Shakespeare: An Illustrated Stage History* (1996). Highly readable essays on stage productions from the Renaissance to the present.

Berry, Ralph. *Changing Styles in Shakespeare* (1981). Discusses productions of six plays (*Coriolanus*, *Hamlet*, *Henry V*, *Measure for Measure*, *The Tempest*, and *Twelfth Night*) on the English stage, chiefly 1950–1980.

————. *On Directing Shakespeare: Interviews with Contemporary Directors* (1989). An enlarged edition of a book first published in 1977, this version includes the seven interviews from the early 1970s and adds five interviews conducted in 1988.

Brockbank, Philip, ed. *Players of Shakespeare: Essays in Shakespearean Performance* (1985). Comments by twelve actors, reporting their experiences with roles. See also the entry for Russell Jackson (below).

Bulman, J. C., and H. R. Coursen, eds. *Shakespeare on Television* (1988). An anthology of general and theoretical essays, essays on individual productions, and shorter reviews, with a bibliography and a videography listing cassettes that may be rented.

Coursen, H. P. *Watching Shakespeare on Television* (1993). Analyses not only of TV versions but also of films and videotapes of stage presentations that are shown on television.

Davies, Anthony, and Stanley Wells, eds. *Shakespeare and the Moving Image: The Plays on Film and Television* (1994). General essays (e.g., on the comedies) as well as essays devoted entirely to *Hamlet*, *King Lear*, and *Macbeth*.

Dawson, Anthony B. *Watching Shakespeare: A Playgoer's Guide* (1988). About half of the plays are discussed, chiefly in terms of decisions that actors and directors make in putting the works onto the stage.

Dessen, Alan. *Elizabethan Stage Conventions and Modern Interpretations* (1984). On interpreting conventions such as the representation of light and darkness and stage violence (duels, battles).

Donaldson, Peter. *Shakespearean Films/Shakespearean Directors* (1990). Postmodernist analyses, drawing on Freudianism, Feminism, Deconstruction, and Queer Theory.

Jackson, Russell, and Robert Smallwood, eds. *Players of Shakespeare 2: Further Essays in Shakespearean Performance by Players with the Royal Shakespeare Company* (1988). Fourteen actors discuss their roles in productions between 1982 and 1987.

————. *Players of Shakespeare 3: Further Essays in Shake-

spearean Performance by Players with the Royal Shakespeare Company (1993). Comments by thirteen performers.

Jorgens, Jack. *Shakespeare on Film* (1977). Fairly detailed studies of eighteen films, preceded by an introductory chapter addressing such issues as music, and whether to "open" the play by including scenes of landscape.

Kennedy, Dennis. *Looking at Shakespeare: A Visual History of Twentieth-Century Performance* (1993). Lucid descriptions (with 170 photographs) of European, British, and American performances.

Leiter, Samuel L. *Shakespeare Around the Globe: A Guide to Notable Postwar Revivals* (1986). For each play there are about two pages of introductory comments, then discussions (about five hundred words per production) of ten or so productions, and finally bibliographic references.

McMurty, Jo. *Shakespeare Films in the Classroom* (1994). Useful evaluations of the chief films most likely to be shown in undergraduate courses.

Rothwell, Kenneth, and Annabelle Henkin Melzer. *Shakespeare on Screen: An International Filmography and Videography* (1990). A reference guide to several hundred films and videos produced between 1899 and 1989, including spinoffs such as musicals and dance versions.

Sprague, Arthur Colby. *Shakespeare and the Actors* (1944). Detailed discussions of stage business (gestures, etc.) over the years.

Willis, Susan. *The BBC Shakespeare Plays: Making the Televised Canon* (1991). A history of the series, with interviews and production diaries for some plays.

5. Miscellaneous Reference Works

Abbott, E. A. *A Shakespearean Grammar* (new edition, 1877). An examination of differences between Elizabethan and modern grammar.

Allen, Michael J. B., and Kenneth Muir, eds. *Shakespeare's Plays in Quarto* (1981). One volume containing facsimiles of the plays issued in small format before they were collected in the First Folio of 1623.

Bevington, David. *Shakespeare* (1978). A short guide to hundreds of important writings on the subject.

Blake, Norman. *Shakespeare's Language: An Introduction* (1983). On vocabulary, parts of speech, and word order.

Bullough, Geoffrey. *Narrative and Dramatic Sources of Shakespeare*, 8 vols. (1957–75). A collection of many of the books Shakespeare drew on, with judicious comments.

Campbell, Oscar James, and Edward G. Quinn, eds. *The Reader's Encyclopedia of Shakespeare* (1966). Old, but still the most useful single reference work on Shakespeare.

Cercignani, Fausto. *Shakespeare's Works and Elizabethan Pronunciation* (1981). Considered the best work on the topic, but remains controversial.

Dent, R. W. *Shakespeare's Proverbial Language: An Index* (1981). An index of proverbs, with an introduction concerning a form Shakespeare frequently drew on.

Greg, W. W. *The Shakespeare First Folio* (1955). A detailed yet readable history of the first collection (1623) of Shakespeare's plays.

Harner, James. *The World Shakespeare Bibliography.* See headnote to Suggested References.

Hosley, Richard. *Shakespeare's Holinshed* (1968). Valuable presentation of one of Shakespeare's major sources.

Kökeritz, Helge. *Shakespeare's Names* (1959). A guide to pronouncing some 1,800 names appearing in Shakespeare.

———. *Shakespeare's Pronunciation* (1953). Contains much information about puns and rhymes, but see Cercignani (above).

Muir, Kenneth. *The Sources of Shakespeare's Plays* (1978). An account of Shakespeare's use of his reading. It covers all the plays, in chronological order.

Miriam Joseph, Sister. *Shakespeare's Use of the Arts of Language* (1947). A study of Shakespeare's use of rhetorical devices, reprinted in part as *Rhetoric in Shakespeare's Time* (1962).

The Norton Facsimile: The First Folio of Shakespeare's Plays (1968). A handsome and accurate facsimile of the first collection (1623) of Shakespeare's plays, with a valuable introduction by Charlton Hinman.

Onions, C. T. *A Shakespeare Glossary*, rev. and enlarged by

R. D. Eagleson (1986). Definitions of words (or senses of words) now obsolete.

Partridge, Eric. *Shakespeare's Bawdy*, rev. ed. (1955). Relatively brief dictionary of bawdy words; useful, but see Williams, below.

Shakespeare Quarterly. See headnote to Suggested References.

Shakespeare Survey. See headnote to Suggested References.

Spevack, Marvin. *The Harvard Concordance to Shakespeare* (1973). An index to Shakespeare's words.

Vickers, Brian. *Appropriating Shakespeare: Contemporary Critical Quarrels* (1993). A survey—chiefly hostile—of recent schools of criticism.

Wells, Stanley, ed. *Shakespeare: A Bibliographical Guide* (new edition, 1990). Nineteen chapters (some devoted to single plays, others devoted to groups of related plays) on recent scholarship on the life and all of the works.

Williams, Gordon. *A Dictionary of Sexual Language and Imagery in Shakespearean and Stuart Literature*, 3 vols. (1994). Extended discussions of words and passages; much fuller than Partridge, cited above.

6. Shakespeare's Plays: General Studies

Bamber, Linda. *Comic Women, Tragic Men: A Study of Gender and Genre in Shakespeare* (1982).

Barnet, Sylvan. *A Short Guide to Shakespeare* (1974).

Callaghan, Dympna, Lorraine Helms, and Jyotsna Singh. *The Weyward Sisters: Shakespeare and Feminist Politics* (1994).

Clemen, Wolfgang H. *The Development of Shakespeare's Imagery* (1951).

Cook, Ann Jennalie. *Making a Match: Courtship in Shakespeare and His Society* (1991).

Dollimore, Jonathan, and Alan Sinfield. *Political Shakespeare: New Essays in Cultural Materialism* (1985).

Dusinberre, Juliet. *Shakespeare and the Nature of Women* (1975).

Granville-Barker, Harley. *Prefaces to Shakespeare*, 2 vols. (1946–47; volume 1 contains essays on *Hamlet, King*

Lear, Merchant of Venice, Antony and Cleopatra, and *Cymbeline*; volume 2 contains essays on *Othello, Coriolanus, Julius Caesar, Romeo and Juliet, Love's Labor's Lost*).

———. *More Prefaces to Shakespeare* (1974; essays on *Twelfth Night, A Midsummer Night's Dream, The Winter's Tale, Macbeth*).

Harbage, Alfred. *William Shakespeare: A Reader's Guide* (1963).

Howard, Jean E. *Shakespeare's Art of Orchestration: Stage Technique and Audience Response* (1984).

Jones, Emrys. *Scenic Form in Shakespeare* (1971).

Lenz, Carolyn Ruth Swift, Gayle Greene, and Carol Thomas Neely, eds. *The Woman's Part: Feminist Criticism of Shakespeare* (1980).

Novy, Marianne. *Love's Argument: Gender Relations in Shakespeare* (1984).

Rose, Mark. *Shakespearean Design* (1972).

Scragg, Leah. *Discovering Shakespeare's Meaning* (1994).

———. *Shakespeare's "Mouldy Tales": Recurrent Plot Motifs in Shakespearean Drama* (1992).

Traub, Valerie. *Desire and Anxiety: Circulations of Sexuality in Shakespearean Drama* (1992).

Traversi, D. A. *An Approach to Shakespeare,* 2 vols. (3rd rev. ed, 1968–69).

Vickers, Brian. *The Artistry of Shakespeare's Prose* (1968).

Wells, Stanley. *Shakespeare: A Dramatic Life* (1994).

Wright, George T. *Shakespeare's Metrical Art* (1988).

7. The Comedies

Barber, C. L. *Shakespeare's Festive Comedy* (1959; discusses *Love's Labor's Lost, A Midsummer Night's Dream, The Merchant of Venice, As You Like It, Twelfth Night*).

Barton, Anne. *The Names of Comedy* (1990).

Berry, Ralph. *Shakespeare's Comedy: Explorations in Form* (1972).

Bradbury, Malcolm, and David Palmer, eds. *Shakespearean Comedy* (1972).

Bryant, J. A., Jr. *Shakespeare and the Uses of Comedy* (1986).

Carroll, William. *The Metamorphoses of Shakespearean Comedy* (1985).

Champion, Larry S. *The Evolution of Shakespeare's Comedy* (1970).

Evans, Bertrand. *Shakespeare's Comedies* (1960).

Frye, Northrop. *Shakespearean Comedy and Romance* (1965).

Leggatt, Alexander. *Shakespeare's Comedy of Love* (1974).

Miola, Robert S. *Shakespeare and Classical Comedy: The Influence of Plautus and Terence* (1994).

Nevo, Ruth. *Comic Transformations in Shakespeare* (1980).

Ornstein, Robert. *Shakespeare's Comedies: From Roman Farce to Romantic Mystery* (1986).

Richman, David. *Laughter, Pain, and Wonder: Shakespeare's Comedies and the Audience in the Theater* (1990).

Salingar, Leo. *Shakespeare and the Traditions of Comedy* (1974).

Slights, Camille Wells. *Shakespeare's Comic Commonwealths* (1993).

Waller, Gary, ed. *Shakespeare's Comedies* (1991).

Westlund, Joseph. *Shakespeare's Reparative Comedies: A Psychoanalytic View of the Middle Plays* (1984).

Williamson, Marilyn. *The Patriarchy of Shakespeare's Comedies* (1986).

8. The Romances (*Pericles*, *Cymbeline*, *The Winter's Tale*, *The Tempest*, *The Two Noble Kinsmen*)

Adams, Robert M. *Shakespeare: The Four Romances* (1989).

Felperin, Howard. *Shakespearean Romance* (1972).

Frye, Northrop. *A Natural Perspective: The Development of Shakespearean Comedy and Romance* (1965).

Mowat, Barbara. *The Dramaturgy of Shakespeare's Romances* (1976).

Warren, Roger. *Staging Shakespeare's Late Plays* (1990).

Young, David. *The Heart's Forest: A Study of Shakespeare's Pastoral Plays* (1972).

9. The Tragedies

Bradley, A. C. *Shakespearean Tragedy* (1904).

Brooke, Nicholas. *Shakespeare's Early Tragedies* (1968).

Champion, Larry. *Shakespeare's Tragic Perspective* (1976).

Drakakis, John, ed. *Shakespearean Tragedy* (1992).

Evans, Bertrand. *Shakespeare's Tragic Practice* (1979).

Everett, Barbara. *Young Hamlet: Essays on Shakespeare's Tragedies* (1989).

Foakes, R. A. *Hamlet versus Lear: Cultural Politics and Shakespeare's Art* (1993).

Frye, Northrop. *Fools of Time: Studies in Shakespearean Tragedy* (1967).

Harbage, Alfred, ed. *Shakespeare: The Tragedies* (1964).

Mack, Maynard. *Everybody's Shakespeare: Reflections Chiefly on the Tragedies* (1993).

McAlindon, T. *Shakespeare's Tragic Cosmos* (1991).

Miola, Robert S. *Shakespeare and Classical Tragedy: The Influence of Seneca* (1992).

———. *Shakespeare's Rome* (1983).

Nevo, Ruth. *Tragic Form in Shakespeare* (1972).

Rackin, Phyllis. *Shakespeare's Tragedies* (1978).

Rose, Mark, ed. *Shakespeare's Early Tragedies: A Collection of Critical Essays* (1995).

Rosen, William. *Shakespeare and the Craft of Tragedy* (1960).

Snyder, Susan. *The Comic Matrix of Shakespeare's Tragedies* (1979).

Wofford, Susanne. *Shakespeare's Late Tragedies: A Collection of Critical Essays* (1996).

Young, David. *The Action to the Word: Structure and Style in Shakespearean Tragedy* (1990).

———. *Shakespeare's Middle Tragedies: A Collection of Critical Essays* (1993).

10. The Histories

Blanpied, John W. *Time and the Artist in Shakespeare's English Histories* (1983).

Campbell, Lily B. *Shakespeare's "Histories": Mirrors of Elizabethan Policy* (1947).

Champion, Larry S. *Perspective in Shakespeare's English Histories* (1980).

Hodgdon, Barbara. *The End Crowns All: Closure and Contradiction in Shakespeare's History* (1991).

Holderness, Graham. *Shakespeare Recycled: The Making of Historical Drama* (1992).

————, ed. *Shakespeare's History Plays: "Richard II" to "Henry V"* (1992).

Leggatt, Alexander. *Shakespeare's Political Drama: The History Plays and the Roman Plays* (1988).

Ornstein, Robert. *A Kingdom for a Stage: The Achievement of Shakespeare's History Plays* (1972).

Rackin, Phyllis. *Stages of History: Shakespeare's English Chronicles* (1990).

Saccio, Peter. *Shakespeare's English Kings: History, Chronicle, and Drama* (1977).

Tillyard, E. M. W. *Shakespeare's History Plays* (1944).

Velz, John W., ed. *Shakespeare's English Histories: A Quest for Form and Genre* (1996).

11. *King Lear*

In addition to the readings listed above in Section 9, The Tragedies, see the following: for material concerning the play on the stage and screen, see page 260; for material concerning the texts of the play, see (in addition to the items by Peter Blaney, Michael Warren, and Rene Weis) page 146.

Armstrong, Philip. "Uncanny Spectacles: Psychoanalysis and the texts of *King Lear*." *Textual Practice* 8 (1994): 414–34.

Blaney, Peter. *The Texts of "King Lear" and Their Origins* (1982).

Bonheim, Helmut, ed. *The Lear Perplex* (1960).

Bradley, A. C. *Shakespearean Tragedy* (1904).

Campbell, Lily B. *Shakespeare's Tragic Heroes* (1930).

Colie, Rosalie, and F. T. Flahiff, eds. *Some Facets of "King Lear"* (1974).

Cunningham, J. V. *Woe and Wonder* (1951).

Danby, John F. *Shakespeare's Doctrine of Nature* (1949).

Fraser, Russell A. *Shakespeare's Poetics in Relation to "King Lear"* (1962).

Granville-Barker, Harley. *Prefaces to Shakespeare*. 2 vols. (1946–47); part of the material is reprinted above.

Halio, Jay, ed. *The Tragedy of King Lear* (1992).

Heilman, Robert B. *This Great Stage: Image and Structure in "King Lear"* (1948).

Holland, Norman N., and Sidney Homan and Bernard J. Paris, eds. *Shakespeare's Personality* (1989).

Kahn, Coppélia. "The Absent Mother in *King Lear*." *Rewriting the Renaissance: The Discourses of Sexual Difference in Early Modern Europe*. Ed. Margaret Ferguson, Maureen Quilligan, and Nancy J. Vickers (1986); pp. 33–49.

Lamb, Charles. "On Shakespeare's Tragedies" (1808); rptd. in *Lamb's Criticism*, ed. E. M. W. Tillyard (1923), pp. 43–48.

Lothian, John Maule. *"King Lear": A Tragic Reading of Life* (1950).

Mack, Maynard. *"King Lear" in Our Time* (1965); part of the material is reprinted above.

Moulton, Richard G. *Shakespeare as a Dramatic Artist* (1897).

Novy, Marianne. *Love's Argument: Gender Relations in Shakespeare* (1984).

———.*Women's Re-Visions of Shakespeare: On the Responses of Dickinson, Woolf, Rich, H.D., George Eliot, and Others* (1990).

Perrett, Wilfred. *The Story of King Lear from Geoffrey of Monmouth to Shakespeare* (1904).

Rosen, William. *Shakespeare and the Craft of Tragedy* (1960).

Sewall, Richard B. *The Vision of Tragedy* (1959).

Shakespeare Studies 13 (1960; devoted to *King Lear*).

Stoll, E. E. *Art and Artifice in Shakespeare* (1933).

Taylor, Gary, and Michael Warren, eds. *The Division of the Kingdom: Shakespeare's Two Versions of "King Lear"* (1983).

Thompson, Ann. "Are There Any Women in *King Lear*?" *The Matter of Difference: Materialist Feminist Criticism of Shakespeare*. Ed. Valerie Wayne (1991), pp. 117–28.

Warren, Michael. *The Complete "King Lear" 1608–1623* (1989); unbound photographic facsimiles of Q1, Q2, and F, as well as a bound version of the next title listed.

———.*The Parallel "King Lear" 1608–23* (1989); photographic facsimiles of Q1 and F, in parallel columns, and, in the outer margins, reproductions of corrected states of Q and F.

Weis, René, ed. *"King Lear": A Parallel Text Edition* (1993); prints Q on the left-hand page, F on the right, both in modernized spelling.

Wilson, Richard. *Will Power* (1993).

The Signet Classic Shakespeare Series:

The Comedies

*extensively revised and updated to provide
more enjoyment through a greater
understanding of the texts*

ALL'S WELL THAT ENDS WELL
Sylvan Barnet, ed.
(522613)
THE COMEDY OF ERRORS, *Harry Levin, ed.*
(528395)
LOVE'S LABOR'S LOST, *John Arthos, ed.*
(522672)
MEASURE FOR MEASURE, *S. Nagarajan, ed.*
(527151)
A MIDSUMMER NIGHT'S DREAM
Wolfgang Clemen, ed.
(526961)
MUCH ADO ABOUT NOTHING
David Stevenson, ed.
(526813)
THE TAMING OF THE SHREW, *Sylvan Barnet, ed.*
(526791)
THE TEMPEST, *Robert Langbaum, ed.*
(527127)
TWELFTH NIGHT, *Herschel Baker, ed.*
(526767)
THE WINTER'S TALE, *Frank Kermode, ed.*
(527143)

To order call: 1-800-788-6262